Achieving Equity in School Writing

Paul D. Deane

Achieving Equity in School Writing

Causes and Cures for Opportunity and Achievement Gaps in a Key Twenty-First Century Skill

PETER LANG
Lausanne • Berlin • Bruxelles • Chennai • New York • Oxford

Library of Congress Cataloging-in-Publication Control Number: 2023018676

Bibliographic information published by the **Deutsche Nationalbibliothek**.
The German National Library lists this publication in the German
National Bibliography; detailed bibliographic data is available
on the Internet at http://dnb.d-nb.de.

Cover design by Peter Lang Group AG

ISBN 9781433193989 (paperback)
ISBN 9781433193972 (hardback)
ISBN 9781433193996 (ebook)
ISBN 9781433194009 (epub)
DOI 10.3726/b19194

© 2023 Paul D. Deane
Published by Peter Lang Publishing Inc., New York, USA
info@peterlang.com - www.peterlang.com

All rights reserved.
All parts of this publication are protected by copyright.
Any utilization outside the strict limits of the copyright law, without the permission of the
publisher, is forbidden and liable to prosecution.
This applies in particular to reproductions, translations, microfilming, and storage and
processing in electronic retrieval systems.

This publication has been peer reviewed.

Contents

Acknowledgments ix
Lists of Figures xi
Lists of Tables xiii

Introduction 1
    Evidence of Group Differences in Writing Achievement 2
    Deficits vs. Assets: Or, What Is Really Going On? 4
    Continuities vs. Discontinuities in Writing Development 5
    How to Use This Book 6
    How This Book Is Structured 6
    A Personal Note: Context and Perspective 11
Chapter One Why Writing is Hard 19
    The Cognitive Complexity of Writing 19
    The Sociocultural Complexity of Writing 22
    The Complexity of Learning to Write 24
Chapter Two Writing as Purposeful Action: Motivation for Writing as Cause and Effect 31
    Overview 32
    Group Differences Mediated by Motivation 35
        Self-Efficacy 36

      Beliefs and Attitudes   39
      Goal Orientation   43
      Cost/Benefit Analysis   45

Chapter Three Writing as Self-Regulation: The Mediating Roles of Reading Fluency and Working Memory   79
   Overview   79
   Group Differences Mediated by (Re)reading   82
   Group Differences Mediated by Attention and Working Memory   84
      Group Differences in Working Memory Associated with Gender   84
      Group Differences in Working Memory Associated with Race and Socioeconomic Status   85

Chapter Four Writing as the Formulation of Ideas: The Mediating Effects of Prior Content Knowledge   93
   Overview   93
   Group Differences Mediated by Prior Content Knowledge   95
      Gender Differences in Prior Content Knowledge   95
      Socioeconomic and Cultural Differences in Prior Content Knowledge   96

Chapter Five Writing as Verbal Self-Expression: The Causal Role of Oral Language Skills   105
   Group Differences Mediated by Oral Language Skills   105
      Gender-Based Similarities and Differences in Oral Language Skills   105
      Differences in Writing Achievement Mediated by the Stigmatization of Dialect Features and the Cost of Code-Switching   106
      Differences in Writing Achievement Mediated by Second Language Status   108
      Differences in Writing Achievement Mediated by Socioeconomic Differences in Linguistic Knowledge   109

Chapter Six Writing as Getting Words on the Page: The Effects of Transcription Skills on Writing Development   119
   Overview   120
      Handwriting Fluency   120
      Spelling and Other Orthographic Skills   121
      Keyboarding Fluency   121
   Group Differences Mediated by Transcription Skills   122
      Group Differences in Handwriting   123
      Group Differences in Spelling   124
      Group Differences in Keyboarding   124

Chapter Seven How to Achieve Equity in School Writing ... 135
    Improve Writing Motivation ... 136
        Provide Real Audiences and Authentic Purposes for Writing ... 136
        Make Writing Social and Collaborative ... 137
        Encourage Students to Adopt Mastery Goals ... 138
        Provide Supportive Feedback ... 138
        Give Students Greater Agency and Choice of Writing Topics ... 139
        Welcome Linguistic and Cultural Diversity ... 139
    Improve Writing Self-Regulation ... 140
    Develop Deeper Knowledge about Writing and Writing Strategies ... 141
        Provide Models to Emulate ... 142
        Explicitly Teach Students How to Write in Multiple Genres and Disciplines ... 142
    Improve Idea Generation by Making Time for Prewriting ... 144
    Develop Deeper Content Knowledge ... 144
        Implement Writing to Learn ... 145
        Incorporate Inquiry Learning into Writing Tasks ... 146
    Increase Effective Working Memory Capacity ... 146
        Provide Frequent Opportunities to Practice Writing ... 147
        Support Process Writing ... 147
        Support Alternate Input Formats ... 148
    Strengthen Language Skills ... 149
        Increase Vocabulary Knowledge ... 149
        Develop Syntactic Flexibility ... 150
        Develop Code-Switching and Code-Meshing Abilities ... 151
        Cultivate Metalinguistic Awareness ... 151
    Improve Transcription Skills ... 152
    Improve Reading Skills ... 153

Conclusion ... 163
Index ... 169

Acknowledgments

This book started its life as part of a research project led by Randy E. Bennett at ETS, focusing on causes and cures for group differences in educational outcomes and benefited greatly from his leadership and advice. I would particularly like to acknowledge the generous contributions made by Norbert Elliott, who read and provided detailed commentary on an early version of the manuscript. Any gaps or inaccuracies are, of course, entirely my responsibility.

Lists of Figures

Figure I.1. Theory of Action for Equitable Development of Writing Expertise — 10
Figure 2.1. Major Factors Affecting Writing Motivation — 33
Figure 3.1. Aspects of Self-Regulation — 81

Lists of Tables

Table 1.1	Classification of writing processes by activity type and mode of cognitive representation	21
Table 2.1	Causal Mechanisms Associated with Writing Motivation	57
Table 3.1	Causal Mechanisms Associated with Working Memory	85
Table 4.1	Causal Mechanisms Associated with Group Differences in Content Knowledge	98
Table 5.1	Causal Mechanisms Associated with Group Differences in Working Memory	111
Table 6.1	Causal Mechanisms Associated with Group Differences in Transcription Skills	126

Introduction

Writing is important.

Writing is hard.

Which means that skilled writers have an advantage in school, on the job market, and in their chosen professions.

Writing is a critical 21st-century skill (Yancey, 2009; Perin, 2013). The ability to write well is a crucial in a variety of professional roles (College Board, 2004; Rios, Ling, Pugh, Becker, & Macall, 2020). In college applications, students commonly submit admissions essays. When candidates apply for professional positions, they typically provide application letters. resumes, and often, professional writing samples. On the job, they will draft emails and memoranda, write reports, and create other written products. In short, writing can smooth or hinder entry into the upper tiers of American society.

This fact makes writing an important educational goal. In a democratic society, all citizens should be able to learn the skills they need. And yet many students are not making adequate progress in writing. The National Assessment of Educational Progress (NAEP) provides a snapshot of U.S. student performance. On the 2011 NAEP writing assessment, only 24 % of students were classified as "Proficient", and 3 % as "Advanced", in either 8th or 12th grade. The rest demonstrated at best partial mastery of the writing skills expected at their level (NCES, 2012).[1] In fact, much of the U.S. population (even graduates from 2- and 4-year colleges) appear to enter the workforce inadequately prepared as writers (Casner-Lotto & Barrington, 2006; Kirsch, Braun, Yamamoto, & Sum, 2007; Stewart, Wall, & Marciniec, 2016).

Evidence of Group Differences in Writing Achievement

However, some student groups demonstrate lower levels of writing proficiency than others. In the 2011 NAEP writing assessment, very few students achieved proficient or advanced standing if their families had low socioeconomic status (SES). For instance, in 8th grade, only 12 % of students qualifying for free and reduced lunch scored as proficient or advanced, versus 37 % of the remaining population. This gap—about 30 points on the NAEP scale—is almost one full standard deviation below the mean for the higher-scoring group.

Similar effects can be observed for racial and ethnic groups likely to be poor or suffer from discrimination.[2] Compared to the White population, Black and Hispanic students had lower mean NAEP writing scores. In 8th grade, there was a 26-point gap between White and Black students and a 22-point gap between White and Hispanic students. In 12th-grade, there was a 29-point gap between White and Black students, and a 25-point gap between White and Hispanic students. While some groups (in particular, Asian and multiracial students) performed comparabaly with White students, the general pattern was for students from minority groups to demonstrate lower performance on NAEP writing. This

---

1 Unfortunately, the 2011 NAEP Writing assessment is the most recent nationally representative dataset that provides national information about student writing achievement. The 2017 NAEP Writing Assessment encountered technical difficulties which made it impossible to compare determine whether shifts in student performance were due to levels of student ability or due to shifts in the testing platform, which was administered on tablets for the first time in 2017 (NCES, 2017).

2 Note that throughout this book, I will use categories collected by the U.S. federal government in census forms and educational surveys and assessments. These are the demographic categories analyzed in most of the research literature. The limitations imposed by this scheme must always be taken into account. For example, it will not be possible to say much about smaller, or recently recognized groups. And of course, it is important to resist the temptation to overgeneralize, since there is, almost always, far more variation between individuals within a group than there ever is between groups. Group differences matter because they reveal differences in the support and opportunities afforded to individuals from different backgrounds and communities, not because they suggest or confirm social stereotypes.

pattern develops early and persists. Many students from disadvantaged groups fall steadily behind not only in writing but in other academic subjects (Kuhlfeld, Gershoff, & Paschall, 2018).

There is also a significant gap between male and female students (Kim, Al-Otaiba, Wanzek, & Gatlin, 2015). There is an overall advantage for girls, though boys show greater variability (Bourke & Adams, 2011) and demonstrate specific advantages in some areas such as grammatical complexity (Jones & Myhill, 2007). Boys from minority or low-SES backgrounds are particularly at risk (Engelhard, Walker, Gordon, & Gabrielson, 1994). On the 2011 NAEP writing test, only 6 % of 12th-grade Black males were rated as proficient or advanced, compared to 12 % of Black females, 27 % of White males, and 43 % of White females (NCES, 2012). Similar patterns can be observed for other variables, such as eligibility for free and advanced lunch. Only 7 % of low-SES 12th-grade males were rated as proficient or advanced, compared to 15 % of low-SES females, 26 % of higher-SES males, and 41 % of higher-SES females. Even worse, the male/female achievement gap grows over time (Scheiber, Reynolds, Hajovsky, & Kaufman, 2015). The gender gap for writing is probably greatest among adults (Kaufman, Kaufman, Liu, & Johnson, 2009).

These patterns parallel differences in many other educational statistics: dropout and suspension rates, reading and math achievement, high school graduation rates, and college enrollment/completion (Goldin, Katz, & Kuziemko, 2006; Stoet & Geary, 2020). Across the board, the pattern favors White students over minorities, females over males, and students from affluent backgrounds over students from poorer or immigrant backgrounds (de Brey, Musu, McFarland, Wilkinson-Flicker, Diliberti, Zhang, … & Wang, 2019). On the 2019 NAEP Reading test, 42 % of 12th-grade females, but only 32 % of 12th-grade males tested as Proficient or higher. 47 % of White 12th-grade students, but only 17 % of Black 12th-grade students, tested as Proficient or higher. 48 % of students whose parents had college degrees tested as proficient or higher, but only 20 % of students whose parents did not finish high school (NCES, 2019a, 2019b).

NAEP 2022 Math and Reading results indicate a negative impact of COVID 19 on student performance (NCES, 2022a, 2022b). The average NAEP math score dropped by 5 points for 4th grade, and by 8 points for 8th. The average NAEP reading score dropped by 3 points for both 4th and 8th graders. In both math and reading, score decreases were larger for the lowest-performing students. Math scores for students above the 90th percentile dropped by 2%, but scores for the lowest quartile dropped by 7%. Reading scores for students above the 90th percentile showed no significant change, but lowest quartile reading scores dropped by 5%. In both math and reading, scores showed greater drops for African

American and Hispanic than for White students. State end-of-year tests showed similar patterns. Post-COVD, performance dropped on state math and ELA assessments, and disparities between advantaged and traditionally underserved groups increased (Jack, Halloran, Okun, & Oster, 2022).

This evidence suggests that disparities in writing achievement, as measured by standardized writing assessments, form part of a larger, systemic pattern.

Deficits vs. Assets: Or, What Is Really Going On?

Historically, achievement gaps have often been perceived as evidence that traditionally underserved groups are doing something wrong. Proponents of such "deficit-based" accounts identify features of the disadvantaged group that they view as causally responsible for lower performance—such as family structure (Moynihan, 1965), the way parents talk to their children (Hart & Risley, 1995), or class-based differences in dialect and register (Bernstein, 1960). Deficit-based models have been broadly criticized on the grounds that they ignore the funds of knowledge and other cultural assets that students from minority groups have at their disposal (Flores, Cousin, & Diaz, 1991; Moll, Amanti, Neff, & Gonzalez, 1992; Scales, Benson, Leffert, & Blyth, 2000) and prevent educators from adopting more effective "asset-based" educational methods that build on student strengths rather than highlighting weaknesses (Ladson-Billings, 1995; Scales et al., 2000), thereby providing more equitable opportunities to learn (Moss, Pullin, Gee, Haertel, & Young, 2008).

Over the past 20 to 30 years, these criticisms have been amplified in various ways. For instance, some critics have argued that the educational system creates structural impediments for students from traditionally underserved groups (Alemán, 2009), for instance, by imposing upper-middle-class cultural norms and disciplining students who do not conform to those norms (Skiba & Williams, 2014; Mallett, 2017). More generally, Khalifa, Gooden, and Davis (2016) argue that "it is deleterious for students to have their cultural identities rejected in school and unacknowledged as integral to student learning." Other critics have focused on standardized assessments, including standardized writing assessments, and criticized the idea that they can be truly neutral, advocating instead for more culturally responsive forms of assessment that reflect and respect cultural context (Gordon & Bonilla-Bowman, 1996; Hood, 1998; Nortvedt, Wiese, Brown, Burns … & Taneri, 2020; Randall, 2021).

Recommendations for culturally relevant (Gutiérrez & Rogoff, 2003), culturally responsive (Gay, 2010), and culturally sustaining (Paris, 2012) pedagogies focus on changing classroom dynamics. They advocate training teachers to:

- engage with the communities from which their students are drawn
- respect community norms and cultural practices
- motivate and engage students by connecting academic work with local cultural contexts and practices
- empower students to engage with issues of concern to themselves and their communities and develop deeper, critically informed perspectives.

Emerging evidence indicates that such pedagogies can help students from diverse backgrounds learn more effectively (Piazza, Rao, & Protacio, 2015; Byrd, 2016; Larson, Pas, Bradshaw, Rosenberg, & Day-Vines, 2018; Mackay & Strickland, 2018).

However, there is a difference between arguing for a general educational philosophy and mapping out how to improve educational outcomes for a specific skill. It is important to understand how writing achievement gaps develop and to determine the causal mechanisms that help students from diverse backgrounds become effective writers. What writing skills do students need to develop? What circumstances make writing skills easier, or harder, to acquire, and how are those circumstances affected by cultural, social, and psychological variables? How can cultural strengths and assets be used to empower students as writers? More generally, what instructional practices will motivate and engage student writers from diverse backgrounds? To answer these questions, we need to understand how writing works, how it is learned, and how it can be equitably taught. That is what this book is about.

Continuities vs. Discontinuities in Writing Development

This book assumes that writing is fundamentally a single construct. But as students move through the American educational system, they pass through discrete institutions—elementary and middle schools, high schools, colleges and universities—with discrete goals and expectations. At each level, the writing construct is defined differently, and different instructional goals are set. For instance, at the elementary level, writing instruction emphasizes transcription skills (i.e., handwriting and spelling). Elementary writing assessment methods, such as curriculum-based measurement of writing (CBM-W) reflect this emphasis (Dockrell, Connelly, Walther, & Critten, 2015). By contrast, college level construct definitions, such as the CCCC position statement, Principles for the Postsecondary Teaching of Writing (CCCC Executive Committee, 2015), focus on the rhetorical and social nature of writing and emphasize deliberation and critical thinking. And yet, even in elementary school, writing is (or at least, should be) a meaningful, communicative act (Green & Steber, 2021). Conversely, even at the college level, transcription fluency can have a major impact on writing quality (Lovett, Lewandowski, Berger, & Gathje, 2010). This book argues that common factors affect writing achievement from elementary school to college. As students move through the educational system, the relative importance of these factors may vary, but at any level, it would be a grave mistake to ignore them. A more balanced, integrated approach to writing instruction is needed to produce equitable outcomes and maximize student chances of success.

How to Use This Book

This book is intended to help educators, school and district leaders, and policymakers make evidence-based curricular decisions. Chapter One looks at the challenges that make writing a particularly difficult skill for students to master or for teachers to teach. Chapters Two through Six highlight critical causal factors and explore how these factors affect students from different backgrounds. Chapters Seven reviews best practices in writing instruction and discusses critical issues that arise when those practices are implemented in schools. The chief purpose of this book is to inform educators about why students from diverse backgrounds may perform well or poorly on school writing tasks and to show them when, why, and how educational best practices are likely to work.

Note, however, that this book is not intended as a practical guide to implementing best practices. Such resources exist and are referenced where appropriate. But before educators decide to implement a particular pedagogical approach, they need to understand why common practices can have inequitable outcomes and develop a clear understanding of how to provide a systematic and effective response.

How This Book Is Structured

This book is structured as follows:

> **Chapter One: Why writing is hard.** This chapter reviews the factors that make writing a complex skill. Writers need to manage a hierarchy of goals (social, rhetorical, conceptual, linguistic, and orthographic). Each of these goals is

associated with different standards for quality, which means that writers are constantly balancing the demands imposed by competing standards while managing multiple, competing writing processes. These processes include the need to plan, produce, monitor, and revise one's own writing, and (depending on the specific requirements of specific discourse communities) to evaluate and respond to the writing of others.

It is useful to distinguish between everyday forms of writing (where fast, efficient production is prioritized over maximizing text quality to facilitate direct communication with an audience) and more formal, often professional forms of writing (where complex planning, review, and revision processes may be enforced to maximize the quality of published texts). While formal writing demands greater, more sustained efforts than everyday writing, all writing requires fluency, and fluency presupposes prerequisite knowledge and skills. These prerequisite demands are subject to variation both among individuals and between groups and mediate both learning and achievement. They scale up steadily, especially at the transitions from primary to secondary school, secondary school to college, and from college to postgraduate or professional training.

Chapter Two: Writing as Purposeful Action: Motivation for writing as cause and effect. This chapter explores connections between motivation, social identity formation, and writing achievement. Writing achievement can be affected by what an individual believes about writing, by their personal sense of self-efficacy, and by how writing fits (or does not fit) their developing sense of social identity. When school genre norms clash with the rhetorical norms and values of specific cultural or ethnic groups, this dynamic can lead to group disparities in writing achievement. Negative outcomes are particularly likely when the subjects valued in school differentially engage the interest of students from different groups, or when the school culture creates unhealthy and often inequitable forms of competition.

Chapter Three: Writing as Self-Regulation: The role of attention and working memory. This chapter explores the link between self-regulation, executive control, working memory, and writing achievement. Writing takes careful management even in everyday writing where there is relatively little effort devoted to planning, revision, and editing. The writer must juggle *ideation* (idea generation and planning), *translation* (sentence composition), *transcription* (handwriting or typing), and *monitoring* (rereading to identify needs for corrections and revisions) . These processes compete with one another and other cognitive processes for attentional resources. Anything which reduces attention and working memory capacity therefore reduces writing performance. This can lead to disparities in writing achievement. Sophisticated, flexible reading skills are a critical prerequisite to effective self-regulation strategies for writing. As a result, students from groups with weaker average reading achievement may also fall behind in writing. Economic and family stress—or stressful school situations—also make it harder to focus on complex writing tasks. Poverty-induced anxiety and stereotype threats pose a particular threat to students from poorer communities and from communities of color.

Chapter Four: Writing as the Formulation of Ideas: The mediating effects of prior content knowledge. This chapter reviews evidence that content knowledge facilitates writing performance. In general, students with relevant topic knowledge produce stronger texts for less effort than students with weaker topic knowledge, while showing evidence of greater fluency. There are obvious links to socioeconomic status and gender: low socioeconomic status is associated with weaker knowledge about the topics students are usually asked to write about in school, even if they know more about subjects less likely to be assessed. Students may be perceived as weak writers on school tasks yet write effectively in other contexts. Links between prior knowledge and gender are less clear. However, literacy instruction in the early grades tends to emphasize narrative and avoid writing that explores specific, factual content, which may align early school writing tasks with stereotypically female-gendered content.

Chapter Five: Writing as Verbal Self-Expression: The causal role of oral language skills. In the early stages of writing development, writing performance is largely driven by oral language skills plus transcription (e.g., handwriting and spelling). Low oral language skills are thus associated with lower academic performance, and specifically weaker writing. Control of oral language can be a particular issue for second language learners and students with secondary language impairment. Everyday experience with academic vocabulary and formal registers can also give students whose home dialect is upper-middle-class English an advantage on academic writing tasks. A critical issue is whether schools value flexibility in language use and encourage students to adapt their speaking and writing styles to a variety of social and cultural contexts.

Chapter Six: Writing as Getting Words on the Page: The effects of transcription skills on writing development. Transcription occurs when writers use pen or keyboard to physically (or digitally) inscribe their texts. Transcription combines motor skills (handwriting or typing) with linguistic skills (e.g., spelling), and as such, requires focused attention and practice. There are significant group differences in handwriting and spelling achievement, which may reflect differences in the quality of instruction, differences in access to technology, or differences in support for at-home and community literacy practices associated with community SES. Students with weak transcription skills spend more time and effort just getting words on the page, which increases cognitive load and reduces the time and attention they can devote to idea generation, planning, and revision. This dynamic guarantees that students with early advantages in transcription and spelling will find writing tasks significantly easier. Such advantages tend to compound over time.

Chapter Seven: How to Achieve Equity in School Writing. This chapter reviews the literature on best practices in writing instruction. When best instructional practices are reframed to focus on achieving equity in writing instruction, we obtain the following theory of action (Figure I.1). The rest of this book explains how these pieces fit together.

As this figure suggests, improving writing instruction—and achieving equity in student writing achievement—requires a holistic, integrated approach. Nine different causal factors must be considered. To improve student writing, it is necessary to (1) increase writing motivation; (2) improve self-regulation of writing; (3) develop deeper knowledge about writing and writing strategies; (4) develop deeper content knowledge; (5) improve idea generation; (6) increase effective working memory capacity; (7) strengthen language skills, (8) improve transcription skills, and (9) improve reading skills. Each of these mechanisms is supported by a variety of studies, including meta-analyses that establish the efficacy of specific interventions.

The model hypothesizes multiple causal connections, some of them recursive. Higher levels of writing motivation are likely to cause people to work harder and devote more attention to writing, thereby increasing their working memory capacity and enabling more effective self-regulation. When students develop deeper knowledge about writing and writing strategies, they have an easier time generating ideas and implementing specific writing strategies. When students acquire deeper content knowledge, they will find it more interesting and generate ideas more fluently. And of course, fluent idea generation and strong self-regulation produce stronger writing performance.

Moving to the other side of Figure I.1, effective working memory capacity plays a key role. It can be increased by building motivation, self-regulation, content knowledge, idea generation, and foundational literacy skills (including oral

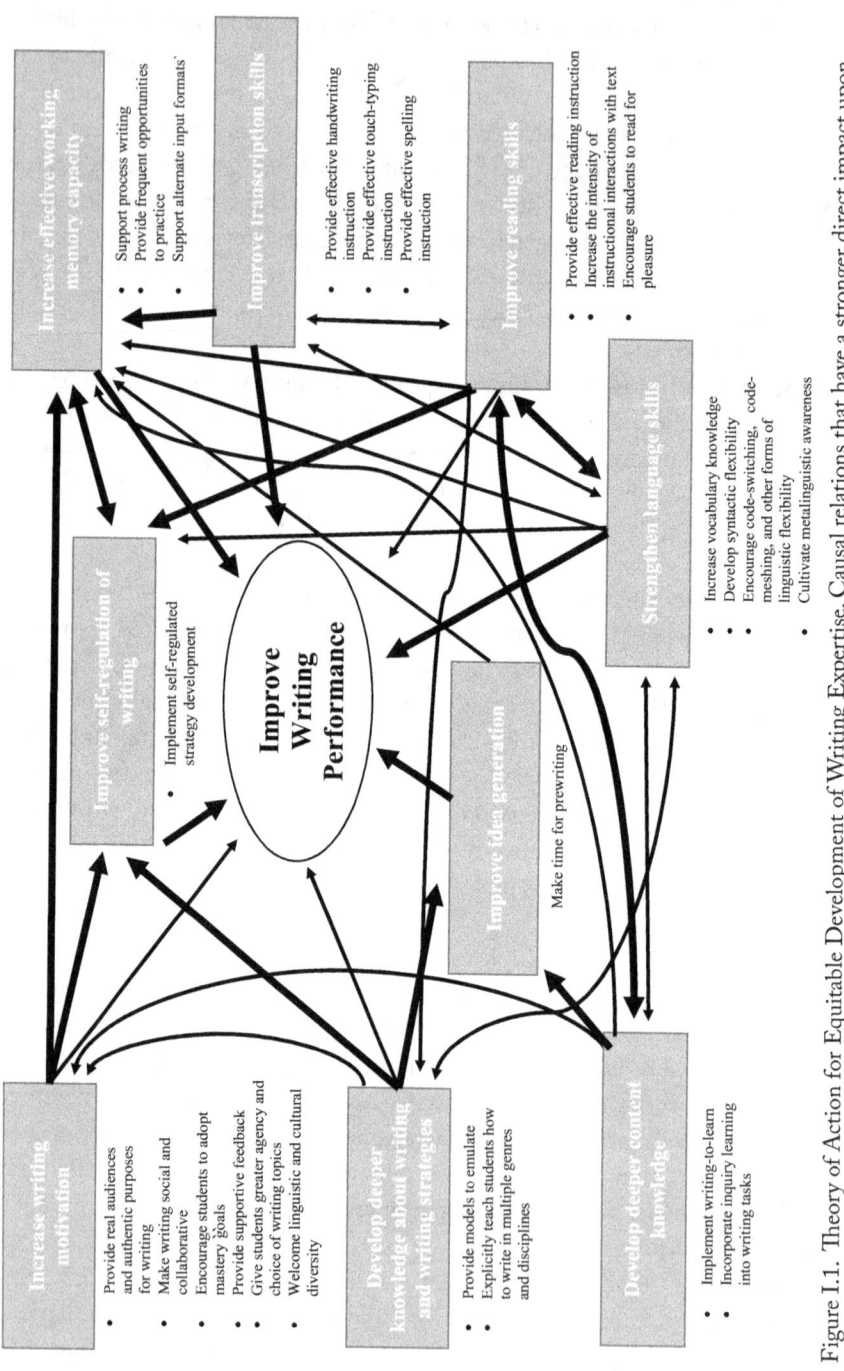

Figure I.1. Theory of Action for Equitable Development of Writing Expertise. Causal relations that have a stronger direct impact upon writing performance are shown with wider arrow

language, reading, and transcription). Foundational skills are mutually reinforcing, and (through extensive interaction with texts), causally associated with increases in content knowledge. They critically affect higher-order processes, especially through their impact on effective working memory capacity.

The rest of this book motivates this theory of action, showing how the causal mechanisms described in Figure I.1 play out when schools continue instructional business as usual, and identifying how schools can adjust instruction to teach writing both effectively and equitably.

A Personal Note: Context and Perspective

Much recent work on literacy emphasizes context and perspective. It is therefore appropriate to pause at this point to provide some personal context and perspective about who I am, what background I bring to this work, what perspectives I take as an author—and thus what I bring to the table as an interpreter of the evidence on writing skill development.

I obtained my Ph.D. in theoretical linguistics at the University of Chicago in the mid-1980s, during the cognitive turn in psychology and the social sciences. The Chicago linguistics program had an interdisciplinary focus; I studied under professors in the linguistics, psychology, anthropology, and Near Eastern Studies departments. In my early work, I focused on how word meanings develop and the cognitive mechanisms that enable people to extend them flexibly in context. I observed interesting connections between those mechanisms and standard problems in transformational grammar. In *Grammar in Mind and Brain: Explorations in Cognitive Syntax* (Deane, 1986), I drew on evidence from linguistics, psycholinguistics, and neuropsychology to link grammatical theory to how the brain manages attention. At the time, I was working in a university English department, where first-year composition classes accounted for half my course load. As I learned how to teach writing, I also began to see connections between psycholinguistic and cognitive theories and the learning needs of developing writers.

A series of career turns brought me into industry, first as a lexicographer, then as a computational linguist, where I worked for startup companies trying to build search engines that would be sensitive to meaning. When I joined Educational Testing Service (ETS) as a research scientist, I entered an environment built around interdisciplinary collaboration in multicultural teams, where I worked regularly with teachers, assessment developers, statisticians, cognitive scientists, and education researchers from a variety of countries, languages, and social backgrounds.

At ETS, I have worked on computational applications, such as e-rater®, ETS' automated writing evaluation engine, innovative approaches to literacy assessment, and foundational literacy research. I have studied innovative approaches to writing assessment (Deane, Wilson, Zhang, Li, Guo, … & Richter, 2021), ways to use vocabulary assessment to support instruction (McKeown, Deane, Scott, Krovetz, & Lawless, 2017), and led the development of frameworks for describing, scaffolding, and measuring literacy learning and linking it to effective classroom practices (Deane & Song, 2014; Deane, Sabatini, Feng, Sparks, Song, Fowles, … & Foley, C., 2015; O'Reilly, Deane, & Sabatini, 2015; Sparks & Deane, 2015; Bennett, Deane, & van Rijn, 2016)

One of my graduate program professors, who had worked on the American Dialect Atlas, was one of the few people to place my (very general American) accent correctly: and what he said was, "Third generation immigrant, upwardly mobile, suburban." Which is fair enough: my parents were first generation college students, and my father's parents were immigrants from the Caribbean. My life and cultural background thus fall solidly within the typical arc of members of the Baby Boomer generation who came from immigrant backgrounds, but from communities that encountered few barriers to their assimilation into the dominant culture. As such, I cannot and do not claim to speak for people from communities with different experiences, but my training, background, and work experience have prepared me very well for dealing with the complexities, both cognitive and sociolinguistic, of writing in the 21st century.

What I bring to the subject of writing development, more than anything else, is a deeply interdisciplinary perspective, generally sociocognitive in orientation (Mislevy, 2018). I have long developed the habit of looking for links and causal connections across disciplinary boundaries, which is to say: by integrating multiple perspectives. I hope this book will help its readers to make those kinds of connections among the various disciplines concerned with writing.

Reference List

Alemán Jr, E. (2009). LatCrit educational leadership and advocacy: Struggling over Whiteness as property in Texas school finance. *Equity & Excellence in Education, 42*(2), 183–201. https://doi.org/10.1080/10665680902744246

Bennett, R. E., Deane, P., & van Rijn, P. W. (2016). From cognitive-domain theory to assessment practice. *Educational Psychologist, 51*(1), 82–107. https://doi.org/10.1080/00461520.2016.1141683

Bernstein, B. (1960). Language and social class. *The British Journal of Sociology, 11*(3), 271–276. https://doi.org/10.2307/586750

Bourke, L., & Adams, A.-M. (2011). Is it differences in language skills and working memory that account for girls being better at writing than boys? *Journal of Writing Research, 3*(3), 249–277. https://doi.org/10.17239/jowr-2012.03.03.5

Byrd, C. M. (2016). Does culturally relevant teaching work? An examination from student perspectives. *SAGE Open, 6*(3), 1–10. https://doi.org/10.1177/2158244016660744

Casner-Lotto, J., & Barrington, L. (2006). *Are They Really Ready to Work? Employers' Perspectives on the Basic Knowledge and Applied Skills of New Entrants to the 21st Century US Workforce.* Partnership for 21st-Century Skills. https://files.eric.ed.gov/fulltext/ED519465.pdf

CCCC Executive Committee. (2015). Principles for the postsecondary teaching of writing. *National Council of Teachers of English.* https://cccc.ncte.org/cccc/resources/positions/postsecondarywriting

College Board. (2004). *Writing: A Ticket to Work ... or a Ticket Out. A Survey of Business Leaders.* National Commisssion on Writing. https://archive.nwp.org/cs/public/download/nwp_file/21479/writing-ticket-to-work.pdf?x-r=pcfile_d

de Brey, C., Musu, L., McFarland, J., Wilkinson-Flicker, S., Diliberti, M., Zhang, A., ... & Wang, X. (2019). *Status and Trends in the Education of Racial and Ethnic Groups 2018 (NCES 2019–038).* National Center for Education Statistics. https://eric.ed.gov/?id=ED592833

Deane, P. D. (1986). *Grammar in Mind and Brain: Explorations in Cognitive Syntax.* Mouton De Gruyter. https://doi.org/10.1515/9783110886535

Deane, P., & Song, Y. (2014). A case study in principled assessment design: Designing assessments to measure and support the development of argumentative reading and writing skills. *Psicología Educativa, 20*(2), 99–108. https://doi.org/10.1016/j.pse.2014.10.001

Deane, P. D., Sabatini, J., Feng, G., Sparks, J., Song, Y., Fowles, M., ... Foley, C. (2015). *Key Practices in the English Language Arts (ELA): Linking Learning Theory, Assessment, and Instruction* (RR-15-24). Educational Testing Service. https://doi.org/10.1002/ets2.12063

Deane, P. D., Wilson, J., Zhang, M., Li, C., van Rijn, P., Guo, H., ... & Richter, T. (2021). The sensitivity of a scenario-based assessment of written argumentation to school differences in curriculum and instruction. *International Journal of Artificial Intelligence in Education, 31*(1), 57–98. https://doi.org/10.1007/s40593-020-00227-x

Dockrell, J. E., Connelly, V., Walter, K., & Critten, S. (2015). Assessing children's writing products: the role of curriculum-based measures. *British Educational Research Journal, 41*(4), 575–595. https://doi.org/10.1002/berj.3162

Engelhard, G., Walker, E. V. S., Gordon, B., & Gabrielson, S. (1994). Writing tasks and gender: Influences on the writing quality of Black and White students. *Journal of Educational Research, 87*(4), 197–209. https://doi.org/10.1080/00220671.1994.9941244

Flores, B., Cousin, P. T., & Diaz, E. (1991). Transforming deficit myths about learning, language, and culture. *Language Arts, 68*(5), 369–379.

Gay, G. (2010). *Culturally Responsive Teaching: Theory, Research, and Practice.* Teachers College Press.

Goldin, C., Katz, L. F., & Kuziemko, I. (2006). The homecoming of American college women: The reversal of the college gender gap. *The Journal of Economic Perspectives, 20*(4), 133–156. https://doi.org/10.1257/jep.20.4.133

Gordon, E. W., & Bonilla-Bowman, C. (1996). Chapter II: Can performance-based assessments contribute to the achievement of educational equity? *Teachers College Record, 97*(5), 32–51. https://doi.org/10.1177/016146819609700502

Green, J., & Steber, K. (2021). The evolution of an elementary writing workshop: Fostering teacher efficacy and authentic authorship in young writers. *Teaching/Writing: The Journal of Writing Teacher Education, 10*(1), Article 3. https://scholarworks.wmich.edu/wte/vol10/iss1/3

Gutiérrez, K., & Rogoff, B. (2003). Cultural ways of learning: Individual traits or repertoires of practice. *Educational Researcher, 32*(5), 19–25. https://doi.org/10.3102/0013189X032005019

Hart, B., & Risley, T. R. (1995). *Meaningful Differences in the Everyday Experience of Young American Children.* Paul H Brookes.

Hood, S. (1998). Culturally responsive performance-based assessment: Conceptual and psychometric considerations. *Journal of Negro Education, 67*(3), 187–196. https://doi.org/10.2307/2668188

Jack, R., Halloran, C., Okun, J., & Oster, E. (2022). *Pandemic Schooling Mode and Student Test Scores: Evidence from US School Districts* (NBER Working Paper 29497). National Bureau of Economic Research. https://doi.org/10.3386/w29497

Jones, S., & Myhill, D. (2007). Discourses of difference? Examining gender differences in linguistic characteristics of writing. *Canadian Journal of Education / Revue Canadienne de L'Éducation, 30*(2), 456–482. https://doi.org/10.2307/20466646

Kaufman, A. S., Kaufman, J. C., Liu, X., & Johnson, C. K. (2009). How do educational attainment and gender relate to fluid intelligence, crystallized intelligence, and academic skills at ages 22–90 years? *Archives of Clinical Neuropsychology, 24*(2), 153–163. https://doi.org/10.1093/arclin/acp015

Khalifa, M. A., Gooden, M. A., & Davis, J. E. (2016). Culturally responsive school leadership: A synthesis of the literature. *Review of Educational Research, 86*(4), 1272–1311. https://doi.org/10.3102/0034654316630383

Kim, Y.-S., Al-Otaiba, S., Wanzek, J., & Gatlin, B. (2015). Toward an understanding of dimensions, predictors, and the gender gap in written composition. *Journal of Educational Psychology, 107*(1), 79–95. https://doi.org/10.1037/a0037210

Kirsch, I., Braun, H., Yamamoto, K., & Sum, A. (2007). *America's Perfect Storm: Three Forces Changing Our Nation's Future.* Educational Testing Service. https://files.eric.ed.gov/fulltext/ED496620.pdf

Kuhlfeld, M., Gershoff, E., & Paschall, K. (2018). The development of racial/ethnic and socioeconomic achievement gaps during the school years. *Journal of Applied Developmental Psychology*, (57), 62–73. https://doi.org/10.1016/j.appdev.2018.07.001

Ladson-Billings, G. (1995). But that's just good teaching! The case for culturally relevant pedagogy. *Theory Into Practice*, *34*(3), 159–165. https://doi.org/10.1080/00405849509543675

Larson, K. E., Pas, E. T., Bradshaw, C. P., Rosenberg, M. S., & Day-Vines, N. L. (2018). Examining how proactive management and culturally responsive teaching relate to student behavior: Implications for measurement and practice. *School Psychology Review*, *47*(2), 153–166. https://doi.org/10.17105/SPR-2017-0070.V47-2

Lovett, B. J., Lewandowski, L. J., Berger, C., & Gathje, R. A. (2010). Effects of response mode and time allotment on college students' writing. *Journal of College Reading and Learning*, *40*(2), 64–79. https://doi.org/10.1080/10790195.2010.10850331

Mackay, H., & Strickland, M. J. (2018). Exploring culturally responsive teaching and student-created videos in an at-risk middle school classroom. *Middle Grades Review*, *4*(1), 1–15. Retrieved from https://scholarworks.uvm.edu/mgreview/vol4/iss1/7

Mallett, C. A. (2017). The school-to-prison pipeline: Disproportionate impact on vulnerable children and adolescents. *Education and Urban Society*, *49*(6), 563–592. https://doi.org/10.1007/s10560-015-0397-1

McKeown, M. G., Deane, P. D., Scott, J. A., Krovetz, R., & Lawless, R. R. (2017). *Vocabulary Assessment to Support Instruction: Building Rich Word Learning Experiences*. Guilford.

Mislevy, R. J. (2018). *Sociocognitive Foundations of Educational Measurement*. Routledge.

Moll, L. C., Amanti, C., Neff, D., & Gonzalez, N. (1992). Funds of knowledge for teaching: Using a qualitative approach to connect homes and classrooms. *Theory into Practice*, *31*(2), 132–141. https://doi.org/10.1080/00405849209543534

Moss, P. A., Pullin, D. C., Gee, J. P., Haertel, E. H., & Young, L. J. (Eds.). (2008). *Assessment, equity, and opportunity to learn*. Cambridge University Press.Moynihan, D. P. (1965). *The Negro Family: The Case for National Action*. United States Department of Labor, Office of Policy Planning and Research. https://www.blackpast.org/african-american-history/moynihan-report-1965/

NCES. (2012). *The Nation's Report Card: Vocabulary Results from 2009 and 2011 NAEP Reading Assessments* (NCES 2013–452). U.S. Department of Education, National Center for Education Statistics. https://nces.ed.gov/nationsreportcard/pdf/main2011/2013452.pdf

NCES. (2017). *Technical Summary of Preliminary Analyses of NAEP 2017 Writing Assessments*. U.S. Department of Education, National Center for Education Statistics. https://nces.ed.gov/nationsreportcard/subject/writing/pdf/2017_writing_technical_summary.pdf

NCES. (2019a). *The Nation's Report Card: 2019 NAEP Reading Assessment* [4th and 8th Grades]. U.S. Department of Education, National Center for Education Statistics. https://www.nationsreportcard.gov/highlights/reading/2019/

NCES. (2019b). *The Nation's Report Card: 2019 NAEP Reading Assessment* [12th Grade]. U.S. Department of Education, National Center for Education Statistics. https://www.nationsreportcard.gov/highlights/reading/2019/g12/

NCES. (2022a). *The Nation's Report Card: 2022 Reading Assessment* [4th and 8th Grades]. U.S. Department of Education, National Center for Education Statistics. https://www.nationsreportcard.gov/highlights/reading/2022/

NCES. (2022b). *The Nation's Report Card: 2022 Reading Assessment* [12th Grade]. U.S. Department of Education, National Center for Education Statistics. https://www.nationsreportcard.gov/highlights/mathematics/2019/g12/

Nortvedt, G. A., Wiese, E., Brown, M., Burns, D., McNamara, G., O'Hara, J., ... & Taneri, P. O. (2020). Aiding culturally responsive assessment in schools in a globalising world. *Educational Assessment, Evaluation and Accountability, 32*(1), 5–27. https://doi.org/10.1007/s11092-020-09316-w

O'Reilly, T., Deane, P., & Sabatini, J. (2015*). Building and Sharing Knowledge Key Practice: What Do You Know, What Don't You Know, What Did You Learn?* (RR-15-24). Educational Testing Service. https://doi.org/10.1002/ets2.12074

Paris, D. (2012). Culturally sustaining pedagogy: A needed change in stance, terminology, and practice. *Educational Researcher, 41*(3), 93–97. https://doi.org/10.3102/0013189X12441244

Perin, D. (2013). Best practices in teaching writing for college and career readiness. In S. Graham, C. A. MacArthur, & J. Fitzgerald (Eds.), *Best Practices in Writing Instruction* (pp. 48–72). Guilford.

Piazza, S. V., Rao, S., & Protacio, M. S. (2015). Converging recommendations for culturally responsive literacy practices: Students with learning disabilities, English language learners, and socioculturally diverse learners. *International Journal of Multicultural Education, 17*(3), 1–20. https://doi.org/10.18251/ijme.v17i3.1023

Randall, J. (2021). "Color-Neutral" is not a thing: Redefining construct definition and representation through a justice-oriented critical antiracist lens. *Educational Measurement: Issues and Practice, 40*(4), 82–90. https://doi.org/10.1111/emip.12429

Rios, J. A., Ling, G., Pugh, R., Becker, D., & Bacall, A. (2020). Identifying critical 21st-century skills for workplace success: A content analysis of job advertisements. *Educational Researcher, 49*(2), 80–89. https://doi.org/10.3102/0013189X19890600

Scales, P. C., Benson, P. L., Leffert, N., & Blyth, D. A. (2000). Contribution of developmental assets to the prediction of thriving among adolescents. *Applied Developmental Science, 4*(1), 27–46. https://psycnet.apa.org/doi/10.1207/S1532480XADS0401_3

Scheiber, C., Reynolds, M. R., Hajovsky, D. B., & Kaufman, A. S. (2015). Gender differences in achievement in a large, nationally representative sample of children and adolescents. *Psychology in the Schools, 52*(4), 335–348. https://doi.org/10.1002/pits.21827

Skiba, R. J., & Williams, N. T. (2014). Are Black kids worse? Myths and facts about racial differences in behavior. *The Equity Project at Indiana University.* https://www.justice4all.org/wp-content/uploads/2016/04/Are-Black-Kids-Worse-Myths-and-Facts-About-Racial-Differences-in-Behavior.pdf

Sparks, J. R., & Deane, P. (2015). *Cognitively Based Assessment of Research and Inquiry Skills: Defining a Key Practice in the English Language Arts* (RR-15–35). Educational Testing Service. https://doi.org/10.1002/ets2.12082

Stewart, C., Wall, A., & Marciniec, S. (2016, July). Mixed signals: Do college graduates have the soft skills that employers want? *Competition Forum, 14*(2), 276–281. https://www.researchgate.net/profile/Alison-Wall/publication/316066488_Mixed_Signals_Do_College_Graduates_Have_the_Soft_Skills_That_Employers_Want/links/5ae86b62aca2725dabb40a10/Mixed-Signals-Do-College-Graduates-Have-the-Soft-Skills-That-Employers-Want.pdf

Stoet, G., & Geary, D. C. (2020). Gender differences in the pathways to higher education. *Proceedings of the National Academy of Sciences, 117*(25), 14073–14076. https://doi.org/10.1073/pnas.2002861117

Yancey, K. B. (2009). *Writing in the 21st Century*. National Council of Teachers of English. https://cdn.ncte.org/nctefiles/press/yancey_final.pdf

CHAPTER ONE

Why Writing is Hard

Writing is complex. It is an act of communication, takes place in a social context, follows social norms, and often requires collaboration. It draws on prior knowledge (to select and organize content) but also relies on critical-thinking and problem-solving skills. It requires the writer to present information effectively, structuring the text to accomplish rhetorical goals. Whatever the writer wants to say, it must be expressed, word by word, and sentence by sentence, to produce a coherent text that will communicate the author's message clearly and effectively. The writer must also transcribe the text onto the page, or enter it on a keyboard, following English orthographic conventions. This complex bundle of tasks must be planned and executed without exceeding the limits of working memory, all the while monitoring progress, and if necessary, working recursively to correct errors, edit language, or revise content.

The Cognitive Complexity of Writing

Some of my earlier work reviews the cognitive complexities of writing (Deane, 2011, 2013; Deane, Odendahl, Quinlan, Fowles, Welsh, & Bivens-Tatum, 2008). For an internal ETS research initiative, "Cognitively Based Assessments of, for, and as Learning" (CBAL), I undertook a wide-ranging series of literature reviews focused on understanding how writing skills develop and how their development can be supported. The most striking result of that research, at least for me, was the sheer complexity of what counted as high-quality writing. This fact shows up in standard rubrics for assessing writing. For instance, the National Writing Project's Writing Continuum assessment system holds writers accountable for:

- *content* (that is, the quality and clarity of ideas)
- *structure* (the use of text structures to communicate those ideas in a unified and coherent manner)
- *stance*, *style*, and *tone* (social and emotional framing of those ideas, expressed through a variety of linguistic choices)
- *sentence fluency* (linguistic structure, crafted to communicate ideas clearly and with appropriate emphasis and rhythm)
- *diction* (making word choices that communicate meaning precisely and powerfully)
- *conventions* (adhering to conventional expectations for grammar, usage, and mechanics)

(Bang, 2013)

Such standards are commonplace for writing instructors. But they implicate entirely different modes of thought: social and emotional, rational and logical, rhetorical and linguistic, creative and conventional.

Table 1.1 presents an array of skills implicated in writing. It captures salient distinctions from the cognitive psychology of writing processes (Flower & Hayes, 1980; Alamargot & Chanquoy, 2001; Hayes, 2012), including planning, translating (expressing ideas in words), transcribing (keyboarding or handwriting), and monitoring, while distinguishing between writing activities that implicate different forms of cognitive representation.

Coordinating this complex array of processes can be a challenge, since each process competes for limited working memory resources and makes heavy demands on the central executive system. When writers must devote too much to transcription and translation, their capacity to engage in planning and monitoring necessarily suffers (McCutchen, 1996; Kellogg, 2001; Kellogg, Whiteford, Turner, Cahill, & Mertens, 2013).

Such limitations are particularly problematic for novice writers, who typically take a knowledge-telling approach to writing (Bereiter & Scardamalia, 1987), in which they focus on retrieving and writing down what they know about a subject, with little effort to rethink or reconceptualize the content. Mastering writing is like developing other complex performance skills: it requires deliberate practice. More sophisticated writers switch focus strategically among writing subgoals. They avoid working memory limitations by adopting a more complex and recursive writing process. Their deeper knowledge of writing enables them to choose and orchestrate a sequence of effective writing strategies (Kellogg, 1999; McCutchen, 2011; Kellogg & Whiteford, 2012; Schriver, 2012).

Table 1.1 Classification of Writing Processes by Activity Type and Mode of Cognitive Representation[1]

	Plan before	Execute	Monitor during	Evaluate and Revise after
Social	Create a rhetorical plan	Control overall writing process to keep content, organization, style, and tone consistent with one's rhetorical purpose.	Track progress toward rhetorical goals and adjust subgoals as needed	Evaluate overall writing success; Rethink purpose, audience, and task, and revise accordingly
Conceptual	Set goals for information gathering	Recall or gather necessary information and organize what one knows about the subject	Track how well content fits overall goals; as needed, generate additional content or delete existing material.	Evaluate and revise for accuracy, completeness of information presented; validity of arguments, etc.
Text-Structural	Choose an organizational template appropriate to the task and genre	Organize the text appropriately, providing appropriate cues to help the reader keep track of the intended structure	Monitor and correct text-structure cues as needed	Evaluate and revise text to improve and more accurately signal the intended structure
Verbal	Plan how to present ideas, sentence by sentence, clause by clause, and phrase by phrase	Express one's ideas in words	Monitor and correct expression as needed to make sure that the text accurately conveys intended message	Evaluate and edit language to make sure that it is clear, unambiguous, and precise.
Orthographic	Access words; retrieve spellings and other orthographic details	Produce each word, letter by letter, whether on a keyboard or by hand	Monitor and correct typos, spelling errors, and other orthographic errors as needed.	Proofread an existing text and correct it as needed.

1 This table is replicated from Deane (2011) and is reproduced with permission from ETS.

The Sociocultural Complexity of Writing

Discussions of how people learn to write in social and cultural contexts suggest a similar level of complexity. For example, the National Council of Teachers of English' Guiding Principles for Understanding and Teaching Writing postulate the following principles:

- Writing is social and rhetorical
- Writing serves a variety of purposes
- Everyone is a writer
- Writers bring multiliteracies, and they bring cultural and linguistic assets to whatever they do
- Writers compose using different modes and technologies
- Writers compose inside and outside the classroom
- Writers grow within a context / culture / community of feedback
- Writers grow when they broaden their repertoire, and when they refine their judgment in making choices with their repertoire
- Assessment should be transparent and contextual, and it should provide opportunities for writers to take risks and grow.
- Writers grow when they have a range of writing experiences and in-depth writing experiences.

(Adler-Kassner, Baca, & Fredericksen, 2018)

Layered within these statements is a world of complexity, a world in which writers must juggle multiple forms and contexts for writing, become participants in multiple discourse communities, and learn how to manage a complex writing process in which feedback and collaboration are central. As Deborah Brandt argues in *Literacy in American Lives* (2001) and *The Rise of Writing* (2014), this complexity has arisen in large part due to economic changes that have driven the successive development of new literacies. During the 20th and early 21st centuries, the rise of mass media, the modern corporation, and the administrative state, the development of mainframe and personal computers, the advent of the world-wide web, and the development of social media have created new economic reasons for people to write as part of their jobs, and, increasingly, as part of their everyday lives. These changes have happened quickly, layering new contexts for writing on top of existing social structures. Much of the writing that people do at work is writing on behalf of someone else or for a corporation or government agency—as ghostwriters, speechwriters, as preparers of briefs, reports, training or technical manuals, white papers, press releases, emails, or social media posts—and is subject to review and revision by supervisors or collaborators before being released for public consumption.

However, writing is also embedded in a variety of everyday activities—recipes, shopping lists and sticky notes, personal notes and letters, entries in diaries and journals, text messages, chats, emails, and posts to social networking sites and personal blogs, to name a representative sample (Barton & Hamilton, 2000; Hull & Schultz, 2001). Individuals who do not identify as writers may be proficient in a variety of everyday writing activities (Hansford & Adlington, 2009; Brown, 2015). Writing thus ranges in complexity and immediacy. On one end of the scale, people may compose short texts quickly and fluently, in forms they are intimately familiar with, addressing topics they know well, to communicate with people who form an immediate part of their personal social network. At the other end of the scale, people may draft and revise complex texts with considerable effort, in consultation with collaborators, editors, reviewers, or supervisors, in genres they are still acquiring, addressing topics they need to research in depth, to communicate with an audience they have never met and may never meet in person and who may have values and assumptions very different than their own.

For convenience, I will refer to tasks toward the lower end of this scale as "everyday writing", and tasks toward the higher end of this scale as "professional writing". Of course, what counts as everyday or professional writing varies from person to person, from context to context, and across the lifespan (Bazerman, Applebee, Berninger, Brandt, Graham, Jeffery, ... & Wilcox, 2018). The social media post that a teenager creates in five minutes may draw upon skills that that same student developed with great effort as an elementary school student. The cheat sheet another student posts to an online forum, giving directions about how to beat a particular boss in an online RPG, may reflect knowledge and skills acquired from hundreds of hours spent playing and discussing the game in an online gaming community. The questions or comments that college students quickly draft and post to a class bulletin board may draw upon skills they developed—against, potentially after considerable instruction and effort—in middle school and high school. The email one of those students might quickly write and send to a friend, soliciting participation in a political protest, might be deeply rooted in cultural or community traditions. The memo that a business analyst dashes off for a supervisor, suggesting a particular sales strategy, may reflect both college writing experiences and years of training and professional development. Some older Americans, adapting to the need to compose digitally, might use voice-to-speech technology much as they used dictation during their business career (Yancey, 2020).

The sheer variety of contexts for writing and the rapid pace of technical change in writing practices and technologies mean that writers must acquire both general expertise and flexibility and control over a large repertoire of written genres.

The Complexity of Learning to Write

Learning to write is no simple process. As students move from school to college, and from college into the workplace, their repertoire, and more and more writing tasks require an elaborated process. Rhetorical goals become more complex and varied, and less immediately personal. Content becomes more abstract and less familiar. Text structure and diction may become specialized or academic and reflect a greater variety of social contexts and communities of practice (Wardle & Roozen, 2012). The escalating requirements of school and academic writing function are part of the process of socializing writers into professional and disciplinary communities (Prior, 1998; Duff, 2010) and typically happens on the job, as a form of cognitive apprenticeship (Beaufort, 2000; Leijten, Van Waes, Schriver, & Hayes, 2014).

At the highest levels of expertise, writing can be an elaborate process involving multiple collaborators, multiple drafts, multiple reviews, multiple revisions, and an extended editing process (Henry, 2000; Beaufort, 2008) . At this level, different aspects of the writing process define entire families of writing genres. Professional writers may produce task definition documents, such as calls for submissions and requests for proposals. They may submit book proposals and formal outlines. They may write content and editorial reviews. Along the way, they will deal with copyeditors and proofreaders, activities that require specialized forms of feedback and markup (Greco, Milliot, & Wharton, 2014; Ware & Mabe, 2015).

Historically, only a small percentage of people have become professional writers (though far more people need these skills than ever before). However, professional writing processes resemble recommended best practices in writing pedagogy (Graves, 1983; Pritchard & Honeycutt, 2007; Graham & Sandmel, 2011)[2]. In fact, as more and more writing practices have shifted online, it has

---

2 These pedagogies mostly originated as part of the "process" movement in composition studies (Graves, 1983). Process approaches have been criticized by postprocess theorists as being too quick to impose generalizations on the plethora of actual writing practices enacted by individual writers across a variety of writing contexts (Lotier, 2021). This critique should be born in mind, since there is much to criticize in a too-rigid instructional practice that forces students to go through stages of the writing process in lockstep, without consideration of the actual rhetorical context and the needs of individual students.

become clear that digital writing tools can provide effective pedagogical supports (Purcell, Buchanan, & Friedrich, 2013; Anderson, Mitchell, Thompson, & Trefz, 2014; Hazelton, Nastel, Elliott, Burstein, & McCaffrey, 2021), mostly because they make aspects of writing and the writing process collaborative and visible.

Brandt (2019) argues that writing is fundamentally a craft skill—meaningful because it supports meaningful work, and which is best therefore taught by a practitioner. This view of writing is fundamentally driven by the need to prepare students to thrive in a world where professional writing is a fact of life. In such a world, people need to learn how to navigate unfamiliar writing tasks and genres, familiarize themselves with new tools and technologies, gather the information they will need to write with confidence, evaluate how well their writing meets community expectations, and manage complex writing processes.

Higher engagement. Greater effort. Deeper reflection. Richer collaboration. This is what craft-based pedagies require. But if they set up some students to fail, they can be counterproductive. Students who have consistently received high-quality education -- whose parents work in the new information economy, and therefore have rich access to technology—who have organic access to "sponsors", as Brandt (2001) terms them, who can ease their transition into professional work—these are the students who will move smoothly from home to school and from school to the 21st-century workplace.

Consider, for a moment, the kinds of writing processes that are characteristic of everyday and professional writing—understanding, of course, that the distinction between everyday and professional writing is a heuristic that will match some writing practices better than others. More or less by definition, everyday writing involves the production of short texts for a well-defined, familiar purpose, about a well-understood topic, without the need for advance planning. Such texts are typically produced quickly with minimal editing or revision.

There is a name for this kind of process: it is called *knowledge-telling* (Bereiter & Scardamalia, 1987; Hayes, 2012). Since the 1980s, writing pedagogies have tried to teach students the strategies that will enable them to enact a more complex writing process, what Bereiter & Scardamalia term "knowledge-transforming", characterized by iterative, often cyclical or interleaved phrases of planning, drafting, review, and revision. Many of these stages include a significant role for evaluation and feedback by third parties. This sort of intensive, highly reflective writing process is what Kellogg (2008) calls *knowledge-crafting.*

However, in many contexts, knowledge-telling is not a sign of weak writing skill. It is simply the most efficient way to work. No one uses knowledge-crafting to write a shopping list, draft a short text message to a friend, or take notes during a lecture. If writers already know what kind of text to produce and have a clear mental outline of what they want to say and how they want to say it, planning and revision are a waste of time. The professional writing process is designed for exactly the opposite situation: when one is not certain what to say, or how to say it, or whether it will be good enough to satisfy external standards for quality. Which is, paradoxically, the situation that novice writers find themselves in, most of the time.

One of the great dangers for novice writers is that they may learn how to write effectively for some purposes and then get stuck: for example, by defaulting to knowledge telling when only knowledge crafting will do. This is an easy trap to fall into, since American school often emphasize reading over writing and primarily assess students' ability to recall and understand the content of what they read. School writing tasks often require students to produce short texts (less than a page), focus on demonstrating content knowledge, with the teacher as primary audience (Applebee, 1983; Applebee & Langer, 2011; Brandt, 2019). When writing mostly consists of note taking, question answering, and summarization, knowledge-telling is an efficient strategy. By contrast, expert writers have learned when to employ knowledge telling strategies and when to employ some other, more complex process. They deploy planning, reviewing, and revision strategies as needed, and engage the full suite of knowledge-crafting practices only in contexts that demand them.

Knowledge telling may be simpler than knowledge-crafting, but it is still a complex skill. At the very least, it requires the ability to generate ideas and express them in writing (Juel, Griffith, & Gough, 1986). Specifically, knowledge-telling requires:

1. Motivation to undertake the task
2. Self-regulation to manage the writing task effectively
3. Knowledge of the content to be communicated
4. Control over oral language, to put their ideas into words
5. Transcription skills to convert oral language into written text
6. The ability to read (and therefore monitor, evaluate, and improve) what they have written.

These are among the factors listed in Figure I.1 in the introduction. Other factors listed there—e.g., self-regulation and knowledge about writing—come most strongly into play when writers need to shift from knowledge-telling to knowledge-transforming or knowledge-crafting strategies.

All of the factors listed in Figure I.1 are subject to individual and group variation. Some students enjoy writing and identify as writers. Others do not.

Some students can write about a topic off the top of their heads; others struggle to generate ideas. Some students stay on task effortlessly; others are easily distracted or discouraged. Some students find the right words fluently; others may be tongue-tied, self-conscious, or inarticulate. Some students handwrite or type quickly and accurately; others struggle to write anything at all or have difficulty writing legibly. Some students can scan what they have written and quickly determine how to improve it; others can do so only with significant effort and support.

A basic problem in education is the "Matthew Effect" (Merton, 1995), in which the rich get richer, and the poor get poorer. As students move through school, and they encounter more varied and more complex tasks, advantages and disadvantages compound. Students who accomplish everyday school writing tasks fluently and effectively are also likely to have the motivation, executive control, knowledge, and fluency they need to succeed at more complex writing tasks. Conversely, students who struggle over everyday school writing tasks are unlikely to succeed at more challenging assignments.

In this book, I will argue that these mechanisms account for writing achievement gaps. For example, the writing gender gap can be traced back to factors that make female students more likely to have the interest, school-relevant topic knowledge, attentional focus, verbal control, and transcription fluency that makes knowledge-telling an effective writing strategy. As a result, they are more likely to have the bandwidth, interest, and engagement to acquire more sophisticated writing strategies.

It is important not to read too much into the existence of achievement gaps in school. There is often a tension between the actual contexts of everyday writing (where writing is undertaken to accomplish well-defined goals that are immediately relevant to the writer), and the way writing skills are taught in school (where the value and meaning of writing may be far less evident.) People who demonstrate weak writing performance in school may communicate effectively outside the school context, or may achieve writing proficiency later in life, in contexts where they have the necessary motivation and opportunity. But such people are, by definition, poorly served by an education that has failed to prepare them to enter the workforce on an equal footing.

Reference List

Adler-Kassner, L., Baca, I., & Fredericksen, J. (2018). *Understanding and Teaching Writing: Guiding Principles.* National Councl of Teachers of English. https://ncte.org/statement/teaching composition/

Alamargot, D., & Chanquoy, L. (2001). *Through the Models of Writing*. Springer. https://doi.org/10.1007/978-94-010-0804-4

Anderson, R. S., Mitchell, J. S., Thompson, R. F., & Trefz, K. D. (2014). Supporting young writers through the writing process in a paperless classroom. In R. S. Anderson & C. Mims (Eds.), *Handbook of Research on Digital Tools for Writing Instruction in K-12 Settings* (pp. 337–362). IGI Global. https://doi.org/10.4018/978-1-4666-5982-7

Applebee, A. N. (1983). *Writing in the Secondary School: English and the Content Areas* (Report No. 21). National Council of Teachers of English. https://doi.org/10.2307/357415

Applebee, A. N., & Langer, J. A. (2011). "EJ" Extra: A snapshot of writing instruction in middle schools and high schools. *The English Journal, 100*(6), 14–27. https://www.jstor.org/stable/23047875

Bang, H. J. (2013). Reliability of national writing project's analytic writing continuum assessment system. *Journal of Writing Assessment, 6*(1). https://escholarship.org/uc/item/03g148gh

Barton, D., & Hamilton, M. (2000). Literacy practices. In D. Barton, M. Hamilton, & R. Ivanic (Eds.), *Situated Literacies: Reading and Writing in Context* (pp. 7–15). Routledge. https://doi.org/10.4324/9780203984963

Bazerman, C., Applebee, A. N., Berninger, V. W., Brandt, D., Graham, S., Jeffery, J. V., ... & Wilcox, K. C. (2018). *The Lifespan Development of Writing*. National Council of Teachers of English. https://wac.colostate.edu/books/ncte/lifespan-writing

Beaufort, A. (2000). Learning the trade a social apprenticeship model for gaining writing expertise. *Written Communication, 17*(2), 185–223. https://doi.org/10.1177/0741088300017002002

Beaufort, A. (2008). Writing in the professions. In C. Bazerman (Ed.), *Handbook of Research on Writing: History, Society, School, Individual, Text* (pp. 221–236). Lawrence Erlbaum. https://doi.org/10.4324/9781410616470

Bereiter, C. B., & Scardamalia, M. (1987). *The Psychology of Written Composition*. Lawrence Earlbaum.

Brandt, D. (2001). *Literacy in American Lives*. Cambridge University Press.

Brandt, D. (2014). *The Rise of Writing: Redefining Mass Literacy*. Cambridge University Press. Brandt, D. (2019). The problem of writing in mass education. *Utbildning & Demokrati Tidskrift för didaktik och utbildningspolitik, 28*(2), 37–54. https://doi.org/10.48059/uod.v28i2.1120

Brown, D. W. (2015). *These Heads Are Packed with Stories: The Out-of-School Writing Experiences of Elementary Age Boys*. [Doctoral dissertation, Georgia State University]. Scholarworks. http://scholarworks.gsu.edu/cgi/viewcontent.cgi?article=1007&context=mse_diss

Deane, P. D. (2011). *Writing Assessment and Cognition* (RR-11-14). Educational Testing Service. https://doi.org/10.1002/j.2333-8504.2011.tb02250.x

Deane, P. D. (2013). Covering the construct: An approach to automated essay scoring motivated by a socio-cognitive framework for defining literacy skills. In M. Shermis & J. Burstein

(Eds.), *Handbook of Automated Essay Evaluation: Current Applications and New Directions* (pp. 298–312). Routledge. https://doi.org/10.4324/9780203122761

Deane, P. D., Odendahl, N., Quinlan, T., Fowles, M., Welsh, C., & Bivens-Tatum, J. (2008). *Cognitive Models of Writing: Writing Proficiency as a Complex Integrated Skill* (RR-08–55). Educational Testing Service. https://doi.org/10.1002/j.2333-8504.2008.tb02141.x

Duff, P. A. (2010). Language socialization into academic discourse communities. *Annual Review of Applied Linguistics, 30*, 169–192. https://doi.org/10.1017/S0267190510000048

Flower, L., & Hayes, J. R. (1980). A cognitive process theory of writing. *College Composition and Communication, 32*(4), 365–387. https://doi.org/10.2307/356600

Graham, S., & Sandmel, K. (2011). The process-writing approach: A meta-analysis. *The Journal of Educational Research, 104*(6), 396–407. https://doi.org/10.1080/00220671.2010.488703

Graves, D. H. (1983). *Writing Teachers and Children at Work*. Heinemann.

Greco, A. N., Milliot, J., & Wharton, R. M. (2014). *The Book Publishing Industry*. Routledge. https://doi.org/10.4324/9780203834565

Hansford, D., & Adlington, R. (2009). Digital spaces and young people's online authoring: challenges for teachers. *Australian Journal of Language and Literacy, 32*(1), 55–68. https://search.informit.org/doi/10.3316/ielapa.584398231565216

Hayes, J. R. (2012). Modeling and remodeling writing. *Written Communication, 29*(3), 369–388. https://doi.org/10.1177/0741088312451260

Hazelton, L., Nastal, J., Elliot, N., Burstein, J., & McCaffrey, D. F. (2021). Formative automated writing evaluation: A standpoint theory of action. *Journal of Response to Writing, 7*(1), Article 3. https://scholarsarchive.byu.edu/journalrw/vol7/iss1/3/

Henry, J. (2000). *Writing Workplace Cultures: An Archeology of Professional Writing*. Southern Illinois University Press.

Hull, G., & Schultz, K. (2001). Literacy and learning out of school: A review of theory and research. *Review of Educational Research, 71*(4), 575–611. https://doi.org/10.3102/00346543071004575

Juel, C., Griffith, P. L., & Gough, P. B. (1986). Acquisition of literacy: A longitudinal study of children in first and second grade. *Journal of Educational Psychology, 78*(4), 243–255. https://doi.org/10.1037/0022-0663.78.4.243

Kellogg, R. T. (1999). Training advanced writing skills: The case for deliberate practice. *Educational Psychologist, 44*(4), 250–266. https://doi.org/10.1080/00461520903213600

Kellogg, R. T. (2001). Competition for working memory among writing processes. *American Journal of Psychology, 114*(2), 175–191. https://doi.org/10.2307/1423513

Kellogg, R. T. (2008). Training writing skills: A cognitive developmental perspective. *Journal of Writing Research, 1*(1), 1–26. https://doi.org/10.17239/jowr-2008.01.01.1

Kellogg, R. T., & Whiteford, A. P. (2012). The development of writing expertise. In E. Grigorenko, E. Mambrino, & D. Preiss (Eds.), *Writing, A Mosaic of New Perspectives* (pp. 109–124). Psychology Press. https://doi.org/10.4324/9780203808481

Kellogg, R. T., Whiteford, A. P., Turner, C. E., Cahill, M., & Mertens, A. (2013). Working memory in written composition: An evaluation of the 1996 model. *Journal of Writing Research, 5*(2), 159–190. https://doi.org/10.17239/jowr-2013.05.02.1

Leijten, M., Van Waes, L., Schriver, K., & Hayes, J. R. (2014). Writing in the workplace: Constructing documents using multiple digital sources. *Journal of Writing Research, 5*(3), 285–337. https://doi.org/10.17239/jowr-2014.05.03.3

Lotier, K. M. (2021). *Postprocess Postmortem.* WAC Clearing House/Unversity of Colorado Press. https://doi.org/10.37514/PER-B.2021.1268.

McCutchen, D. (1996). A capacity theory of writing: Working memory in composition. *Educational Psychology Review, 8,* 299–325. https://doi.org/10.1007/BF01464076

McCutchen, D. (2011). From novice to expert: Implications of language skills and writing-relevant knowledge for memory during the development of writing skill. *Journal of Writing Research, 3*(1), 51–68. https://doi.org/10.17239/jowr-2011.03.01.3

Merton, R. K. (1995). The Thomas theorem and the Matthew effect. *Social Forces, 74*(2), 379–422. https://doi.org/10.2307/2580486

Prior, P. (1998). *Writing/Disciplinarity: A Sociohistoric Account of Literate Activity in the Academy.* Lawrence Erlbaum. https://doi.org/10.4324/9780203810651

Pritchard, R. J., & Honeycutt, R. L. (2007). Best practices in implementing a process approach to teaching writing. In C. A. MacArthur, S. Graham, & J. Fitzgerald (Eds.), *Best Practices in Writing Instruction* (pp. 28–49). Guilford.

Purcell, K., Buchanan, J., & Friedrich, L. (2013). *The Impact of Digital Tools on Student Writing and How Writing Is Taught in Schools.* Pew Research Center. https://www.pewresearch.org/internet/2013/07/16/the-impact-of-digital-tools-on-student-writing-and-how-writing-is-taught-in-schools/

Schriver, K. (2012). What we know about expertise in professional communication. In V. W. Berninger (Ed.), *Past, Present, and Future Contributions of Cognitive Writing Research to Cognitive Psychology* (pp. 275–312). Psychology Press. https://doi.org/10.4324/9780203805312

Wardle, E., & Roozen, K. (2012). Addressing the complexity of writing development: Toward an ecological model of assessment. *Assessing Writing, 17*(2), 106–119. https://doi.org/10.1016/j.asw.2012.01.001

Ware, M., & Mabe, M. (2015). *The STM Report: An Overview of Scientific and Scholarly Journal Publishing.* Digital Commons. https://digitalcommons.unl.edu/cgi/viewcontent.cgi?article=1008&context=scholcom

Yancey, K. B. (2020). The composing of seniors. In Elliott, N. & Horning, A. S. (Eds.), *Talking Back: Senior Scholars and Their Colleagues Deliberate the Past, Present, and Future of Writing Studies* (pp. 376–387). Colorado Univ. Press.

CHAPTER TWO

Writing as Purposeful Action: Motivation for Writing as Cause and Effect

School can be a profoundly alienating, hence demotivating experience. Many of the variables that drive such alienation have nothing to do with writing *per se*, and everything to do with disconnects—between teachers and students, between school and community, or between educational settings and the assumptions of curriculum and assessment designers. But when students write, the social context matters. Some students start out highly engaged and motivated, but others do not. As students learn, their prior experiences motivate (or discourage them). The resulting feedback loop affects all the skills that writers need to master, from foundational skills like handwriting and spelling all the way up to applied critical thinking skills, such as conducting research and building an academic argument. Since writing motivation affects student performance and subsequent academic placements (for example, placement in regular vs. basic first-year university writing courses), the consequences can be substantial (Shaughnessy, 1979; Molloy, Fonville, & Salam, 2020).

There are many reasons why students may not be motivated to write, but one is intrinsic. School is the primary context in which students learn to write. During the early stages of learning, necessary supporting skills have not yet been mastered. In that context, writing can require great effort for little apparent benefit. As a result, writing motivation is a significant predictor of writing quality, at school entrance (Dunsmuir & Peter, 2004), in the early grades (Steve Graham, Berninger,

& Fan, 2007), and beyond (Mavrogenes & Bezruczko, 1993; Knudson, 1995; Lam & Law, 2007; Troia, Harbaugh, Shankland, Wolbers, & Lawrence, 2013), for second-language learners as well as for native speakers (Hashemian & Heidari, 2013). Lack of motivation may be a rational response when students perceive little value in writing—or consider success unlikely, and unlikely to be rewarded.

Of course, school is one context among many. Students who are reluctant writers in academic settings may be enthusiastic writers outside of school (Witte, 2007; Jacobs, 2008; Lenhart, Arafeh, Smith, & Macgill, 2008; Dredger, Woods, Beach, & Sagstetter, 2013; Gardner, 2013; Stewart, 2014). For instance, online affinity spaces, such as fan fiction sites, afford a variety of opportunities to participate in rich online writing activities (Hansford & Adlington, 2009; Buck, 2012; Lammers, Curwood, & Magnifico, 2012; Curwood, Magnifico, & Lammers, 2013; Magnifico, Curwood, & Lammers, 2015). But that is cold comfort, since the whole point of having schools is to make sure that everyone obtains the education they need—not just those who naturally gravitate to specific interests.

Students are more likely to have positive attitudes toward reading and writing (and stronger reading and writing performances) in classroom environments where the teaching style, classroom management, communication strategies, and presentation of content maximize student engagement (Bogner, Raphael, & Pressley, 2002). The challenge of teaching writing in school is thus, in large part, the challenge of convincing students to put in the effort needed to become skilled writers, and of providing the support they need to succeed.[1]

Overview

Motivation is a complex construct, involving the interaction of decision-making processes with personal priorities, beliefs, values, and feelings. Figure 2.1 outlines the major factors involved, in line with general motivation theory (Eccles & Wigfield, 2002) and the literature on writing motivation (Boscolo & Hidi, 2007; Troia, Shankland, & Wolbers, 2012; MacArthur, Philippakos, & Graham, 2016; Ling, Elliott, Burstein, McCaffrey, MacArthur, & Graham, 2021; Graham, Harbaugh-Schattenkirk, Aitken, Harris, Ng, Ray, ... & Wdowin, 2022).

---

1 I discuss this and related issues, at length in my paper, "The Challenges of Writing in School" (2018).

WRITING AS PURPOSEFUL ACTION: MOTIVATION FOR WRITING | 33

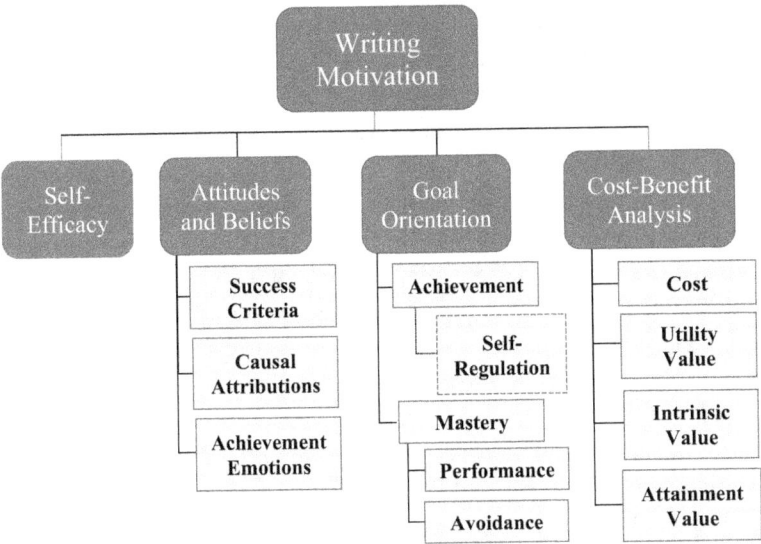

Figure 2.1 Major Factors Affecting Writing Motivation[2]

Self-efficacy defines how well someone believes they can perform (Bandura, 1997; Troia et al., 2012). Someone with strong self-efficacy can work confidently and persist in the face of difficulties. Conversely, people with weak self-efficacy may invest minimal effort and give up when they encounter difficulties.

Self-efficacy emerges from experience. It comprises the attitudes and beliefs that people develop from experience. These include:

- the *success criteria*, or implicit standards, they have learned to apply (McMillan & Hearn, 2008)
- the *causal attributions* (beliefs about the causes of failure or success) that they have come to accept (Weiner, 1985), and
- the *achievement emotions* (positive or negative feelings toward the task and their own task performance) that they have developed (Huang, 2011).

---

2   Figure 2.1 was inspired both by the general literature and specific research on writing motivation, particularly the model presented in Figure 1 of Ling, Elliott, Burstein, McCaffrey, MacArthur, and Graham (2021). However, I have organized the major categories somewhat differently. I believe that there are important connections between beliefs about writing and emotions (which Ling et al. treat as a major bullet under the heading, 'feelings'), and have therefore placed emotions and beliefs about writing together under the heading 'Attitudes and Beliefs'. I have also retained the categories of expectancy-value theory, under the heading 'Cost/Benefit Analysis', as I believe they capture the way motivation depends critically on a balance between effort and desire.

The way people experience a task is strongly affected by their *goal orientation*—the lens through which they interpret success or failure (Nicholls, 1984; Dweck & Leggett, 1988). Goal orientation has a significant impact both on what do people during a task and what they decide to do after the task has been completed. If people are oriented toward *achievement*, they may work toward *performance goals*, where they try to maximize their chances of receiving praise, or toward *avoidance* goals, where they try to minimize their chances of being criticized or shamed. If they are oriented toward *mastery*, they will respond to success (or perhaps even more importantly, failure) as an opportunity to learn. Students who adopt mastery goals are likely to improve even if they perform poorly at first. Students with low self-efficacy who adopt achievement goals are less likely to perform well or to learn from experience (Elliott & Dweck, 1988). Mastery orientation highlights the importance of self-control, that is, of *self-regulation* (Robson, Allen, & Howard, 2020). Self-regulation is particularly important in complex literacy tasks like writing (Kaplan, Lichtinger, & Gorodetsky, 2009).

Self-efficacy, motivational beliefs and attitudes, and goal orientation affect the implicit cost/benefit analyses that define motivation in specific situations. Four factors directly affect such analyses (Wigfield, 1994):

- *Cost* (how much time, attention, and energy a task is likely to require)
- *Utility value* (how much completing a task will advance someone's personal goals)
- *Intrinsic value* (how valuable and interesting a task seems to be for its own sake)
- *Attainment value* (how important a task is to someone's conception of their identity, ideals, or competence in a specific domain).

If someone judges that a task is important, useful, worthwhile, interesting, and easy to perform, they should be highly motivated. Conversely, if a person judges a task to be unimportant, uninteresting, of little personal relevance, and hard, they may not even try.

This is a general theory of motivation; it applies to writing because writing is goal-directed behavior (Hayes, 1996). However, specific measures of writing motivation have been developed. Codling and Gambrell (1997) developed the Motivation to Write Profile for elementary school teachers, a combined survey and interview instrument designed to measure writing attainment value and self-efficacy. Hamilton, Nolen, and Abbott (2013) developed measures focusing on self-efficacy and mastery goals. They found that the structure of writing motivation shifted during the elementary years, with a stronger focus on mastery goals in the upper grades. MacArthur, Philippakos, and Graham (2016) developed a writing motivation instrument with seven subscales. They found that higher and lower-performing students differed on almost every dimension.

Motivation is a psychological construct, but it is also social and cultural (McInerney, Walker, & Liem, 2011). In the social and cultural context defined by a local school, student motivation is strongly affected by teacher attitudes and practices (Mills & Clyde, 1991). For instance, learning is enhanced by mastery goals, but students are less likely to adopt mastery goals in a competitive classroom environment (Ames, 1992) or in one in which they do not feel respected and valued (Kumar, Karabenick, & Burgoon, 2015).

Group Differences Mediated by Motivation

Figure 2.1 suggests that writing achievement gaps can emerge in several different ways:

1. **Self-Efficacy.** If members of a group perceive themselves as likely to fail, they will probably show low self-efficacy. Why put hard work into a challenging writing task when experience indicates you will not succeed?
2. **Success Criteria.** If schools emphasize success criteria that make it harder for some groups to succeed, achievement gaps may result. For example, if writing is primarily judged by adherence to the norms for Standard Academic English (SAE), students from upper-middle class, White families may be advantaged over students who grew up speaking some other language variety, such as African American Vernacular English, or AAVE (Baker-Bell, 2020).
3. **Causal Attribution.** If classroom practices encourage students to attribute high or low performance to ability, and some groups are (for whatever reason) likely to have higher performance than others, it becomes much easier for members of the disadvantaged group to give up. Why should they do more than they must if they do not expect their efforts to matter?
4. **Achievement Emotions.** If members of one group consistently have frustrating, emotionally negative writing experiences, their motivation will be reduced. If writing is an unpleasant experience, it is only natural to do as little as possible.
5. **Goal Orientation.** If specific groups are more strongly inclined toward performance goals, or if they attend schools where the classroom environment favors performance goals, lower-performing members of the

group may be disadvantaged. For example, gender stereotypes for males may favor a competitive approach (Niederle & Vesterlund, 2011), but competitive attitudes may be less conducive to learning than mastery goals (Ames, 1992), especially for struggling students.

6. **Cost.** If writing takes more effort, on average, for members of some groups than for others, the relative *cost* will be higher, reducing group motivation levels. For example, most people find it harder to write in a second language than in their native tongue.

7. **Utility Value.** If writing helps students from some groups achieve meaningful personal goals more often, on average, than for students from other groups, their relative utility value will be higher. For example, most people find it easier to write on a subject that matters personally, addressing an audience they know, whose opinion matters to them. Conversely, if students have no compelling reason to engage, their performance may hinge on their (real or perceived) willingness to comply with teacher expectations.

8. **Intrinsic Value.** If specific writing tasks are more engaging for members of some groups than for others, they will experience those tasks as having higher intrinsic interest and value. For instance, when asked to write about a stereotypically male task, such as football (Yu, Zuo, Blum, Tolman, Kågesten, Mmari, ... & Lou, 2017), students whose identity and interests align with the stereotype may be more highly motivated.

9. **Attainment Value.** If assigned writing tasks are more familiar, more highly valued, or more important in specific cultural traditions, they may have higher attainment value for students who identify with those traditions (Eccles & Wigfield, 2020). It is easier to imitate a model you believe is meant for you.

In the sections that follow, I examine each of these mechanisms in turn.

Self-Efficacy

Overview

Self-efficacy plays a critical role in writing motivation and writing performance (Pajares, 2003; Bruning & Kauffman, 2015). Lower self-efficacy leads to greater writing apprehension (Daly & Miller, 1975a, 1975b; Pajares & Valiante, 1997; though see Muhammad & Latif, 2019) and correlates positively with other measures of motivation. It accounts for much of the variance in writing performance associated with motivational factors (Graham, Daley, Aitken, Harris, & Robinson,

2018). Self-efficacy is usually measured using survey instruments (Pajares, Hartley, & Valiante, 2001; Pajares, 2007).

Students who are stronger writers not only tend to have higher levels of writing self-efficacy but to assume that writing outcomes are primarily determined by effort. Weaker writers are more likely to attribute writing outcomes to factors outside their control, such as luck or ability (Shell, Colvin, & Bruning, 1995; Sanders-Reio, Alexander, Reio, & Newman, 2014). High self-efficacy increases the likelihood that a writer will persist in a writing task and is associated with higher writing quality (Zimmerman & Bandura, 1994; Ling, Elliot, Burstein, McCaffrey, MacArthur, & Holtzman, 2021). Conversely, low self-efficacy tends to lead to high levels of apprehension and avoidance (Wolters, 2003; Zhou, Lam, & Zhang, 2022) or minimal effort (Pajares & Valiante, 2006).

Since writing is a complex skill, students can have high self-efficacy for some parts of the writing construct, but not others. Pajares (2007) distinguishes at least three subtypes of writing self-efficacy: *self-efficacy for ideation*, *self-efficacy for conventions*, and *self-efficacy for writing strategies*. Similar multi-factor models were confirmed by O'Mahony, Dempsey, and Killeen (2008) and Bruning, Dempsey, and Kim (2013), who found the same three factors, and by Dempsey (2013), whose data primarily distinguished self-efficacy for ideation and self-efficacy for conventions. Self-efficacy may improve as students acquire effective self-regulation strategies that help them to manage the writing process (Schunk & Swartz, 1993). Strikingly, Zumbrunn, Broda, Varier, and Conklin (2019) found that teacher reports of student self-regulation were only significantly correlated with self-efficacy for conventions. Self-efficacy for idea generation and self-efficacy for self-regulation were not.

Students do not always accurately self-assess. Student groups with lower mean writing performance, including students with learning disabilities, sometimes have higher self-efficacy than other, more able groups (Klassen, 2008). Over time, students tend to develop more accurate self-assessments, which means that writing self-efficacy tends to decrease in the higher grades, especially for lower-performing students (Meece & Miller, 2001). This presents a challenge for teachers, who must provide weaker students with experiences that will simultaneously increase their writing skills, their ability to evaluate their own writing accurately, and their self-efficacy (Walker, 2003; Bruning & Kauffman, 2015). However, instruction can reduce self-efficacy. Intervention studies with control groups sometimes find that writing self-efficacy decreases within the control group following business-as-usual instruction (Duijnhouwer, Prins, & Stokking, 2012; Chung, Chen, & Booth Olson, 2021).

Group Differences in Writing Self-Efficacy

Gender-Based Differences in Self-Efficacy

Females tend to show higher writing self-efficacy than males (Pajares, Miller, & Johnson, 1999; Cordeiro, Castro, & Limpo, 2018), though not all studies show such differences, possibly due to differences in measurement methods (Shell, Colvin, & Bruning, 1995; Pajares & Johnson, 1996; Villalón, Mateos, Cuevas, 2015). The strength of gender effects is linked to the strength of identification with stereotypical gender roles (Pajares, Valiante, & Cheong, 2006). Higher levels of female self-efficacy for writing are linked to lower levels of writing apprehension and to a greater likelihood that writing tasks will be perceived as useful (Pajares & Valiante, 1997; Villalón, Mateos, & Cuevas, 2015). Strategy-based writing interventions can increase self-efficacy more for females than for males. Andrade, Wang, Du, and Akawi (2010) observed this kind of interaction on a rubric-based writing intervention. García and Fidalgo (2008) observed a similar effect in an intervention that focused on self-directed strategy development. Likely causes of gender differences in writing self-efficacy will be examined in later chapters. However, higher levels of female self-efficacy for writing must reflect significant differences in the way they experience writing in school. It means that females are more likely to experience school writing positively, as a locus of control and achievement, rather than as a context in which they experience feelings of frustration, boredom, powerlessness, and shame.

Socioeconomic Differences in Self-Efficacy

There is relatively little literature that focuses specifically on the relationship between writing self-efficacy and socioeconomic status, race, or ethnicity, though we would expect to see (and do see) the same general relations between writing self-efficacy and writing achievement for low-SES students as we see in the general population (Martin, 2016). In a study focusing on boys' writing motivation, Collie, Martin, and Curwood (2016) found that students with more highly educated parents tended to have higher self-efficacy. In a study conducted in Israel, Korat and Schiff (2005) observed that children attending high SES schools had higher writing self-efficacy than children attending low SES schools. They also observed that degree of print exposure also predicted higher writing self-efficacy, but only in the low-SES schools. Results like these imply that students from upper-middle-class backgrounds are more likely to have more positive school writing experiences, leading to a positive, rather than a negative motivation cycle.

Racial and Ethnic Differences in Self-Efficacy

Usher and Pajares (2006) found that social relationships played a stronger role in the formation of writing self-efficacy for African American students than for White students. Otherwise, relatively little literature directly addresses racial or ethnic differences in writing self-efficacy.

Causal Implications

Overall, this scattering of results is consistent with what we would expect based on our theory of action. Writing self-efficacy is an outcome of experience, but once established, it reinforces existing achievement patterns by raising writing motivation for higher-performing students, and decreasing it for everyone else (Troia et al., 2012). This effect can be increased when the school environment encourages competitive attitudes (Chan & Lam, 2008). The negative feedback cycles associated with low performance and low self-efficacy present a critical educational challenge.

Beliefs and Attitudes

Success Criteria

Attitudes toward tasks are heavily influenced by what people want to accomplish. In a simple task, success criteria are obvious. But writing is anything but simple (White & Bruning, 2005).

As discussed in Chapter One, standard rubrics for writing quality reference multiple standards. Some are rhetorical, focusing on the author's purpose. Others are cognitive, focusing on the quality of reasoning. Others are text-structural, dealing with methods of organizing and presenting information. Yet others are linguistic, dealing with clarity, preciseness, and conciseness of verbal expression. And finally, there are formal, orthographic standards, dealing with such things as spelling, punctuation, capitalization, and the correct form for handwritten letters. Diederich, French, and Carlton (1961) found that when teachers were asked to evaluate writing quality, they often prioritized different standards. The situation for students can be even more challenging Unlike (at least some) teachers, they have not spent years reading, evaluating, and providing feedback on other people's writing. They must, instead, infer success criteria from their classroom writing experience.

The situation is complicated further by the fact that the success criteria for writing change as students move through school. In the early grades, success is closely linked to the development of transcription skills—handwriting, spelling, punctuation. Theoretical accounts of early writing often adopt the so-called "Simple View of Writing" (Berninger & Graham, 1998; Berninger, 2000), in which writing is equated with oral language skills plus transcription. Classrooms focused on teaching transcription skills naturally emphasize fluency and accuracy. But this means that as students move into higher grades, they need to modify their internal definitions of successful writing. But they may not. Not all students master spelling, punctuation, and grammar when the curriculum says they should.

MacArthur, Philippakos, and Graham's (2016) results are particularly interesting when viewed in this light. They found two clusters of beliefs about writing. One focused on content; the other, on adherence to written conventions. Content beliefs led students to agree with statements like, "Writing is one of the best ways to explore new ideas", "Writing helps me make my ideas clearer", or "Revising helps me clarify my ideas". Conventions beliefs led students to agree with statements like "Good writers do not make errors in grammar", "Writing quickly is an important part of good writing", or "Good writers need little revision because they get it right the first time." Lower-performing writers tended to agree more strongly with Conventions beliefs. Philippakos, Wang, and MacArthur (2021) and Ling, Elliott, Burstein, McCaffrey, MacArthur, and Graham (2021) found similar results.

Consider, for a moment, how writing may be addressed in a traditional classroom. The student is given an assignment, turns an essay in, then gets it back with a grade and teacher comments and corrections—stereotypically, written directly on the student's paper in red ink. Lower performing students, who are more likely to produce conventions errors, get lower grades and many red marks. In this context, lower-performing students will naturally conclude that good writing is writing without errors and make it their highest priority to get fewer red marks—which is an avoidance and not a mastery goal. If teachers perceive the language of minority students or second language students as particularly error-prone, students from those groups are likely to be disproportionately affected.

Of course, the "traditional classroom" is a stereotype. Real classrooms vary on many dimensions. But success criteria matter. Emphasizing formal correctness over communicative success is likely to discourage precisely those students who are already struggling.

Causal Attribution

People think constantly about why they succeed or fail. Under the best of circumstances, failure will induce people to reflect on the reasons for failure, in order to improve their chances for future success. But people often attribute success or failure to ability and luck (Weiner, 1985). This can lead to self-reinforcing spirals in which both teachers and students attribute low performance to low ability, resulting in reduced effort and less motivation to learn.

This mechanism clearly plays a role in group achievement gaps. The proof of it can be seen in the impact of social-psychological interventions that give students new ways to think about success and failure (Yeager & Walton, 2011), which can have dramatic effects. For example, Wilson and Linville (1985) conducted a study with struggling first-year college students. Students in the study watched videos of upper-year students describing how at first, they struggled, but their grades improved with time. A week later, the same students showed improved scores on a standardized assessment. A year later, they had higher GPAs than students in the control condition and a much lower dropout rate (a decrease of 80 %). Blackwell, Trzesniewski, and Dweck (2007) conducted a study with 7th grade, low income African American and Latino students. Over an eight-week period, students in the experimental group participated in workshops that focused both on teaching study skills and on explaining how brain function can improve when people work hard on difficult tasks. Students in the control group only had lessons on study skills. At the end of the academic year, students in the experimental group had math grades nearly 1/3 higher than students in the control group. According to Oyserman, Bybee, and Terry (2006), low income African American and Latino 8th-grade students had ten sessions in which they completed assignments and wrote essays designed to make them envision a future in which high academic performance was both practically attainable and consistent with their racial identity. A control group took standard elective classes, instead. The students in the treatment group were 60 % less likely to repeat 8th grade. Two years later, they had higher grades (an increase of +.28), higher attendance, were subject to fewer disciplinary interventions, and were less likely to repeat 8th grade.

Similar results have been found with specifically with writing. Self-Regulated Strategy Development (SRSD) is one of the most effective writing pedagogies in the literature. It explicitly targets motivation, while providing students with explicit instruction in writing strategies (Graham & Harris, 1989). Limpo and Alves (2014) developed and validated a scale that measured the extent to which students believed that writing was a malleable skill, rather than a fixed ability, and examined the relationship between a SRSD intervention and students' beliefs on this scale. They not only found that students in the SRSD treatment group had stronger writing performance than students in the control group, but that there were larger improvements when students accepted the idea that writing is a malleable skill.

Of course, causal attributions are not, in and of themselves, the primary cause of group differences in writing achievement. They are likely to be shaped by a complex combination of teacher feedback, peer attitudes, and individual histories of failure and success. However, once students discover that—for whatever reason—they consistently perform poorly on writing tasks, ability seems like the obvious explanation. If students just don't do very well on writing assignments, they may (falsely) conclude, it wasn't their fault. There was nothing they could do.

Achievement Emotions, Feedback, and Student/Teacher Relationships

When people succeed or fail at writing tasks, they experience positive (or negative) emotions. Over time, their emotional reactions consolidate into a general feeling or attitude (Bruning & Horn, 2000). This process is largely driven by feedback. Fong, Williams, Williamson, Lin, Kim, and Schallert (2017) outline the emotions students report after receiving writing feedback, ranging from shame, anger, and hopelessness to pride, enjoyment, and hope (with boredom taking pride of place in the middle). Critically, Fong and his colleagues found that different types of feedback elicited different emotional reactions, depending not only on the tenor and quality of the feedback, but on the student's relationship with the person providing feedback. Negative emotions were often associated with the perception that the feedback provider did not care, did not respect the student, or failed to provide useful feedback. But negative feelings could also be associated with self-blaming. Students reported feeling anger and shame both when they realized what they did wrong and when they concluded that they had no idea how to improve their performance.

These results highlight the importance of teacher/student (and student/student) relationships in a feedback context. Marrs, Zumbrunn, McBride, and Stringer (2016) analyzed 867 elementary students' self-reports about the emotional impact of writing feedback. While most expressed positive feelings about feedback, about 12% indicated strong emotional resistance. Their explanations often focused on the attitude of the person providing the feedback, as evidenced by such statements as "It's not nice," "They're mean," or "I think they will give bad comments about it." Zumbrunn, Marrs, & Mewborn (2016) report similar results for junior high students.

Such comments suggest conflicted student/teacher relationships. Critically, teacher/student conflict is a greater risk for some groups than for others. Spilt and Hughes (2015) analyzed an ethnically diverse sample of 657 first-grade students. They found that after controlling for other variables, African American students were the most likely to experience teacher/student conflict. While their data focused on first grade, before writing is the focus of the curriculum, it strongly suggests that negative teacher feedback may contribute to lower performance for some groups, if a supportive student/teacher relationship is absent.

Goal Orientation

Motivation is affected not only by what people are trying to do (their success criteria). What they are trying to do also matter (their goal orientation). People who focus on achievement goals typically care most about what other people think, so they seek to win praise and avoid shame. Atkinson (1957) worked out a mathematical model of how achievement goals interact with success and failure to predict motivation. If someone strongly desires to succeed—and they have a decent chance of succeeding—it makes sense to work hardest when success is uncertain. Such people are said to have *performance goals*. On the other hand, if someone is afraid of failure—and have a decent chance of failing—it makes sense to put in the most effort when success is either certain or impossible (in which case, failure will be entirely due to circumstance). Such people are said to have *avoidance goals*.

When people focus on performance goals, prior experience colors their reactions to success or failure (Weiner, 1985). People with a history of success may attribute success to ability and failure to circumstances outside their control. People with a history of failure are likely to attribute failure to their personal lack of ability and success to unexpectedly favorable circumstances. On other hand, when students are focused on *mastery goals* even low-performing students are likely to find ways to improve. Pajares, Britner, and Valiante (2000) confirmed these predictions for children's writing.

Whether students adopt achievement or mastery goals is strongly affected by classroom structure (Ames, 1992; Meece and Miller, 1999, 2001). Classrooms are most conducive to learning when meaningful and challenging tasks are assigned, when appropriate scaffolding is supplied, when the teacher's authority is used to encourage student participation and enable them to work independently, and when work is evaluated privately, with a focus on individual improvement that allows students to make mistakes and correct them as a normal part of the learning process. These are the classroom practices that encourage a mastery orientation and build intrinsic rather than extrinsic motivation (Deci, Betley, Kahle, Abrams, & Porac, 1981).

Unfortunately, not all classrooms are like this. The percentage of classrooms that encourage mastery goals decreases as students move from elementary school to middle school and from middle school to high school, and so does the average level of writing motivation (Wigfield, Eccles, Schiefele, Roeser, & Davis-Kean, 2006). Pajares and Cheong (2003) specifically observed a drop in writing motivation from elementary school to middle school, though with partial recovery in high school. Collie, Martin, and Curwood (2016) report that writing motivation decreases for male students during the high school years. These results suggest that students may often be in less-supportive classrooms during middle school and high school, despite (or perhaps, because of) escalating expectations for student writing.

The Role of Competition in Exacerbating Group Performance Differences

One of the most obvious ways that classrooms can encourage performance, rather than mastery goals, is by encouraging students to compete. A competitive classroom in which students are constantly comparing their work is likely to have serious consequences for low-performing students, both socially (Gasser, Grütter, Torchetti, & Buholzer, 2017) and in terms of their academic achievement (Kaplan, Lichtinger, & Gorodetzky, 2009).

There are significant gender linked differences in goal structure. Girls are more likely to adopt mastery goals (Pajares, Britner, & Valiante, 2000; Pajares & Cheong, 2003; Pajares, Johnson, & Usher, 2007). Conversely, performance-approach goals are associated with stronger writing motivation for boys but not for girls (Pajares & Valiante, 2001). As a result, competitive classrooms may have a particularly negative effect on the performance of low-performing boys.

A similar case can be made for the interaction between classroom structure and student motivation for students from specific racial or ethnic groups. Kaplan and Maehr (1999) argued that the kinds of classroom structures that Ames (1992) recommends might improve performance for African American students in multiethnic schools. The argument—to be discussed later in this chapter under the heading of attainment value—is that supportive classroom environments make learning easier for students from all backgrounds. This is, of course, an important supposition of culturally responsive pedagogy (Ladson-Billings, 1995; Gay, 2010).

The Role of Self-Regulation in Motivation and Learning

Self-regulation refers to the ways people modify their own behavior, through goal setting, self-monitoring, and other adaptive activities (Inzlicht, Werner, Briskin, & Roberts, 2021). Since writing is a complex skill that requires the integration of multiple processes, and a great deal of metacognitive awareness, self-regulation plays an important role in the development of writing proficiency (Graham, Harris, MacArthur, & Santangelo, 2017), even in the early grades (Puranik & Li, 2022).

Mastery goal orientation is strongly associated with the acquisition of self-regulation skills for writing (Kaplan, Lichtinger, & Gorodetsky, 2009). Schunk and Zimmerman (2007) review evidence that indicates that self-regulation and self-efficacy for writing can be increased by targeted writing strategy instruction. For instance, cooperative writing assignments improve both writing performance and writing self-efficacy, since they provide less-skilled students with engaging models of effective writing strategies without providing negative feedback (Razmjoo & Hoomanfard, 2012).

Since self-regulation is closely associated with mastery goal orientation, we might expect to find greater self-regulation among females. This appears to be the case both at school entry (Matthews, Ponitz, & Morrison, 2009) and later (Meece & Painter, 2012), specifically including writing tasks (Weis, Heikamp, & Trommsdorff, 2013). Conversely, there is evidence that childhood poverty can reduce children's ability to self-regulate, primarily by exposing them to a variety of physical and psychosocial sources of stress (Greene, 2017; Evans & Kim, 2013). If some groups—for whatever reason—tend to have higher levels of self-regulation, that is likely to be a significant advantage in learning how to write, given the cognitive complexity of writing.

Cost/Benefit Analysis

Ultimately, motivation consists in an implicit cost-benefit analysis. When people decide how much energy to invest in a task, they are balancing multiple factors, including cost, utility value, attainment value, and intrinsic value (along with its close relative, interest).

Cost

There is a sense in which Figure 2.1 is misleading, because it puts all the ways in which a task can be difficult under a single heading, "Cost". But writing is complex on multiple dimensions, as is the process of learning to write. Writing in school is particularly challenging because students are still acquiring supporting skills, on multiple dimensions, which makes the writing process much more effortful for younger, less literate writers. Cost cannot, therefore, be addressed in a single subsection of a single chapter. Instead, Chapters Three through Seven will separately discuss distinct aspects of writing that impose cognitive costs.

Utility Value

Overview

Writing is a form of communication, and as such, its utility value depends upon audience, on content, and on how the writer relates to both. Motivation is not likely to be a problem if a writer wishes to communicate important content to a valued audience in a context that affirms the worth of their participation and their worth as a participant (Pressick-Kilborn & Walker, 2002; Magnifico, 2010; Camacho, Alves, & Boscolo, 2021). Recommendations for effective literacy (reading and writing) instruction emphasize the importance of creating a supportive classroom environment in which students are afforded agency and are given authentic tasks with meaningful content and real, preferably responsive audiences (Cleary, 1991; Purcell-Gates, Duke, & Martineau, 2007; Young & Ferguson, 2020).

When a teacher assigns, collects, and grades a writing task, the primary goal may cease to be communication, even with the teacher. For instance, Dredger, Woods, Beach, and Sagstetter (2013) report that in a survey of attitudes toward writing, middle school students primarily identified grades, and not communication as their motivation for writing in school. They identified communication and self-expression as motivations for out-of-school writing. Fulfilling school requirements may be sufficiently motivating for students who treat academic achievement as a core element in their self-concept, but if students do not perceive school writing tasks as relevant, they may disengage (Hawthorne, 2008). A critical issue is whether schools foster a sense of social connection; lack of a sense of relatedness is likely to lead to a general disengagement from academic work (Furrer & Skinner, 2003; Isaac, Sansone, & Smith, 1999).

The basic problem is that students often write only because the teacher assigned a writing task. Such tasks may not seem real; they are often only simulations, opportunities to practice skills that may one day be used. But for the student, that day is not this day ... which means that utility value will seem be very low. In this context, school writing becomes an act of compliance, like filling out a worksheet, to be done and gotten over with.

Group Differences Mediated by Low Utility Value

Gender Effects. To the extent that writing becomes an act of compliance, social expectations and associated personality trait distributions may partially explain gender differences in writing achievement The proposed causal mechanism is a feedback loop in which gender differences (in particular, relative frequency of negative attitudes toward compliance with school requirements) exacerbate other educational issues. School or teacher reactions to academic disengagement may also elicit different consequences, based upon gendered identity (Disenhaus, 2015; Myers, 2018).

That there are male/female differences in interest and motivation, and not just writing performance is well established (Knudson, 1995; Reilly, Neumann, & Andrews, 2019). For instance, Daly and Miller (1975b) observed greater apprehension about writing in teenage boys than girls. Similarly, Graham, Berninger, and Abbott (2012), and Graham, Harris, Kiuhara, & Fishman (2017) found that girls had more positive attitudes toward reading and writing than boys. In their review of the literature, Meece, Glienke, and Burg (2006) concluded that boys expect to do well in mathematics, science, and sports, while girls show more positive motivation toward language arts skills, including reading and writing. Critically, they observe that gender motivation differences in mathematics and science tend to lessen with age, whereas females remain consistently more strongly motivated than males in the language arts. Burušić and Serić (2015) note that these differences in attitude link to the general trend in which boys have a slight advantage in numeric and spatial, and girls in verbal abilities, and raise the possibility that these differences may also be linked to differences in personality. Females may often respond better to academic failure than boys; at least, that is what Troia et al. (2013)'s results suggest, with girls but not boys showing increases in writing achievement motivation if their writing performance was low.

Certain "big five" personality traits, particularly conscientiousness, but also agreeableness, are predictive of academic performance (Poropat, 2009; Furnham, Nuygards, & Chamorro-Premuzic, 2013) and differentially distributed by gender. Bidjerano and Dai (2007) argue that certain combinations of personality traits (e.g., high degrees of conscientiousness, agreeableness, and emotional stability) protect students who might otherwise be at risk of academic failure. Sorić, Penezić, and Burić (2017) argue that conscientiousness and agreeableness increase adoption of mastery and performance-approach goals and decrease the adoption of avoidance goals, thereby increasing academic performance. Schmitt, Realo, Voracek, and Allik (2008) examined personality traits in more than 17,000 individuals in 55 countries and found that male/female personality differences are actually larger in developed countries, where power differences between males and females tend to be smaller. In their overall sample, despite considerable cross-country variation, and in the U.S. sample, women consistently showed higher levels of agreeableness and conscientiousness than men. These differences suggest that a larger proportion of females than males may be protected from academic disengagement because their personality traits, interests, and modes of social interaction may be better adapted to the way particular skills, including writing, are taught in school.

As Alloway (1997, p. 7) puts the case, the language arts curriculum emphasizes "processes of self-disclosure, introspection, empathic response, and personalized and creative expression" within a school context that requires students "to accept inferior status to the teacher, to experience powerlessness in the face of adult rule, to be regulated by the demands of the institution, and to be controlled by the state authority". Females are more strongly expected to comply with such expectations, whereas stereotypical understandings of masculine behavior encourage boys "to concentrate on things outside of self, rather than on the self," and to adopt an identity "more maverick, self-styled and independent than can be expressed within the processes of school regulation". These differences in expectation may favor boys in some contexts, such as oral conversation (Wolfe, 2000), but they may favor women more in many school contexts, where compliance is expected and is more in line with conventional female gender norms (Cleary, 1996; Contestabile, 2014), especially since students are likely to interpret one another's writing in gendered ways, which is likely to reinforce existing norms (Anderson, 2002; Jones, 2012).

Lack of motivation, misbehavior, and resistance to school norms are stereotypically more characteristic of boys than of girls. However, the extent to which teachers subscribe to the stereotypes can matter. Gendered social expectations can lead teachers to focus more on controlling off-task behavior among boys than among girls, where the cues for disengagement are often less salient (Swinson & Harrop, 2009). In fact, Bennett, Gottesman, Rock, and Cerullo (1993) observed that greater numbers of early-primary boys were classified as at risk academically due to behavior, rather than due to performance differences on academic tasks.

When boys' gendered behavior clashes with expected school behavior, especially if school instructional practice is not strongly motivating, a cycle of frustration, boredom, and disengagement may ensue, leading to lower achievement, which is likely to guarantee more frustration, more boredom, and greater disengagement (Sarroub & Pernicek, 2016). This cycle may be exacerbated by peer pressure that devalues academic achievement (Sandra Graham, Taylor, & Hudley, 1998). In fact, boys who show little evidence of strong literacy skills in school may excel in out-of-school literacies that they do not connect with literacy activities in school (Brown, 2015). Such gender effects are particularly problematic when teachers and other school personnel perceive minority boys as noncompliant and unmotivated (Glock & Klapproth, 2017). Perceived misbehaviors may demonstrate disconnects between school and community norms or reflect attempts to transform school-based practices into something more personally meaningful

(Blair & Sanford, 2004; Brozo, 2006). This mechanism may be particularly salient for writing because writing requires greater effort and more sustained attention than most classroom activities, which means that writing differences are more likely to be exacerbated (or controlled) by motivation (Brozo, 2019).

However, neither boys nor girls should be treated as monolithic groups (cf. Disenhaus, 2015). The causal mechanisms I have proposed are unlikely to apply across-the-board, to all boys or all girls: they define a causal sequence that will most strongly affect boys who are already at risk for failure due to other factors, who may compensate for poor school performance by emphasizing an identity in which they can perceive themselves as being neither failures nor powerless (Alloway, 2007; Martino, 1999; Watson, Kehler, & Martino, 2010). Avoiding a monolithic approach is also important because all students are likely to benefit from pedagogical techniques often recommended for boys, such as providing meaningful work that makes connections outside the classroom and making sure that school experiences instill a sense of agency (Assor, Kaplan, & Roth, 2002; Boscolo & Gelati, 2013).

Cultural and Racial Effects. In fact, the mechanisms I have described for male/female differences are likely to interact with other social identities than gender. As Balfanz, Byrne, and Fox (2015) indicate in their review of the data on school suspensions, suspension rates are particularly high among Black, economically disadvantaged, and special education students, and significantly reduces the likelihood that they will graduate or attend a postsecondary institution. In their data (drawn from a sample of more than 24,000 students from Florida schools), high suspension rates were correlated with lower attendance rates and course failures.

High suspension and dropout rates do not happen in a vacuum. They may be caused by punitive attitudes toward minority students (Payne & Welch, 2010). But they may also be caused by higher levels of boredom and frustration. Boredom is frequent enough for all students (Macklem, 2015, chapter 1), and it may be even more frequent for the groups that are likely to show lower levels of writing achievement, e.g., boys, and students from minority groups (Macklem, 2015, chapter 2). According to Pekrun's (2006) control valence theory, boredom occurs most often when students have little control over an activity and perceive it as being of little value (Pekrun, Goetz, Daniels, Stupnisky, & Perry, 2010). It follows that lower writing (or other academic) achievement and higher suspension and dropout rates for African American and Hispanic students may be partly due to higher levels of boredom and frustration. Boredom, in turn, may arise during classroom activities (including writing tasks) that seem purposeless and entirely disconnected from the rest of students' lives.

Divorcing school writing from real audiences, contexts, and purposes may be particularly problematic when combined with issues of race and ethnic diversity. Unfortunately, decontextualized writing instruction is often characteristic of schools serving students from low socioeconomic backgrounds (Becker & Luthar, 2002; Alderman, 2007, chapter 1). In such contexts, writing instruction focuses on short, formulaic assignments or on preparing students for the state accountability examinations (Applebee & Langer, 2011; Graham, 2019). Studies contrasting high- and low-performing schools have observed that lower-performing schools tend to favor teacher- and test-centered, rather than student-centered modes of instruction. In such environments, students are treated as passive recipients of instruction, and teachers emphasize discipline, increasing the likelihood of negative student/teacher interactions (Peabody, 2011; Hirn, Hollo, & Scott, 2018). To the extent that such practices predominate in majority-minority schools, they are likely to reinforce or even worsen achievement gaps in writing.

Intrinsic Value and Interest

The intrinsic value a writer attributes to writing also affects motivation. The literature distinguishes the intrinsic interest that an individual has in a task, from other, more situational sources of motivation, with intrinsic motivation (and greater individual autonomy) having more powerful, and lasting effects (Deci, Vallerand, Pelletier, & Ryan, 1991). There are two forms of intrinsic value that an individual may attach to a writing task: they may be intrinsically interested in the act of writing itself or in the topic about which they are writing.

Overview

Intrinsic interest in writing and development of writerly identities. Over time, as students develop their engagement with writing and their skills as writers, they may become intrinsically interested in writing and define their social identities at least partly around their participation in writing activities. Such interest needs to be developed. Intrinsic interest develops in stages. In the early stages, intrinsic interest and engagement depend critically on situational interest and personality (Schraw & Lehman, 2001). If interest is primarily motivated by extrinsic factors, such as grades, engagement beyond the immediate task is unlikely, and students are unlikely to develop the curiosity that supports long-term intrinsic interest (Thomas & Oldfather, 1997). If students are learning to write in a context that repeatedly creates strong situational interest, individual interest in writing as an activity will emerge, as ongoing, engaged participation will elicit curiosity and independent engagement (Hidi & Anderson, 1992; Hidi & Renninger, 2006; cf. Luria, Shalom, & Levy, 2021).

There is an important relationship between the development of interest and the formation of individual identity. At early stages of interest development, where students do not feel competent, they may be very sensitive to criticism; thus, an instructional approach that emphasizes grades and relative academic performance may undercut writing interest for all but the strongest students (Renninger, 2009). Even social approaches to writing instruction, such as writer's workshop, can have a negative effect on less-confident writers if a competitive environment is allowed to develop (Lipstein & Renninger, 2006). But if social interactions are kept supportive and collaborative, students can provide one another with a literate community with a real audience and purpose, and thus provide the support that students need to develop intrinsic interest in writing (Hidi, Berndorff, & Ainley, 2002; Nolen, 2007; Oldfather & Shanahan, 2007)..

The implications for at-risk groups are significant. If the classroom environment is not engaging and encourages students to focus on performance goals such as grades, motivation and performance are likely to suffer for all but the most advantaged groups and for the highest-performing writers within those groups (Bruning & Horn, 2000; Boscolo & Gelati, 2013).

The role of topic interest. Topic interest helps people focus and sustain attention (Hidi, Renninger, & Krapp, 2004), which can lead to stronger writing performance (Abbott, Mickail, Richards, Renninger, Beers, & Berninger, 2017). There are significant interactions between writing quality, prior knowledge, and interest. Hidi and colleagues (Hidi & McLaren, 1991; Hidi & Anderson, 1992) examined what happens when students have high interest and low knowledge, or low interest and high-knowledge, by assigning writing tasks with or without a tutorial designed to build up topical knowledge. High topic interest did not compensate for a lack of knowledge, whereas deeper post-tutorial knowledge, even in the face of lack of interest, produced higher-quality writing. However, Benton, Corkill, Sharp, Downey, and Khramtsova (1995) found that when prior topic knowledge was present, topical interest predicted additional variance in the writing quality above and beyond the variance predicted by topic knowledge alone.

Complicating the picture still further, Boscolo and colleagues (Boscolo, Del Favero, & Borghetto, 2007; Boscolo, Ariasi, Del Favero, & Ballarin, 2011) examined what happens to interest when students read and then write about informational texts. Their studies indicated complex interrelationships among topic interest, change in topical knowledge, general interest in writing, and writing task type. Harder writing tasks decreased topic interest. Conversely, high levels of general interest in writing increased topic interest, though the effects were stronger for some writing tasks than for others. Situational interest also appears to increase when topics are made more personally meaningful, via connections to previously developed interests (Hidi & Renninger, 2019), personal experience (Böhm, 2017; Bernacki & Walkington, 2018), and other people (Fryer, Shum, Lee, & Lau, 2021).

One implication is that selecting "interesting" topics may not have a straightforward impact on writing quality, due to interactions with students' prior knowledge and interests, their personal attitudes about writing, the social context within which they are writing, and the specific reading and writing tasks assigned.

The Role of Choice. Topic interest is closely allied with topic choice. All other things being equal, we would expect students to select more interesting topics, when given the choice. Having a choice of writing topics has a motivating effect (Turner, 1995; Patall, Cooper, & Robinson, 2008). Topic choice promotes a more positive attitude, elicits greater effort (Flowerday & Schraw, 2003), and sometimes increases writing quality (Patall, 2013; Ryan & Deci, 2017). However, students are more likely to choose a topic they know well than one they are interested in but lack the knowledge to develop (Gradwohl & Schumacher, 1989). In some contexts, writing quality improves when writers are given a choice of writing tasks or topics (Bridgeman, Morgan, & Wang, 1997; Powers & Bennett, 1999; Bonyadi, 2014). In other studies, where the topics were drawn from large scale writing assessments, no difference in performance based on topic choice was observed (Powers, Fowles, Farnum, & Gerritz, 1992; Gabrielson & Gordon, 1995; Jennings, Fox, Graves, & Shohamy, 1999). However, choices within a task can also have a motivating effect. For instance, Aitken, Graham, and McNeish (2022) found that giving students a choice of which side to defend improved student motivation, and Rosenzweig, Harackiewicz, Priniski, Hecht, Canning, Tibbetts, and Hyde (2019) found that giving students in biology course choice of written response format, such as letter vs. essay, led to significantly higher motivation and indirectly, to higher course grades and a higher likelihood of enrollment in a course in the same subject.

Group Differences Mediated by Topic Interest and Topic Choice

Gender Differences. It seems evident that differences in culture, lived experience, and background knowledge between social groups will have a significant impact on what members of those groups are motivated to write about. If we examine the earlier literature on gender differences in topic choice, this is exactly what we find (Graves, 1975; Gray-Schlegel & Gray-Schlegel, 1995). According to Peterson

(2000)'s review of this literature, males tended to differ from females in their choice of topics along the following dimensions:

* *Relationship to the writer's experience.* Girls tended to select story topics situated within "primary territory", dealing with personal situations and emotions. Boys tended to place stories within "tertiary territory", dealing with imaginary or distant situations with no immediate connection to personal experience.
* *Gender of the character in control.* Student writers tended to write about characters of their own gender.
* *Focus on action or violence vs. emotions and relationships.* Males tended more often to include topics that included risk, problem solving, and especially action sequences or violence. Females were more likely to focus on emotions and relationships.

King and Gurian (2006), Scheuer, de la Cruz, Pedrazzini, Iparraguirre, and Pozo (2012) and Gelati (2012) make similar observations about differences between boys' and girls' topic preferences in writing. However, it is important to note that there can be considerable variation in interests among students of the same gender, compared to relatively small average differences between genders (Koutsogiannis & Adampa, 2012).

It is important to recognize that differences in writing topic choice may in part be responses to the expectations of students and teachers (Peterson, 2001, 2002). This may rapidly lead to conflict, particularly for boys, if their topic choices conflict with the topics that their (in all probability, female) teachers consider appropriate and interesting (Beaton, 2010; DeFauw, 2016). Allowing students autonomy as writers necessarily requires teachers to relinquish control, especially since, as Disenhaus (2015) reports, topic choice had a significant impact on boys' motivation for writing.

Social and Cultural Differences. Considering the importance of cultural relevance and cultural responsiveness in recent theorizing, and the frequency with which advocates of culturally relevant and culturally responsive pedagogies advocate giving students topic choice (Montgomery, 2001; Howard, 2011; Lewis Chiu, Carrero, & Lusk, 2017), surprisingly little concrete, empirical information is available about how cultural differences affect topic interest and topic choice in writing. A starting point can be found in computational linguistic studies like Canziani, Esmizdeh, and Nemati (2021) or Gutiérrez, Shutova, Lichtenstein, de Melo, and Gilardi (2016). These studies found that social and cultural differences tend to be correlated with significant differences both in the kinds of topics that people choose to write about and in the way ideas are framed by their linguistic choices.

Overall, the literature on topic interest and topic choice suggests that having topic choice is beneficial when the classroom culture values writing and grants students enough autonomy to develop and write about subjects of deep intrinsic interest (Paris & Turner, 1995). But topic interest and topic choice are unlikely to overcome a lack of topic knowledge or the absence of an authentic audience, purpose, and social context for writing.

Attainment Value

Overview

Attainment value is the importance that people attribute to an activity based on personal identity and values, as opposed to the more immediate, personal sense of usefulness that defines utility value. As such, attainment value is strongly associated with social and cultural values, the role models people admire, and the social groups they actively identify with (Eccles, 2009). The attainment value of school activities is thus strongly influenced by the extent to an activity is valued by the community and by peers, and ultimately, by the extent to which students feel that the activity is appropriate, meaningful, and important for people like themselves. Since students form their social identities while they are being schooled, their response to instruction is partly conditioned by their developing self-concepts, and their self-concepts, in turn, are molded by their school experience (McCarthy, 2001). For writing, the critical issue is whether the texts and writing practices to which they are exposed encourage them to identify as writers.

Group Differences Mediated by Attainment Value and Identity Formation

Writerly Identities and Gender. As someone who wishes not just to be an academic writer, but also a writer of fiction, I have had occasion to attend meetings of a variety of writing groups, including the Society of Children's Book Writers and Illustrators (SCBWI). Attending an SCBWI meeting, or meetings of other, similar groups, is an exercise in gender imbalance. More than 80 % of the people I encounter at such meetings are women—almost exclusively, White and Asian women. This reflects the fact that there are significant gender imbalances in book authorship by genre: more female authors of fiction; more male authors of nonfiction; more female authors of children, young adult, and romance novels; more male authors of science fiction, graphical novels, and comics (Thelwall, 2017). On an online community like Goodreads, we see similar gender imbalances in the genres that people who self-identify as male and female more characteristically review: Female reviewers predominate in such genres as romance, erotica, children's picture books, and paranormal fantasy; male reviewers predominate in such genres as philosophy, politics, history, science fiction, graphic novels, and comics (Thelwall, 2019). These differences correspond to differences in readership, with women generally tending to read more than men, and to read relatively more fiction (Taylor, 2019).

In U.S. schools, three-quarters of teachers are female (Ingersoll, Merrill, Stuckey, & Collins, 2019), and 83 % of English Language Arts teachers (Nguyen & Northrop, 2022). Thus, to the extent that teachers' personal preferences affect their selection and presentation of writing assignments and reading materials, there may be more frequent congruence between girls' developing identities as readers and writers and their classroom experiences.

Writerly Identities and Race. When a minority group has long been discriminated against, existing social and educational practices may perpetuate discriminatory patterns. Various authors have argued that this is exactly what happens when Black students encounter traditional instructional practices. African American discourse is characterized by rhetorical and linguistic patterns derived in part from African cultural traditions, and largely transmitted through a culture centered on African American cultural institutions, including primarily Black church denominations (Smitherman, 1976; Alim & Smitherman, 2012). Many of these patterns may be disvalued in school because they do not match majority community expectations or the educational policies that those expectations inform (Rosa & Flores, 2017; Cushing, 2022), even though they are both appropriate and effective in context (Ball, 1992; Delpit, 2006).

If school practices require students to adopt communicative practices that contradict their everyday norms or require them to abandon their own culture as the price of school success, there is a risk that they will become alienated and not value academic achievement as much as they otherwise would (Ford & Harris, 1995; Fordham & Ogbu, 1986; Gay, 2010). This can lead to in-group peer pressure that discourages a focus on academic achievement (Kaplan & Maehr, 1999; Fryer & Torelli, 2010). This may be particularly an issue for Black males, where the intersection of social issues related to race and gender may have particularly potent effects (Tatum & Gue, 2012; Tatum, Johnson, & McMillon, 2020).

There is much more going on here than the risk that teachers and school staff will display negative attitudes toward African American Vernacular English. If the language, texts and topics assigned to minority students seem to exclude them—to be written by, and for, people who "are not like me"—alienation and disengagement are likely to follow, even if there is no overt bias against any specific accent or dialect. Conversely, students are likely to be more engaged, and to produce stronger writing, when the texts and topics assigned to them have greater cultural relevance (Norment, 1997, 2021).

These points bring us back to issues of culturally relevant (and culturally responsive) pedagogy first broached in Chapter One, but it casts them in a somewhat different light. The point of culturally relevant writing pedagogy is that it can help build identities in which being a writer has high attainment value. When students can imagine writing in terms that resonate with rather than undercut the way they understand themselves and their world, they are more likely to make writing a fundamental part of their identities (Haddix, 2009, 2018).

Writerly Identities, Culture, and Language. The causal mechanisms I described in the preceding sections are not specific to gender or racial groups. Low-SES and immigrant communities may favor modes of discourse that differ significantly from those preferred in upper-middle-class communities, resulting in miscommunication between students and teachers (Crago, Eriks-Brophy, Pesco, & McAlpine, 1977; Au, 2016). Working-class or Hispanic writers who successfully adapt to the academic requirements of school may experience academic writing as a kind of game, in which they create the impression of belonging to communities they do not identify with and whose language (or dialect) they do not speak (Ashley, 2022, pp. 229–254). This may interact with an emphasis on form and correctness (linked to the imposition of standard English) which can limit the extent to which writing instruction focuses on meaningful communication about interesting topics (Douillard, 2006) and causes students to become alienated or disengaged from school (Snell, 2013).

As before, males appear to be particularly at risk. Sandra Graham, Taylor, and Hudley (1998) observed that Latina females tended to admire high-achieving Latina females, whereas Latino males tended to admire low-achieving Latino males, paralleling the higher academic and writing performance for Latinas over Latinos. As before, students may learn to disconnect out-of-school literacy practices from in-school writing (Stewart, 2014), with predictable negative consequences for academic performance (Jackson, 2002). Once again, we observe an interaction between identity formation and learning. Students who feel excluded may develop identities that preclude their self-identification as writers.

Thus far I have focused on the harm that can be caused by a disconnect between student identities and the writing varieties and practices favored in school. But the reverse relationship also holds. Writing instruction for students from low-SES or ESL backgrounds appears to be most effective when the cultural

Table 2.1 Causal Mechanisms Associated with Writing Motivation.

Causal Factor	Gender	SES	Race
Higher self-efficacy produces higher levels of resilience and persistence. However, low performance reduces self-efficacy over time.	Self-efficacy is higher on average for females	Self-efficacy is corelated with SES	
Mastery orientation leads to stronger learning and performance	Girls are more likely to set mastery goals. Boys are more likely to set performance goals.		
Mastery orientation leads to increased self-regulation	Girls tend to show higher levels of self-regulation.		
Competitive classroom environments reduce mastery orientation and increase apprehension.	Low-performing students are more likely to adopt performance avoidance goals and display increased levels of apprehension. Low-performing boys are more likely to develop performance avoidance goals and higher levels of apprehension.		
		Decontextualized writing tasks may be characteristic of low-SES and minority schools.	
Decontextualized writing tasks lead to low utility value, linking performance with compliance attitudes under conditions favoring boredom and disengagement.	Traditional gender roles demand higher levels of female compliance. More females than males show high levels of Agreeableness and Conscientiousness Suspension and dropout rates are higher for boys	Group stereotypes associate poverty and minority groups with lower levels of compliance. Suspension and dropout rates are higher for low-SES students.	Suspension and dropout rates are higher for African American and Hispanic students.

(*Continued*)

Table 2.1 Continued

Causal Factor	Gender	SES	Race
Motivation is increased when students write about topics that they are interested in.	Students are likely to conform with gendered interest patterns, favoring nonfiction for males, most forms of fiction for females School writing is mostly taught in language arts classes that have historically tended to emphasize literary works/narrative over nonfiction.	School writing tasks often fail to draw on the interests and funds of knowledge that students bring with them from working class and minority communities.	
Motivation is increased when students have greater choice and agency.	Boys' motivation for writing increases when they have a choice of topics.	Giving students choice and greater autonomy is strongly advocated by proponents of culturally responsive teaching.	
Student motivation increases if they can treat authority figures as role models.	More than 80 % of teachers are female.	More than 80 % of teachers are White.	
Motivation is increased when students can see how the writing tasks that they are assigned in school will have value in their lives outside school.		The norms and genres of academic writing are more likely to be familiar and meaningful for students from upper-middle-class families.	School tasks impose expectations that clash with literate traditions specific to minority communities (such as "preaching" and "testifying" in African American communities)

differences are understood and welcomed and meaningful connections are made between school literacy and students' home language and culture (Ball, 2006; Au, 2009; Wingate, 2015). People who speak more than one language or language variety have social and cultural assets that can help them think and communicate more effectively. Their home language be easier to use at certain stages of the writing process—for instance, when they are taking notes, or developing a writing plan. Their home language may give them access to texts and literary traditions that are unavailable to monolingual speakers of standard American English. These advantages are invisible in strictly monolingual classrooms, where writers must present themselves in an alien context. In a multicultural context, people may slip fluently from one language to the other—or mix languages within the same communication for expressive purposes—or switch languages mid-stream to communicate concepts that are more clearly expressed in one language than the other. These considerations provide strong motivation for teachers to consider a translingual approach to writing instruction. Both teachers and students can benefit from a pedagogy that builds on the strengths students bring with them from their home languages and cultures (Horner, Lu, Royster, & Trimbur, 2011; Losey & Shuck, 2021; Stewart, Hansen-Thomas, Flint, & Núñez, 2022)

Table 2.1 summarizes the causal mechanisms that are associated with group differences in writing motivation and performance.

Reference List

Abbott, R., Mickail, T., Richards, T., Renninger, K. A., Hidi, S. E., Beers, S., & Berninger, V. International Journal of Educational Methodology.

Aitken, A. A., Graham, S., & McNeish, D. (2022). The effects of choice versus preference on writing and the mediating role of perceived competence. *Journal of Educational Psychology, 114*(8), 1844–1865. https://doi.org/10.1037/edu0000765

Alderman, M. K. (2007). *Motivation for Achievement: Possibilities for Teaching and Learning.* Routledge. https://doi.org/10.4324/9780203823132

Alim, H. S., & Smitherman, G. (2012). *Articulate While Black: Barack Obama, Language, and Race in the U.S.* Oxford University Press.

Alloway, N. (1997). Boys and literacy: Lessons from Australia, gender & education. *Gender and Education, 91*(1), 49–60. https://doi.org/10.1080/09540259721448

Alloway, N. (2007). Swimming against the tide: Boys, literacies, and schooling – an Australian story. *Canadian Journal of Education / Revue Canadienne de l'Éducation, 30*(2), 582–605. https://doi.org/10.2307/20466651

Ames, C. (1992). Classrooms: Goals, structures, and student motivation. *Journal of Educational Psychology, 84*(3), 261–271. https://doi.org/10.1037/0022-0663.84.3.261

Anderson, D. D. (2002). Casting and recasting gender: Children constituting social identities through literacy practices. *Research in the Teaching of English, 36*(3), 391–427.

Andrade, H. L., Wang, X., Du, Y., & Akawi, R. L. (2010). Rubric-referenced self-assessment and self efficacy for writing. *The Journal of Educational Research, 102*(4), 287–302. https://doi.org/10.3200/JOER.102.4.287-302

Applebee, A. N., & Langer, J. A. (2011). "EJ" Extra: A snapshot of writing instruction in middle schools and high schools. *The English Journal, 100*(6), 14–27. https://www.jstor.org/stable/23047875

Ashley, L. (2022). *Highly Discriminating*. Bristol University Press.

Assor, A., Kaplan, H., & Roth, G. (2002). Choice is good, but relevance is excellent: Autonomy-enhancing and suppressing teacher behaviours predicting students' engagement in schoolwork. *British Journal of Educational Psychology, 72*(2), 261–278. https://doi.org/10.1348/000709902158883

Atkinson, J. W. (1957). Motivational determinants of risk-taking behavior. *Psychological Review, 64*(6p1), 359–372. https://psycnet.apa.org/doi/10.1037/h0043445

Au, K. H. (2009). Isn't culturally responsive instruction just good teaching? *Social Education, 73*(4), 179–183. https://www.ingentaconnect.com/content/ncss/se/2009/00000073/00000004/art00008

Au, K. H. (Ed.) (2016). *Multicultural Issues and Literacy Achievement*. Lawrence Erlbaum. https://doi.org/10.4324/9781315045450

Baker-Bell, A. (2020). *Linguistic Justice: Black Language, Literacy, Identity, and Pedagogy*. Routledge.

Balfanz, R., Byrnes, V., & Fox, J. H. (2015). Sent home and put off track. In D. J. Losen (Ed.), *Closing the School Discipline Gap: Equitable Remedies for Excessive Exclusion* (pp. 17–30). Teachers College Press.

Ball, A. F. (1992). Cultural preference and the expository writing of African American adolescents. *Written Communication, 9*(4), 501–532. https://doi.org/10.1177/0741088392009004003

Ball, A. F. (2006). Teaching writing in culturally diverse classrooms. In C. A. MacArthur, S. Graham, & J. Fitzgerald (Eds.), *Handbook of Writing Research* (pp. 293–310). Guilford.

Bandura, A. (1997). *Self-Efficacy: The Exercise of Control*. Freeman.

Beaton, A. M. (2010). Student choice in writing: Reflections on one teacher's inner struggle to relinquish control. *Schools, 7*(1), 111–121. https://doi.org/10.1086/651296

Becker, B. E., & Luthar, S. S. (2002). Social-emotional factors affecting achievement outcomes among disadvantaged students: Closing the achievement gap. *Educational Psychologist, 37*(4), 197–214. https://doi.org/10.1207/S15326985EP3704_1

Bennett, R. E., Gottesman, R. L., Rock, D. A., & Cerullo, F. (1993). Influence of behavior perceptions and gender on teachers' judgments of students' academic skill. *Journal of Educational Psychology, 85*(2), 347–356. https://doi.org/10.1037/0022-0663.85.2.347

Benton, S. L., Corkill, A. J., Sharp, J. M., Downey, R. G., & Khramtsova, I. (1995). Knowledge, interest, and narrative writing. *Journal of Educational Psychology, 87*(1), 66–79. https://doi.org/10.1037/0022-0663.87.1.66

Bernacki, M. L., & Walkington, C. (2018). The role of situational interest in personalized learning. *Journal of Educational Psychology, 110*(6), 864–881. https://doi..org/10.1037/edu0000250

Berninger, V. W. (2000). Development of language by hand and its connections to language by ear, mouth, and eye. *Topics of Language Disorders, 20*(4), 65–84. https://psycnet.apa.org/doi/10.1097/00011363-200020040-00007

Berninger, V. W., & Graham, S. (1998). Language by hand: A synthesis of a decade of research on handwriting. *Handwriting Review, 12,* 11–25.

Bidjerano, T., & Dai, D. Y. (2007). The relationship between the Big-Five model of personality and self-regulated learning strategies. *Learning and Individual Differences, 17*(1), 69–81. https://doi.org/10.1016/j.lindif.2007.02.001

Blackwell, L. A., Trzesniewski, K. H., & Dweck, C. S. (2007). Implicit theories of intelligence and achievement across an adolescent transition: A longitudinal study and an intervention. *Child Development, 78*(1), 246–263. https://doi.org/10.1111/j.1467-8624.2007.00995.x

Blair, H. A., & Sanford, K. (2004). Morphing literacy: Boys reshaping Their school-based literacy practices. *Language Arts, 81*(6), 452–460.

Bogner, K., Raphael, L., & Pressley, M. (2002). How grade 1 teachers motivate literate activity by their students. *Scientific Studies of Reading, 6*(2), 135–165. https://doi.org/10.1207/S15327 99XSSR0602_02

Böhm, M. (2017). *The Influence of Situational Interest on the Appropriate Use of Cognitive Learning Strategies* [Doctoral dissertation, Universität Passau]. OPUS. https://opus4.kobv.de/opus4-uni-passau/files/491/boehm_matthias_influenceSI.pdf

Bonyadi, A. (2014). The effect of topic selection on EFL students' writing performance. *SAGE Open, 4*(3). https://doi.org/10.1177/2158244014547176

Boscolo, P., Ariasi, N., Del Favero, L., & Ballarin, C. (2011). Interest in an expository text: How does it flow from reading to writing?. *Learning and Instruction, 21*(3), 467-480.

Boscolo, P., Del Favero, L., & Borghetto, M. (2006). Writing on an interesting topic: Does writing foster interest?. In Writing and motivation (pp. 71-91). Brill.

Boscolo, P., & Gelati, C. (2013). Best practices in writing motivation. In S. Graham, C. A. MacArthur, & J. Fitzgerald (Eds.), *Best Practices in Writing Instruction* (2nd ed., pp. 284–308). Guilford.

Boscolo, P., & Hidi, S. (2007). The multiple meanings of motivation to write. In P. Boscolo & S. Hidi (Eds.), *Writing and Motivation* (pp. 1–16). Elsevier.

Bridgeman, B., Morgan, R., & Wang, M.. (1997). Choice among essay topics: Impact on performance and validity. *Journal of Educational Measurement, 34*(3), 273–286. https://doi.org/10.1111/j.1745-3984.1997.tb00519.x

Brown, D. W. (2015). *These Heads Are Packed with Stories: The Out-of-School Writing Experiences of Elementary Age Boys.* [Doctoral dissertation, Georgia State University]. Scholarworks. http://scholarworks.gsu.edu/cgi/viewcontent.cgi?article=1007&context=mse_diss

Brozo, W. G. (2006). Bridges to literacy for boys: Boys' passions, hobbies, aspirations, and experiences can spark meaningful literacy development. *Educational Leadership, 64*(1), 71–74.

Brozo, W. G. (2019). *Engaging Boys in Active Literacy: Evidence and Practice.* Cambridge University Press.

Bruning, R. H., Dempsey, M., & Kim, C. (2013). Examining dimensions of self-efficacy for writing. *Journal of Educational Psychology, 105*(1), 35–38. https://doi.org/10.1037/a0029692

Bruning, R. H., & Horn, C. (2000). Developing motivation to write. *Educational Psychology, 35*(1), 25–37. https://doi.org/10.1207/S15326985EP3501_4

Bruning, R. H., & Kauffman, D. F. (2015). Self-efficacy beliefs and motivation in writing development. In C. A. MacArthur, S. Graham, & J. Fitzgerald (Eds.), *Handbook of Writing Research* (pp. 160–173). Guilford.

Buck, A. (2012). Examining digital literacy practices on social network sites. *Research in the Teaching of English, 47*(1), 9–38. https://www.jstor.org/stable/41583603

Burušić, J., & Serić, M. (2015). Girls' and boys' achievements differences in the school context: An overview of possible explanations. *Croatian Journal of Education, 17*(Sp.Ed.4), 137–173. https://doi.org/10.15516/cje.v17i0.800

Camacho, A., Alves, R. A., & Boscolo, P. (2021). Writing motivation in school: A systematic review of empirical research in the early twenty-first century. Educational Psychology Review, 33(1), 213-247.

Canziani, B. F., Esmizadeh, Y., & Nemati, H. R. (2021). Student engagement with global issues: the influence of gender, race/ethnicity, and major on topic choice. *Teaching in Higher Education.* https://doi.org/10.1080/13562517.2021.1955340

Chan, J. C., & Lam, S. F. (2008). Effects of competition on students' self-efficacy in vicarious learning. *British Journal of Educational Psychology, 78*(1), 95–108. https://doi.org/10.1348/000709907X185509

Chung, H. Q., Chen, V., & Booth Olson, C. (2021). The impact of self-assessment, planning and goal setting, and reflection before and after revision on student self-efficacy and writing performance. *Reading and Writing, 34*(7), 1885–1913. https://doi.org/10.1007/s11145-021-10186-x

Cleary, L. M. (1991). Affect and cognition in the writing processes of eleventh graders. *Written Communication, 8*(4), 473–507. https://doi.org/10.1177/0741088391008004003

Cleary, L. M. (1996). "I Think I Know What My Teachers Want Now": Gender and writing motivation. *The English Journal, 85*(1), 50–57. https://doi.org/10.2307/821123

Codling, R. M., & Gambrell, L. B. (1997). *The Motivation to Write Profile: An Assessment Tool for Elementary Teachers.* National Reading Research Center. https://files.eric.ed.gov/fulltext/ED402562.pdf

Collie, R. J., Martin, A. J., & Curwood, J. S. (2016). Multidimensional motivation and engagement for writing: Construct validation with a sample of boys. *Educational Psychology, 36*(4), 771–791. https://doi.org/10.1080/01443410.2015.1093607

Contestabile, N. J. (2014). *Boys' Interest in Writing.* [Master's Thesis, The College at Brockport, State University of New York]. SOAR. https://soar.suny.edu/bitstream/handle/20.500.12648/5544/ehd_theses/350/fulltext%20%281%29.pdf?sequence=1&isAllowed=y

Cordeiro, C., Castro, S. L., & Limpo, T. (2018). Examining potential sources of gender differences in writing: The role of handwriting fluency and self-efficacy beliefs. *Written Communication, 35*(4), 448–473. https://doi.org/10.1177/0741088318788843

Crago, M. B., Eriks-Brophy, A., Pesco, D., & McAlpine, L. (1977). Culturally based miscommunication in classroom interaction. *Language, Speech & Hearing Services in Schools, 28*(3), 245–254. https://doi.org/10.1044/0161-1461.2803.245

Curwood, J. S., Magnifico, A. M., & Lammers, J. C. (2013). Writing in the wild: Writer's motivation in fan-based affinity spaces. *Journal of Adolescent & Adult Literacy, 56*(8), 677–685. https://doi.org/10.1002/JAAL.192

Cushing, I. (2022). Raciolinguistic policy assemblages and White supremacy in teacher education. *The Curriculum Journal, 34*(1), 43–61. https://doi.org/10.1002/curj.173

Daly, J. A., & Miller, M. D. (1975a). The empirical development of an instrument to measure writing apprehension. *Research in the Teaching of English, 9*(3), 242–249.

Daly, J. A., & Miller, M. D. (1975b). Further studies on writing apprehension: SAT scores, success expectations, willingness to take advanced courses and sex differences. *Research in the Teaching of English, 9*(3), 250–256.

Deane, P. D. (2018). The challenges of writing in school: Conceptualizing writing development within a sociocognitive framework. *Educational Psychologist, 53*(4), 280–300, https://doi.org/10.1080/00461520.2018.1513844

Deci, E. L., Betley, G., Kahle, J., Abrams, L., & Porac, J. (1981). When trying to win: Competition and intrinsic motivation. *Personality and Social Psychology Bulletin, 7*(1), 79–83. https://doi.org/10.1177/014616728171012

Deci, E. L., Vallerand, R. J., Pelletier, L. G., & Ryan, R. M. (1991). Motivation and education: The self-determination perspective. *Educational Psychologist, 26*(3–4), 325–346. https://doi.org/10.1080/00461520.1991.9653137

DeFauw, D. L. (2016). Supporting boy writers. *Literacy Practice & Research, 41*(2), 52–53.

Delpit, L. D. (2006). *Other People's Children: Cultural Conflict in the Classroom.* The New Press.

Dempsey, M. S. (2013). *Self-Efficacy for Metalinguistic Control and Its Relationship to Writing Quality.* [Doctoral dissertation, University of Nebraska]. DigitalCommons. https://digitalcommons.unl.edu/cgi/viewcontent.cgi?article=1192&context=cehsdiss..

Diederich, P. B., French, J. W., & Carlton, S. T. (1961). *Factors in Judgments of Writing Ability* (ETS-RB-61–15). Educational Testing Service. https://doi.org/10.1002/j.2333-8504.1961.tb00286.x

Disenhaus, N. (2015). *Boys, Writing, and the Literacy Gender Gap: What We Know, What We Think We Know.* [Doctoral dissertation, The University of Vermont]. ScholarWorks. https://scholarworks.uvm.edu/cgi/viewcontent.cgi?article=1329&context=graddis

Douillard, K. A. (2006). *Examining the Teaching and Learning of Writing in Elementary School.* [Doctoral dissertation, University of California San Diego]. Escholarship.org. https://escholarship.org/content/qt4sq9z648/qt4sq9z648.pdf

Dredger, K., Woods, D., Beach, C., & Sagstetter, V. (2013). Engage me: Using new literacies to create third space classrooms that engage student writers. *Journal of Media Literacy Education, 2*(2), 85–101. https://doi.org/10.23860/jmle-2-2-1

Duijnhouwer, H., Prins, F. J., & Stokking, K. M. (2012). Feedback providing improvement strategies and reflection on feedback use: Effects on students' writing motivation, process, and performance. *Learning and Instruction, 22*(3), 171–184. https://doi.org/10.1016/j.learninstruc.2011.10.003

Dunsmuir, S., & Peter, B. (2004). Predictors of writing competence in 4-to 7-year-old children. *British Journal of Educational Psychology, 74*(3), 461–483. https://doi.org/10.1348/0007099041552323

Dweck, C. S., & Leggett, E. L. (1988). A social-cognitive approach to motivation and personality. *Psychological Review, 95*(2), 256–273. https://doi.org/10.1037/0033-295X.95.2.256

Eccles, J. (2009). Who am I and what am I going to do with my life? Personal and collective identities as motivators of action. *Educational Psychologist, 44*(2), 78–89. https://doi.org/10.1080/00461520902832368

Eccles, J. S., & Wigfield, A. (2002). Motivational beliefs, values, and goals. *Annual Review of Psychology, 53*(1), 109–132. https://doi.org/10.1146/annurev.psych.53.100901.135153

Elliott, E. S., & Dweck, C. S. (1988). Goals: An approach to motivation and achievement. *Journal of Personality and Social Psychology, 54*(1), 5–12. https://doi.org/10.1037/0022-3514.54.1.5

Evans, G. W., & Kim, P. (2013). Childhood poverty, chronic stress, self-regulation, and coping. *Child Development Perspectives, 7*(1), 43–48. https://doi.org/10.1111/cdep.12013

Flowerday, T., & Schraw, G. (2003). Effect of choice on cognitive and affective engagement. *The Journal of Educational Research, 96*(4), 207–215. https://doi.org/10.1080/00220670309598810

Fong, C. J., Williams, K. M., Williamson, Z. H., Lin, S., Kim, Y. W., & Schallert, D. L. (2018). "Inside out": Appraisals for achievement emotions from constructive, positive, and negative feedback on writing. *Motivation and Emotion, 42*(2), 236–257. https://doi.org/10.1007/s11031-017-9658-y

Ford, D. Y., & Harris, J. J. (1995). Perceptions and attitudes of Black students toward school, achievement, and other educational variables. *Child Development, 67*(3), 1141–1152. https://doi.org/10.1111/j.1467-8624.1996.tb01787.x

Fordham, S., & Ogbu, J. U. (1986). Black students' school success: Coping with the "burden of 'acting White'". *The Urban Review, 18*(3), 176–206. https://doi.org/10.1007/BF01112192

Fryer, L. K., Shum, A., Lee, A., & Lau, P. (2021). Mapping students' interest in a new domain: Connecting prior knowledge, interest, and self-efficacy with interesting tasks and a lasting desire to reengage. *Learning and Instruction, (75),* Article 101493. https://doi.org/10.1016/j.learninstruc.2021.101493

Fryer, R. G., & Torelli, P. (2010). An empirical analysis of 'acting White'. *Journal of Public Economics, 94*(5), 380–396. https://doi.org/10.1016/j.jpubeco.2009.10.011

Furnham, A., Nuygards, S., & Chamorro-Premuzic, T. (2013). Personality, assessment methods and academic performance. *Instructional Science, 41*(5), 975–987. https://doi.org/10.1007/s11251-012-9259-9

Furrer, C., & Skinner, E. (2003). Sense of relatedness as a factor in children's academic engagement and performance. *Journal of Educational Psychology, 95*(1), 148–141, 162. https://doi.org/10.1037/0022-0663.95.1.148

Gabrielson, S., & Gordon, B. (1995). The effect of task choice on the quality of writing obtained in a statewide assessment. *Applied Measurement in Education, 8*(4), 273–290. https://doi.org/10.1207/s15324818ame0804_1

García, J.-N., & Fidalgo, R. (2008). Writing self-efficacy changes after cognitive strategy intervention in students with learning disabilities: The mediational role of gender in calibration. *The Spanish Journal of Psychology, 11*(2), 414–432. https://doi.org/10.1017/S1138741600004431

Gardner, P. (2013). Writing in context: Reluctant writers and their writing at home and at school. *English in Australia, 48*(1), 71–81.

Gasser, L., Grütter, J., Torchetti, L., & Buholzer, A. (2017). Competitive classroom norms and exclusion of children with academic and behavior difficulties. *Journal of Applied Developmental Psychology,* (49), 1–11. https://doi.org/10.1016/j.appdev.2016.12.002

Gay, G. (2010). *Culturally Responsive Teaching: Theory, Research, and Practice.* Teachers College Press.

Gelati, Carmen (2012). Female superiority and gender similarity effects and interest factors in writing. Past, present, and future contributions of cognitive writing research to cognitive psychology, 153-174.

Glock, S., & Klapproth, F. (2017). Bad boys, good girls? Implicit and explicit attitudes toward ethnic minority students among elementary and secondary school teachers. *Studies in Educational Evaluation,* (53), 77–86. https://doi.org/10.1016/j.stueduc.2017.04.002

Gradwohl, J. M., & Schumacher, G. M. (1989). The relationship between content knowledge and topic choice in writing. *Written Communication, 6*(2), 181–195. https://doi.org/10.1177/0741088389006002003

Graham, S. (2019). Changing how writing is taught. *Review of Research in Education, 43*(1), 277–303. https://doi.org/10.3102/0091732X18821125

Graham, S., Berninger, V. W., & Abbott, R. (2012). Are attitudes toward writing and reading separable constructs? A study with primary grade children. *Reading & Writing Quarterly, 28*(1), 51–69. https://doi.org/10.1080/10573569.2012.632732

Graham, S., Berninger, V. W., & Fan, W. (2007). The structural relationship between writing attitude and writing achievement in first and third grade students. *Contemporary Educational Psychology, 32*(3), 516–536. https://doi.org/10.1016/j.cedpsych.2007.01.002

Graham, S., Daley, S. G., Aitken, A. A., Harris, K. R., & Robinson, K. H. (2018). Do writing motivational beliefs predict middle school students' writing performance? *Journal of Research in Reading, 41*(4), 642–656. https://doi.org/10.1111/1467-9817.12245

Graham, S., Harbaugh-Schattenkirk, A. G., Aitken, A., Harris, K. R., Ng, C., Ray, A., ... & Wdowin, J. (2022). Writing motivation questionnaire: validation and application as a formative assessment. *Assessment in Education: Principles, Policy & Practice, 29*(2), 238–261. https://doi.org/10.1080/0969594X.2022.2080178

Graham, S., & Harris, K. R. (1989). Components analysis of cognitive strategy instruction: Effects on learning disabled students' compositions and self-efficacy. *Journal of Educational Psychology, 81*(3), 353–361. https://doi.org/10.1037/0022-0663.81.3.353

Graham, S., Harris, K. R., Kiuhara, S. A., & Fishman, E. J. (2017). The relationship among strategic writing behavior, writing motivation, and writing performance with young, developing writers. *The Elementary School Journal, 118*(1), 82–104. https://doi.org/10.1086/693009

Graham, S., Harris, K. R., MacArthur, C., & Santangelo, T. (2017). Self-regulation and writing. In Zimmerman, B. J., & Schunk, D. H. (Eds.), *Handbook of Self-Regulation of Learning and Performance* (pp. 138–152). Routledge.

Graham, S., Taylor, A. Z., & Hudley, C. (1998). Exploring achievement values among ethnic minority early adolescents. *Journal of Educational Psychology, 90*(4), 606–620. https://doi.org/10.1037/0022-0663.90.4.606

Graves, D. H. (1975). An examination of the writing processes of seven year old children. *Research in the Teaching of English, 9*(3), 227–241.

Gray-Schlegel, M. A., & Gray-Schlegel, T. (1995). An investigation of gender stereotypes as revealed through children's creative writing. *Literacy Research and Instruction, 35*(2), 160–169. https://doi.org/10.1080/19388079509558205

Greene, J. A. (2017). *Self-Regulation in Education*. Routledge. https://doi..org/10.4324/9781315537450

Gutiérrez, E. D., Shutova, E., Lichtenstein, P., de Melo, G., & Gilardi, L. (2016). Detecting cross-cultural differences using a multilingual topic model. *Transactions of the Association for Computational Linguistics, 4*, 47–60. https://doi.org/10.1162/tacl_a_00082

Haddix, M. (2009). Black boys can write: Challenging dominant framings of African American adolescent males in literacy research. *Journal of Adolescent & Adult Literacy, 53*(4), 341–343. https://doi.org/10.1598/JAAL.53.4.8

Haddix, M. M. (2018). Writing our lives: Preparing teachers to teach 21st century writers in and out of school. In *Clinical Experiences in Teacher Education* (pp. 137–152). New York: Routledge. https://doi.org/10.4324/9781351116701

Hamilton, E. W., Nolen, S. B., & Abbott, R. D. (2013). Developing measures of motivational orientation to read and write: A longitudinal study. *Learning and Individual Differences, 28*, 151–166. https://doi.org/10.1016/j.lindif.2013.04.007

Hansford, D., & Adlington, R. (2009). Digital spaces and young people's online authoring: challenges for teachers. *Australian Journal of Language and Literacy, 32*(1), 55–68. https://search.informit.org/doi/10.3316/ielapa.584398231565216

Hashemian, M., & Heidari, A. (2013). The relationship between L2 learners' motivation/attitude and success in L2 writing. *Procedia-Social and Behavioral Sciences, 70*, 476–489. https://doi.org/10.1016/j.sbspro.2013.01.085

Hawthorne, S. (2008). *Engaging Reluctant Writers: The Nature of Reluctance to Write and the Effect of a Self-Regulation Strategy Training Programme on the Engagement and Writing Performance of Reluctant Writers in Secondary School English*. [Doctoral dissertation, University of Auckland]. ResearchSpace. https://researchspace.auckland.ac.nz/bitstream/handle/2292/3128/02whole.pdf

Hayes, J. R. (1996). A new framework for understanding cognition and affect in writing. In C. M. Levy & S. Ransdell (Eds.), *The Science of Writing: Theories, Methods, Individual Differences, and Applications* (pp. 1–27). Routledge. https://doi.org/10.4324/9780203811122

Hidi, S. E., & Anderson, V. (1992). Situational interest and its impact on reading and expository writing. In A. Renninger, S. Hidi, & A. Krapp (Eds.), *The Role of Interest in Learning and Development* (pp. 215–238). Psychology Press. https://doi.org/10.4324/9781315807430

Hidi, S. E., Berndorff, D., & Ainley, M. (2002). Children's argument writing, interest, and self-efficacy: An intervention study. *Learning and Instruction, 12*(4), 429–446. https://doi.org/10.1016/S0959-4752(01)00009-3

Hidi, S. E., & McLaren, J. A. (1991). Motivational factors and writing: The role of topic interestingness. *European Journal of Psychology of Education, 6*(2), 187–197. https://doi.org/10.1007/BF03191937

Hidi, S. E., & Renninger, K. A. (2006). The four-phase model of interest development. *Educational Psychologist, 41*(2), 111–127. https://doi.org/10.1207/s15326985ep4102_4

Hidi, S. E., & Renninger, K. (2019). Interest development and its relation to curiosity: needed neuroscientific research. *Educational Psychology Review, 31*(4), 833–852. https://doi.org/10.1007/s10648-019-09491-3

Hidi, S., Renninger, K. A., & Krapp, A. (2004). Interest, a motivational variable that combines affective and cognitive functioning. In D. Y. Dai & R. J. Sternberg (Eds.), *Motivation, Emotion, and Cognition: Integrative Perspectives on Intellectual Functioning and Development* (pp. 89–115). Lawrence Erlbaum.

Hirn, R. G., Hollo, A., & Scott, T. M. (2018). Exploring instructional differences and school performance in high-poverty elementary schools. *Preventing School Failure: Alternative Education for Children and Youth, 62*(1), 37–48. https://doi.org/10.1080/1045988X.2017.1329197

Horner, B., Lu, M.-Z., Royster, J. J., & Trimbur, J. (2011). *Language Difference in Writing: Toward a Translingual Approach*. Faculty Scholarship. https://ir.library.louisville.edu/cgi/viewcontent.cgi?article=1065&context=faculty

Howard, T. C. (2011). Culturally responsive pedagogy. In J. A. Banks (Ed.), *Transforming Multicultural Education and Practice: Expanding Educational Opportunity* (pp. 137–163). Teachers College Press.

Huang, C. (2011). Achievement goals and achievement emotions: A meta-analysis. *Educational Psychology Review, 23*(3), 359–388. https://doi.org/10.1007/s10648-011-9155-x

Ingersoll, R. M., Merrill, E., Stuckey, D., & Collins, G. (2019). *Seven Trends: The Transformation of the Teaching Force—Updated October 2018*. Consortium for Policy Research in Education https://repository.upenn.edu/cpre_researchreports/108

Inzlicht, M., Werner, K. M., Briskin, J. L., & Roberts, B. W. (2021). Integrating models of self-regulation. *Annual Review of Psychology, 72*, 319–345. https://doi.org/10.1146/annurev-psych-061020-105721

Isaac, J. D., Sansone, C., & Smith, J. L. (1999). Other people as a source of interest in an activity. *Journal of Experimental Social Psychology, 35*(3), 239–265. https://doi.org/10.1006/jesp.1999.1385

Jackson, C. (2002). Laddishness' as a self-worth protection strategy. *Gender and Education, 14*(1), 37–50. https://doi.org/10.1080/09540250120098870

Jacobs, G. E. (2008). We learn what we do: Developing a repertoire of writing practices in an instant messaging World. *Journal of Adolescent & Adult Literacy, 52*(3), 203–211. https://doi.org/10.1598/JAAL.52.3.3

Jennings, M., Fox, J., Graves, B., & Shohamy, E. (1999). The test-takers' choice: an investigation of the effect of topic on language-test performance. *Language Testing, 16*(4), 426–456. https://doi.org/10.1177/026553229901600402

Jones, S. (2012). Mapping the landscape: Gender and the writing classroom. *Journal of Writing Research, 3*(3), 163–179.

Kaplan, A., Lichtinger, E., & Gorodetsky, M. (2009). Achievement goal orientations and self-regulation in writing: An integrative perspective. *Journal of Educational Psychology, 101*(1), 51–69. https://doi.org/10.1037/a0013200

Kaplan, A., & Maehr, M. L. (1999). Enhancing the motivation of African American students: An achievement goal theory perspective. *Journal of Negro Education, 68*(1), 23–41. https://doi.org/10.2307/2668207

King, K., & Gurian, M. (2006). With boys in mind / Teaching to the minds of boys. *Educational Leadership, 64*(1), 56–61. Retrieved from https://www.ascd.org/el/articles/teaching-to-the-minds-of-boys

Klassen, R. M. (2008). The optimistic self-efficacy beliefs of students with learning disabilities. *Exceptionality Education International, 18*(1), 93–112. https://doi.org/10.5206/eei.v18i1.7617

Knudson, R. E. (1995). Writing experiences, attitudes, and achievement of first to sixth graders. *The Journal of Educational Research, 89*(2), 90–97. https://doi.org/10.1080/00220671.1995.9941199

Korat, O., & Schiff, R. (2005). Do children who read more books know "What is Good Writing" Better than children who read less? a comparison between grade levels and SES groups. *Journal of Literacy Research, 37*(3), 289–324. https://doi.org/10.1207/s15548430jlr3703_2

Koutsogiannis, D., & Adampa, V. (2012). Girls, identities and agency in adolescents' digital literacy practices. *Journal of Writing Research, 3*(3), 217–247. https://doi.org/10.17239/jowr-2012.03.03.4

Kumar, R., Karabenick, S. A., & Burgoon, J. N. (2015). Teachers' implicit attitudes, explicit beliefs, and the mediating role of respect and cultural responsibility on mastery and performance-focused instructional practices. *Journal of Educational Psychology, 107*(2), 533. https://psycnet.apa.org/doi/10.1037/a0037471

Ladson-Billings, G. (1995). But that's just good teaching! The case for culturally relevant pedagogy. *Theory Into Practice, 34*(3), 159–165. https://doi.org/10.1080/00405849509543675

Lammers, J. C., Curwood, J. S., & Magnifico, A. M. (2012). Toward an affinity space methodology: Considerations for literacy research. *English Teaching, 11*(2), 44–58. http://files.eric.ed.gov/fulltext/EJ973940.pdf

Lam, S. F., & Law, Y. K. (2007). The roles of instructional practices and motivation in writing performance. *Journal of Experimental Education, 75*(2), 145–164. https://doi.org/10.3200/JEXE.75.2.145-164

Lenhart, A., Arafeh, S., Smith, A., & Macgill, A. R. (2008). *Writing, Technology and Teens*. Pew Research Center. https://www.pewresearch.org/internet/2008/04/24/writing-technology-and-teens/

Lewis Chiu, C., Carrero, K. M., & Lusk, M. E. (2017). Culturally responsive writing instruction for secondary students with emotional and behavioral disorders. *Beyond Behavior, 26*(1), 28–35. https://doi.org/10.1177/1074295617694406

Limpo, T., & Alves, R. A. (2014). Implicit theories of writing and their impact on students' response to a SRSD intervention. *British Journal of Educational Psychology, 84*(4), 571–590. https://doi.org/10.1111/bjep.12042

Ling, G., Elliot, N., Burstein, J. C., McCaffrey, D. F., MacArthur, C. A., & Holtzman, S. (2021). Writing motivation: A validation study of self-judgment and performance. *Assessing Writing, (48)*, Article 100509. https://doi.org/10.1016/j.asw.2020.100509

Lipstein, R., & Renninger, K. A. (2006). Putting things into words': The development of 12–15-year-old students' interest for writing. In S. E. Hidi & P. Boscolo (Eds.), *Motivation and Writing: Research and School Practice* (pp. 113–140). Elsevier.

Losey, K. M., & Shuck, G. (2021). Plurilingualism for US writing classrooms. In *Plurilingual Pedagogies for Multilingual Writing Classrooms* (pp. 1–11). Routledge. https://doi.org/10.4324/9781003257370

Luria, E., Shalom, M., & Levy, D. A. (2021). Cognitive neuroscience perspectives on motivation and learning: revisiting self-determination theory. *Mind, Brain, and Education, 15*(1), 5-17.

MacArthur, C. A., Philippakos, Z. A., & Graham, S. (2016). A multicomponent measure of writing motivation with basic college writers. *Learning Disability Quarterly, 39*(1), 31–43. https://doi.org/10.1177/0731948715583115

Macklem, G. L. (2015). *Boredom in the Classroom: Addressing Student Motivation, Self-Regulation, and Engagement in Learning.* Springer. https://psycnet.apa.org/doi/10.1007/978-3-319-13120-7

Magnifico, A. M. (2010). Writing for whom? Cognition, motivation, and a writer's audience. Educational psychologist, 45(3), 167-184.

Magnifico, A. M., Curwood, J. S., & Lammers, J. C. (2015). Words on the screen: broadening analyses of interactions among fanfiction writers and reviewers. *Literacy Research: Theory, Method, and Practice, 49*(3), 158–166. https://doi.org/10.1111/lit.12061

Marrs, S., Zumbrunn, S., McBride, C., & Stringer, J. K. (2016). Exploring elementary student perceptions of writing feedback. *I-Manager's /Journal on Educational Psychology, 10*(1), 16–28. Retrieved from https://files.eric.ed.gov/fulltext/EJ1131811.pdf

Martin, M. S. (2016). *Examining the Writing Motivation and Achievement of At-Risk Elementary-Aged Students.* [Doctoral dissertation, University of Tennessee]. TRACE (Tennessee Research and Creative Exchange). https://trace.tennessee.edu/cgi/viewcontent.cgi?article=5117&context=utk_graddiss

Martino, W. (1999). 'Cool boys', 'party animals', 'squids' and 'poofters': Interrogating the dynamics and politics of adolescent masculinities in school. *British Journal of Sociology of Education, 20*(2), 239–263. https://doi.org/10.1080/01425699995434

Matthews, J. S., Ponitz, C. C., & Morrison, F. J. (2009). Early gender differences in self-regulation and academic achievement. *Journal of Educational Psychology, 101*(3), 689–704. https://doi.org/10.1037/a0014240

Mavrogenes, N. A., & Bezruczko, N. (1993). Influences on writing development. *Journal of Educational Research, 86*(4), 237–245. https://doi.org/10.1080/00220671.1993.9941835

McCarthy, S. J. (2001). Identity construction in elementary readers and writers. *Reading Research Quarterly, 36*(2), 122–151. https://doi.org/10.1598/RRQ.36.2.2

McInerney, D. M., Walker, R. A., & Liem, G. A. D. (2011). *Sociocultural Theories of Learning and Motivation: Looking Back, Looking Forward.* Information Age Publishing.

McMillan, J. H., & Hearn, J. (2008). Student self-assessment: The key to stronger student motivation and higher achievement. *Educational Horizons, 87*(1), 40–49. http://files.eric.ed.gov/fulltext/EJ815370.pdf

Meece, J. L., Glienke, B. B., & Burg, S. (2006). Gender and motivation. *Journal of School Psychology, 44*(5), 351–373. https://doi.org/10.1016/j.jsp.2006.04.004

Meece, J. L., & Miller, S. D. (1999). Changes in elementary school children's achievement goals for reading and writing: Results of a longitudinal and an intervention study. *Scientific Studies of Reading, 3*(3), 207–229. https://doi.org/10.1207/s1532799xssr0303_2

Meece, J. L., & Miller, S. D. (2001). A longitudinal analysis of elementary school students' achievement goals in literacy activities. *Contemporary Educational Psychology, 26*(4), 454–480. https://doi.org/10.1006/ceps.2000.1071

Meece, J. L., & Painter, J. (2012). Gender, self-regulation, and motivation. In D. H. Schunk & B. J. Zimmer (Eds.), *Motivation and Self-Regulated Learning* (pp. 351–380). Routledge.

Mills, H., & Clyde, J. A. (1991). Children's success as readers and writers: It's the teacher's beliefs that make the difference. *Young Children, 46*(2), 54–59. https://doi.org/10.1177/0094306114531284r

Molloy, S., Fonville, S., & Salam, A. (2020). "Root and branch": Resisting a basic writing legacy system. *Journal of Basic Writing/, 39*(1), 5–35. https://www.jstor.org/stable/27027819

Montgomery, W. (2001). Creating culturally responsive, inclusive classrooms. *Teaching Exceptional Children, 33*(4), 4–9. https://doi.org/10.1177/004005990103300401

Muhammad, M. M., & Latif, A. (2019). Unresolved issues in defining and assessing writing motivational constructs: A review of conceptualization and measurement perspectives. *Assessing Writing,* (42). https://doi.org/10.1016/j.asw.2019.100417

Myers, K. (2018). Gendered Interactions in School. In B. J. Risman, C. M. Froyum, & W. J. Scarborough (Eds.), *Handbook of the Sociology of Gender* (pp. 199–214). Springer.

Nguyen, T. D., & Northrop, L. (2022). Examining English Language Arts teachers: Evidence from national data. *Teachers College Record, 123*(10), 213–242. https://doi.org/10.1177/01614681211058994

Nicholls, J. G. (1984). Achievement motivation: Conceptions of ability, subjective experience, task choice, and performance. *Psychological Review, 91*(3), 328–346. https://doi.org/10.1037/0033-295X.91.3.328

Niederle, M., & Vesterlund, L. (2011). Gender and competition. *Annual Review of Economics, 3*(1), 601–630. https://doi.org/10.1146/annurev-economics-111809-125122

Nolen, S. B. (2007). The role of literate communities in the development of children's interest in writing. In S. Hidi & P. Boscolo (Eds.), *Writing and Motivation* (pp. 241–255). Elsevier.

Norment, N. (1997). Some effects of culture-referenced topics on the writing performance of African-American students. *Journal of Basic Writing, 16*(2), 17–45. https://wac.colostate.edu/docs/jbw/v16n2/norment.pdf

Norment, N. (2021). The black ink project. *Composition Forum, 47* (Fall, 2021). https://compositionforum.com/issue/47/black-ink-project.php

O'Mahony, P., Dempsey, M., & Killeen, H. (2008). Handwriting speed: Duration of testing period and relation to socio-economic disadvantage and handedness. *Occupational Therapy International, 15*(3), 165–177. https://doi.org/10.1002/oti.255

Oldfather, P., & Shanahan, C. H. (2007). A cross-case study of writing motivation as empowerment. In S. Hidi & P. Boscolo (Eds.), *Writing and Motivation* (pp. 258–279). Emerald Group.

Oyserman, D., Bybee, D., Terry, K. (2006). Possible selves and academic outcomes: How and when possible selves impel action. *Journal of Personality and Social Psychology, 91*(1), 188–204. https://psycnet.apa.org/doi/10.1037/0022-3514.91.1.188

Pajares, F. (2003). Self-efficacy beliefs, motivation, and achievement in writing: A review of the literature. *Reading & Writing Quarterly, 19*(2), 139–158. https://doi.org/10.1080/10573560308222

Pajares, F. (2007). Empirical properties of a scale to assess writing self-efficacy in school contexts. *Measurement and Evaluation in Counseling and Development, 39*(4), 239–249. https://doi.org/10.1080/07481756.2007.11909801

Pajares, F., Britner, S. L., & Valiante, G. (2000). Relation between achievement goals and self-beliefs of middle school students in writing and science. *Contemporary Educational Psychology, 25*(4), 406–422. https://doi.org/10.1006/ceps.1999.1027

Pajares, F., & Cheong, Y. F. (2003). Achievement goal orientations in writing: A developmental perspective. *International Journal of Educational Research, 39*(4), 437–455. https://doi.org/10.1016/j.ijer.2004.06.008

Pajares, F., Hartley, J., & Valiante, G. (2001). Response format in writing self-efficacy assessment: Greater discrimination increases prediction. *Measurement and Evaluation in Counseling and Development, 33*(4), 214–221. https://doi.org/10.1080/07481756.2001.12069012

Pajares, F., & Johnson, M. J. (1996). Self-efficacy beliefs and the writing performance of entering high school students. *Psychology in the Schools, 33*(2), 163–175. https://doi.org/10.1002/(SICI)1520-6807(199604)33:2%3C163::AID-PITS10%3E3.0.CO;2-C

Pajares, F., Johnson, M. J., & Usher, E. L. (2007). Sources of writing self-efficacy beliefs of elementary, middle, and high school students. *Research in the Teaching of English, 42*(1), 104–120.

Pajares, F., Miller, M. D., & Johnson, M. M. (1999). Gender differences in writing self-beliefs of elementary school students. *Journal of Educational Psychology, 91*(1), 50–61. https://doi.org/10.1037/0022-0663.91.1.50

Pajares, F., & Valiante, G. (1997). Influence of self-efficacy on elementary students' writing. *The Journal of Educational Research, 90*(6), 353–360. https://doi.org/10.1080/00220671.1997.10544593

Pajares, F., & Valiante, G. (2001). Gender differences in writing motivation and achievement of middle school students: A function of gender orientation? *Contemporary Educational Psychology, 26*(3), 366–381. https://doi.org/10.1006/ceps.2000.1069

Pajares, F., & Valiante, G. (2006). Self-efficacy beliefs and motivation in writing development. In C. A. MacArthur, S. Graham, & J. Fitzgerald (Eds.), *Handbook of Writing Research* (pp. 158–170). Guilford.

Pajares, F., Valiante, G., & Cheong, Y. F. (2006). Writing Self-Efficacy and Its Relation to Gender, Writing Motivation and Writing Competence: A Developmental Perspective. In S. Hidi & P. Boscolo (Eds.), *Writing and Motivation* (pp. 141–159). Emerald Group.

Paris, S. G., Turner, J. C., Muchmore, J., & Perry, N. (1995). Teachers' and students' perceptions of portfolios. *Journal of Cognitive Education, 5*(1), 6-40.

Patall, E. A. (2013). Constructing motivation through choice, interest, and interestingness. *Journal of Educational Psychology, 105*(2), 522–534. https://psycnet.apa.org/doi/10.1037/a0030307

Patall, E. A., Cooper, H., & Robinson, J. C. (2008). The effects of choice on intrinsic motivation and related outcomes: a meta-analysis of research findings. *Psychological Bulletin, 134*(2), 270–300. https://doi.org/10.1037/0033-2909.134.2.270

Payne, A. A., & Welch, K. (2010). Modeling the effects of racial threat on punitive and restorative school discipline practices. *Criminology, 48*(4), 1019–1062. https://doi.org/10.1111/j.1745-9125.2010.00211.x

Peabody, D. (2011). Beliefs and instructional practices among secondary teachers within selected high-and low-performing high schools. *Florida Journal of Educational Administration & Policy, 4*(2), 181–192. http://files.eric.ed.gov/fulltext/EJ931152.pdf

Pekrun, R. (2006). The control-value theory of achievement emotions: Assumptions, corollaries, and implications for educational research and practice. *Educational Psychology Review, 18*(4), 315–341. https://doi.org/10.1007/s10648-006-9029-9

Pekrun, R., Goetz, T., Daniels, L. M., Stupnisky, R. H., & Perry, R. P. (2010). Boredom in achievement settings: Exploring control-value antecedents and performance outcomes of a neglected emotion. *Journal of Educational Psychology, 102*(3), 531–549. https://doi.org/10.1037/a0019243

Peterson, S. S. (2000). Fourth, sixth, and eighth graders' preferred writing topics and identification of gender markers in stories. *The Elementary School Journal, 101*(1), 79–100. https://doi.org/10.1086/499660

Peterson, S. S. (2001). Gender identities and self-expression in classroom narrative writing. *Language Arts, 78*(5), 451–457. https://www.jstor.org/stable/41483175

Philippakos, Z. A., Wang, C., & MacArthur, C. (2021). Writing motivation of college students in basic writing and first-year composition classes: Confirmatory factor analyses of scales on goals, self-efficacy, beliefs, and affect. *Journal of Learning Disabilities, 56*(1), 72–92. https://doi.org/10.1177/00222194211053238

Poropat, A. E. (2009). A meta-analysis of the five-factor model of personality and academic performance. *Psychological Bulletin, 135*(2), 322–338. https://doi.org/10.1037/a0014996

Powers, D. E., & Bennett, R. E. (1999). Effects of allowing examinees to select questions on a test of divergent thinking. *Applied Measurement in Education, 12*(3), 257–279. https://doi.org/10.1207/S15324818AME1203_3

Powers, D. E., Fowles, M. E., Farnum, M., & Gerritz, K. (1992). *Giving a Choice of Topics on a Test of Basic Writing Skills: Does It Make Any Difference?* (RR-92-19). Educational Testing Service. https://doi.org/10.1002/j.2333-8504.1992.tb01450.x

Pressick-Kilborn, K., & Walker, R. (2002). The social construction of interest in a learning community. Research on sociocultural influences on motivation and learning, 2, 153-182.

Puranik, C., & Li, H. (2022). Self-regulation and early writing: A longitudinal examination from preschool through first grade. *Journal of Experimental Child Psychology, 220*, August 2022, Article 105420. https://doi.org/10.1016/j.jecp.2022.105420

Purcell-Gates, V., Duke, N. K., & Martineau, J. A. (2007). Learning to read and write genre-specific text: Roles of authentic experience and explicit teaching. *Reading Research Quarterly, 42*(1), 8–45. https://doi.org/10.1598/RRQ.42.1.1

Razmjoo, S. A., & Hoomanfard, M. H. (2012). On the effect of cooperative writing on students' writing ability, WTC, self-efficacy, and apprehension. *World Journal of English Language, 2*(2), 19.

Reilly, D., Neumann, D. L., & Andrews, G. (2019). Gender differences in reading and writing achievement: Evidence from the National Assessment of Educational Progress (NAEP). *American Psychologist, 74*(4), 445–458. https://doi.org/10.1037/amp0000356

Renninger, K. A. (2009). Interest and identity development in instruction: An inductive model. *Educational Psychologist, 44*(2), 105–118. https://doi.org/10.1080/00461520902832392

Robson, D. A., Allen, M. S., & Howard, S. J. (2020). Self-regulation in childhood as a predictor of future outcomes: A meta-analytic review. *Psychological bulletin, 146*(4), 324. https://doi.org/10.1037/bul0000227

Rosa, J., & Flores, N. (2017). Unsettling race and language: Toward a raciolinguistic perspective. *Language in Society, 46*(5), 621–647. https://doi.org/10.1017/S0047404517000562

Rosenzweig, E. Q., Harackiewicz, J. M., Priniski, S. J., Hecht, C. A., Canning, E. A., Tibbetts, Y., & Hyde, J. S. (2019). Choose your own intervention: Using choice to enhance the effectiveness of a utility-value intervention. *Motivation Science, 5*(3), 269–276. https://psycnet.apa.org/doi/10.1037/mot0000113

Ryan, R. M., & Deci, E. L. (2017). *Self-Determination Theory: Basic Psychological Needs in Motivation, Development, and Wellness*. Guilford.

Sanders-Reio, J., Alexander, P. A., Reio, T. G., & Newman, I. (2014). Do students' beliefs about writing relate to their writing self-efficacy, apprehension, and performance? *Learning and Instruction, 33*, 1–11. https://doi.org/10.1016/j.learninstruc.2014.02.001

Sarroub, L. K., & Pernicek, T. (2016). Boys, books, and boredom: A case of three high school boys and their encounters with literacy. *Reading & Writing Quarterly, 32*(1), 27–55. https://doi.org/10.1080/10573569.2013.859052

Scheuer, N., de la Cruz, M., Pedrazzini, A., Iparraguirre, M. S., & Pozo, J. I. (2012). Children's gendered ways of talking about learning to write. *Journal of Writing Research, 3*(3), 181–216. https://doi.org/10.17239/jowr-2012.03.03.3

Schmitt, D. P., Realo, A., Voracek, M., & Allik, J. (2008). Why can't a man be more like a woman? Sex differences in Big Five personality traits across 55 cultures. *Journal of Personality and Social Psychology, 94*(1), 168–182. https://doi.org/10.1037/0022-3514.94.1.168

Schraw, G., & Lehman, S. (2001). Situational interest: A review of the literature and directions for future research. *Educational Psychology Review, 13*(1), 23–52. https://doi.org/10.1023/A:1009004801455

Schunk, D. H., & Swartz, C. W. (1993). Goals and progress feedback: Effects on self-efficacy and writing achievement. *Contemporary Educational Psychology, 18*(3), 337–354. https://doi.org/10.1006/ceps.1993.1024

Schunk, D. H., & Zimmerman, B. J. (2007). Influencing children's self-efficacy and self-regulation of reading and writing through modeling. *Reading and Writing Quarterly, 23*(1), 7–25. https://doi.org/10.1080/10573560600837578

Shaughnessy, M. P. (1979). *Errors and Expectations*. Oxford University Press.

Shell, D. F., Colvin, C., & Bruning, R. (1995). Self-efficacy, attribution, and outcome expectancy mechanisms in reading and writing achievement: Grade-level and achievement-level differences. *Journal of Educational Psychology, 87*(3), 386–398. https://doi.org/10.1037/0022-0663.87.3.386

Smitherman, G. (1976). *Talkin and Testifyin: The Language of Black America*. Wayne State University Press.

Snell, J. (2013). Dialect, interaction, and class positioning at school: From deficit to difference to repertoire. *Language and Education, 27*(2), 110–128. https://doi.org/10.1080/09500782.2012.760584

Sorić, I., Penezić, Z., & Burić, I. (2017). The Big Five personality traits, goal orientations, and academic achievement. *Learning and Individual Differences, 54*, 126–134. https://doi.org/10.1016/j.lindif.2017.01.024

Spilt, J. L., & Hughes, J. N. (2015). African American children at risk of increasingly conflicted teacher–student relationships in elementary school. *School Psychology Review, 44*(3), 306–314. https://doi.org/10.17105/spr-14-0033.1

Stewart, M. A. (2014). I don't want to write for them.: An at-risk Latino youth's out-of-school literacy practices. *NABE Journal of Research and Practice, 5*(2), 197–229. https://doi.org/10.1080/26390043.2014.12067779

Stewart, M. A., Hansen-Thomas, H., Flint, P., & Núñez, M. (2022). Translingual disciplinary literacies: Equitable language environments to support literacy engagement. *Reading Research Quarterly, 57*(1), 181–203. https://doi.org/10.1002/rrq.381

Swinson, J., & Harrop, A. (2009). Teacher talk directed to boys and girls and its relationship to their behaviour. *Educational Studies, 35*(5), 515–524. https://doi.org/10.1080/03055690902883913

Tatum, A., & Gue, V. (2012). The Sociocultural Benefits of Writing for African American Adolescent Males. *Reading & Writing Quarterly, 28*(2), 132–142. https://doi.org/10.1080/10573569.2012.651075

Tatum, A. W., Johnson, A., & McMillon, D. (2021). The state of Black Male literacy research, 1999–2020. *Literacy Research: Theory, Method, and Practice, 70*(1), 129–151. https://doi.org/10.1177/23813377211038368

Taylor, H. (2019). *Why Women Read Fiction: The Stories of Our Lives*. Oxford University Press.

Thelwall, M. (2017). Book genre and author gender: Romance>paranormal romance to autobiography>memoir. *Journal of the Association for Information Science and Technology, 68*(5), 1212–1223. https://doi.org/10.1002/asi.23768

Thelwall, M. (2019). Reader and author gender and genre in Goodreads. *Journal of Librarianship and Information Science, 51*(2), 1–28. https://doi.org/10.1177/0961000617709061

Thomas, S., & Oldfather, P. (1997). Intrinsic motivations, literacy, and assessment practices: That's my grade. That's me. *Educational Psychologist, 32*(2), 107–123. https://doi.org/10.1207/s15326985ep3202_5

Troia, G. A., Harbaugh, A. G., Shankland, R. K., Wolbers, K. A., & Lawrence, A. M. (2013). Relationships between writing motivation, writing activity, and writing performance: effects of grade, sex, and ability. *Reading and Writing, 26*(1), 17–44. https://doi.org/10.1007/s11145-012-9379-2

Troia, G. A., Shankland, R. K., & Wolbers, K. A. (2012). Motivation Research in Writing: Theoretical and Empirical Considerations. *Reading & Writing Quarterly, 28*(1), 5–28. https://doi.org/10.1080/10573569.2012.632729

Turner, J. C. (1995). The influence of classroom contexts on young children's motivation for literacy. *Reading Research Quarterly, 30*(3), 410–441. https://doi.org/10.2307/747624

Usher, E. L., & Pajares, F. (2006). Sources of academic and self-regulatory efficacy beliefs of entering middle school students. *Contemporary Educational Psychology, 31*(2), 125–141. https://doi.org/10.1016/j.cedpsych.2005.03.002

Villalón, R., Mateos, M., & Cuevas, I. (2015). High school boys' and girls' writing conceptions and writing self-efficacy beliefs: What is their role in writing performance? *Educational Psychology, 35*(6), 6563–6674. https://doi.org/10.1080/01443410.2013.836157

Walker, B. J. (2003). The cultivation of student self-efficacy in reading and writing. *Reading & Writing Quarterly, 19*(2), 173–187. https://doi.org/10.1080/10573560308217

Watson, A., Kehler, M., & Martino, W. (2010). The problem of boys' literacy underachievement: Raising some questions. *Journal of Adolescent & Adult Literacy, 53*(5), 356–361. https://doi.org/10.1598/JAAL.53.5.1

Weiner, B. (1985). An attributional theory of achievement motivation and emotion. *Psychological Review, 92*(4), 548–573. https://doi.org/10.1037/0033-295X.92.4.548

Weis, M., Heikamp, T., & Trommsdorff, G. (2013). Gender differences in school achievement: The role of self-regulation. *Frontiers in Psychology, 4*, Article 442. https://doi.org/10.3389/fpsyg.2013.00442

White, M. J., & Bruning, R. (2005). Implicit writing beliefs and their relation to writing quality. *Contemporary Educational Psychology, 30*(2), 166–189. https://doi.org/10.1016/j.cedpsych.2004.07.002

Wigfield, A. (1994). Expectancy-value theory of achievement motivation: A developmental perspective. *Educational Psychology Review, 6*(1), 49–78, https://doi.org/10.1007/BF02209024

Wigfield, A., Eccles, J. S., Schiefele, U., Roeser, R. W., & Davis-Kean, P. (2006). Development of achievement motivation. In W. Damon, R. M. Lerner, & N.-. Eisenberg (Eds.), *Handbook of Child Psychology: Social, Emotional and Personality Development* (Vol. 3, pp. 933–1002). Wiley. http://doi.org/10.1002/9780470147658

Wilson, T. D., & Linville, P. W. (1985). Improving the performance of college freshmen with attributional techniques. *Journal of Personality and Social Psychology, 49*(1), 287–293. https://psycnet.apa.org/doi/10.1037/0022-3514.49.1.287

Wingate, U. (2015). *Academic Literacy and Student Diversity: The case for inclusive practice.* Multilingual Matters. https://doi.org/10.21832/9781783093496

Witte, S. (2007). "That's online writing, not boring school writing": Writing with blogs and the Talkback Project. *Journal of Adolescent & Adult Literacy, 51*(2), 92–96. https://doi.org/10.1598/JAAL.51.2.1

Wolfe, J. (2000). Gender, ethnicity, and classroom discourse communication patterns of Hispanic and White students in networked classrooms. *Written Communication, 17*(4), 491–519. https://doi.org/10.1177/0741088300017004003

Wolters, C. A. (2003). Understanding procrastination from a self-regulated learning perspective. *Journal of Educational Psychology, 95*(1), 179–187. https://doi.org/10.1037/0022-0663.95.1.179

Yeager, D. S., & Walton, G. M. (2011). Social-psychological interventions in education: They're not magic. *Review of Educational Research, 81*(2), 267–301. https://doi.org/10.3102/0034654311405999

Young, R., & Ferguson, F. (2020). *Writing for Pleasure: Theory, Research, and Practice*. Routledge. https://doi.org/10.4324/9780429268984

Yu, C., Zuo, X., Blum, R. W., Tolman, D. L., Kågesten, A., Mmari, K., ... & Lou, C. (2017). Marching to a different drummer: A cross-cultural comparison of young adolescents who challenge gender norms. *Journal of Adolescent Health, 61*(4), S48–S54. https://doi.org/10.1016/j.jadohealth.2017.07.005

Zhou, M., Lam, K. K. L., & Zhang, Y. (2022). Metacognition and academic procrastination: A meta-analytical examination. *Journal of Rational-Emotive & Cognitive-Behavior Therapy, 40*(2), 334–368. https://doi.org/10.1007/s10942-021-00415-1

Zimmerman, B. J., & Bandura, A. (1994). Impact of self-regulatory influences on writing course attainment. *American Educational Research Journal, 31*(4), 845–862. https://doi.org/10.3102/00028312031004845

Zumbrunn, S., Broda, M., Varier, D., & Conklin, S. (2019). Examining the multidimensional role of self-efficacy for writing on student writing self-regulation and grades in elementary and high school. *British Journal of Educational Psychology, 90*(3), 580–603. https://doi.org/10.1111/bjep.12315

Zumbrunn, S., Marrs, S., & Mewborn, C. (2016). Toward a better understanding of student perceptions of writing feedback: A mixed methods study. *Reading and Writing, 29*(2), 349–370. https://doi.org/10.1007/s11145-015-9599-3

CHAPTER THREE

Writing as Self-Regulation: The Mediating Roles of Reading Fluency and Working Memory

Overview

Self-regulation helps writers break complex tasks into manageable subtasks. Instead of juggling multiple goals and standards, they tackle one subtask at a time, achieve their immediate goals, and move to the next.

Zimmerman and Risemberg (1997: 79) describe several mechanisms by which writers manage and modify their writing behaviors:

- *Environmental*
  - *Environmental structuring* (Choose the conditions under which one writes: where, when, with what resources and distractions)
  - *Self-selected models* (Seek out mentors or mentor texts and use them as models)
- *Behavioral*
  - *Self-monitoring* (Track writing progress against specific milestones or goals)
  - *Self-consequenting* (Give oneself rewards or punishments to maximize writing motivation, based on the results of self-monitoring)
  - *Self-verbalizations* (Put reflections about one's own writing into words, either orally, or in the form of comments or notes)

- *Personal/Covert*
  - *Time planning and management* (Decide what writing tasks to work on when, and how much time and effort to devote to specific activities and goals)
  - *Goal setting* [and goal shifting] (Set long- and short-term goals for writing, including personal targets for writing quality, length, and text content).
  - *Self-evaluative standards* (Determine when writing is "good enough" and when it needs to be revised)
  - *Use* [and revision] *of cognitive strategies* (Manage specific phases of the writing process, such as task definition, idea generation, planning, and revision)
  - *Use of mental imagery* (to support idea generation)

These mechanisms are coordinated in a self-reflective feedback loop (Sommers, 1980), which Flower and Hayes (1980) and Hayes (2012) term *monitoring* (see Figure 3.1). Monitoring and self-evaluation require writers to reread what they have written. Interventions that target self-selected models, goal setting, self-evaluative standards, cognitive strategies, and mental imagery are known to produce significant writing improvements (Santangelo, Harris, & Graham, 2016), in part because self-regulation frees working memory (McCutchen, 1996; Kellogg, 2001a).

Monitoring and self-evaluation are intrinsically challenging. They require a particularly sophisticated form of reading—highly purpose driven, evaluative, and metacognitive (Hacker, 2018). Even worse, they require multiple *kinds* of metacognitive and metalinguistic knowledge (see Table 1.1 in Chapter One). This suggests that effective writers are fluent, sophisticated, and flexible readers (Fitzgerald & Shanahan, 2000). Finally, self-regulation processes compete with other writing processes for working memory.

This competition is central to the capacity theory of writing (McCutchen, 1996, 2011; Kellogg, 2001a). High demand on working memory first degrades, then disrupts writing performance (Lea & Levy, 1999; Ransdell & Levy, 2002). Conversely, high working memory capacity supports implementation of effective writing strategies (Ransdell, 1999; Alamargot, Caporossi, Chesnet, & Ros, 2011; McCutchen, 2011). Working memory capacity is linked to brain pathways that support executive control (Berninger & Richards, 2012). It is thus particularly important for prewriting, planning, monitoring and revision processes (Torrance & Jeffery, 1999; Olive, 2004; Piolat, Roussey, Olive, & Amada, 2004; Vandenberg & Swanson, 2007).

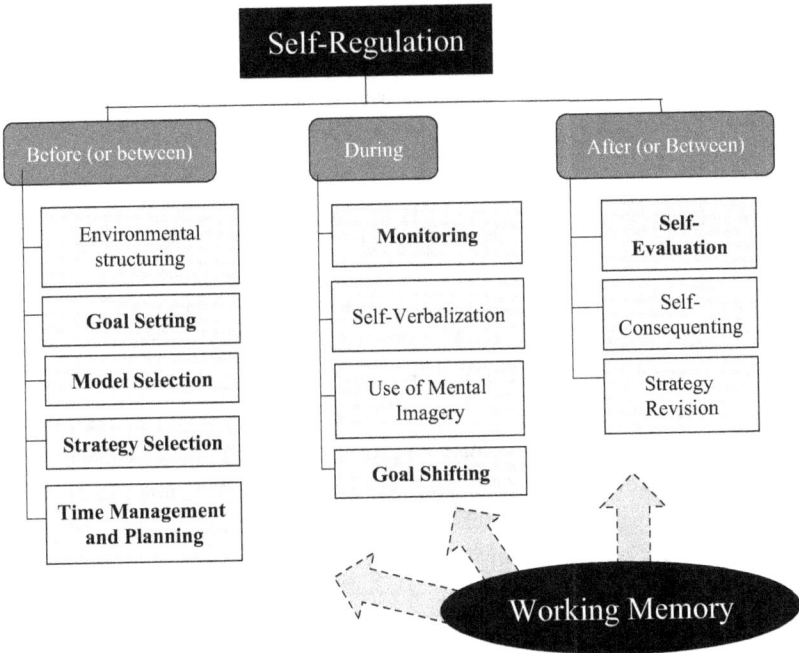

Figure 3.1 Aspects of Self-Regulation. Exercising Self-Regulation Shifts Which Processes Are in the Focus of Attention, and Thus Requires Working Memory Resources. Categories in bold are those for which Santangelo, Harris, and Graham (2016) reported significant effects.

Effective working memory capacity can be extended by drawing on prior knowledge and providing external cues. Cuing specific concepts enables rapid access to knowledge in long-term memory (McCutchen, 2000; Kellogg, 2001b). Graphic organizers, outlines, and rereading the text produced to date thus help reduce working memory load (Kellogg, 1996; Olive & Passerault, 2012).

The moderating role of working memory has been confirmed at every age, from kindergarten to college (Kellogg, 2004; Hoskyn & Swanson, 2003; Berninger, Abbott, Swanson, Lovitt, Trivedi, Lin, . . . & Amtman, 2010; Bourke, Davies, Sumner, & Green, 2014). Without explicit instruction, writing self-regulation may develop more rapidly among stronger readers and more fluent, less distracted writers.[1] Yet self-regulation skills are teachable. Given their role in generating achievement gaps, it is particularly important to develop these skills

---

1 Note that writers who are still mastering the language or acquiring foundational writing skills such as handwriting, keyboarding, or spelling, will have to focus attention on text-generation and transcription, which necessarily reduces the time and energy they can put into self-regulation. This point will be examined in depth in chapters Five and Six.

among struggling writers (Gillespie & Graham, 2014). Because transcription dysfluency reduces working memory and hence self-regulation, teachers must aim both to increase transcription fluency and to provide supports for self-regulation (Berninger, 1999; McCutchen, 2011).

Group Differences Mediated by (Re)reading

Rereading is reading. There are significant reading achievement gaps, both for racial and socioeconomic groups (Kuhlfeld, Gershoff, & Paschall, 2018) and for gender (Reilly, Neumann & Andrews, 2019). Since reading comprehension is an important predictor of writing quality (Ahmed & Wagner, 2020), reading difficulties may prevent some writers from applying sophisticated writing strategies.

To support such strategies, writers read and reread differently at different points in the writing process (Beers, Quinlan, & Harbaugh, 2010). This supports both idea generation and text production (Nottbusch, 2010). Sometimes, writers reread to identify and correct errors (Van Waes, Leijten, & Quinlan, 2010). Rereading during the final stages of drafting is associated with goal-setting and self-instruction behaviors, which require metacognitive evaluation of text quality (Breetvelt, Van den Bergh, & Rijlaarsdam, 1996).

Few studies have examined group differences in rereading and monitoring. Perhaps the most important is Beers (2004), who used eye-tracking to measure reading behaviors during writing. This study observed significant gender differences. Boys spent 70 % of their time rereading the portion of text that they just wrote. They reread previously written text portions only 6 % of the time, which implies a focus on linear text production. Their rereading and monitoring patterns were not affected by genre; similar patterns obtained for narrative and persuasive prompts. Girls showed a different pattern: more time spent rereading previously written stretches of text (15 % on narratives, 18 % on essays); on the persuasive prompt, less time spent monitoring the text just produced; and a combination of higher drafting fluency and slower typing speed, which implies they spent more time editing and revising.

The point of rereading previously written text is to determine whether revisions or edits are necessary; thus, more time spent rereading should correspond to more frequent editing and revision. Keystroke studies indicate that temporal patterns are different by gender during editing (Deane, Roth, Liz, Goswami, Steck, Lewis, & Richter, 2018). In general, higher-performing writers and typically higher-performing groups edit more frequently (Deane & Zhang, 2015; Zhang, Zhu, Deane, & Guo, 2017). Females edit their texts more frequently than males (Zhang,

Bennett, Deane & van Rijn, 2019; Bennett, Zhang, & Sinharay, 2021), even after controlling for text quality (Guo, Zhang, Deane, & Bennett, 2019). Guo, Zhang, Deane, and Bennett (2019) found racial/ethnic differences in pause times associated with editing, with typically higher scoring groups showing greater latency before editing.

Rereading competes with other uses of the eyes during writing. Visual attention is necessary to guide and plan handwriting (Sita & Taylor, 2015). Less experienced writers may focus on tracking hand and pen (Maldarelli, Kahrs, Hunt, & Lockman, 2015), preventing rereading during writing. Similar observations apply to keyboarding. Novice typists often adopt "hunt and peck" methods in which they search visually for each character and use one or a few fingers to press the keys (Logan, Ulrich, & Lindsey, 2016). Hunt and peck typists can become just as fast and accurate as well-trained touch typists, but touch typists can reread more easily without interrupting text production (Feit, Weir, & Oulasvirta, 2016). As a result, touch typists and self-taught typists end up with very different typing habits (Johansson, Wengelin, Johansson, & Holmqvist, 2010), even when both groups are equally fluent typists.

As Tate, Warschauer, and Abedi (2016) report, prior computer use is predictive of writing quality, weakly positively correlated with parental education, and weakly negatively correlated with SES. To the extent that computer use leads to fluency, this suggests a disadvantage for low-SES students. Historically, formal touch-typing instruction was not introduced until middle or even high school (Knox, 2003), and remains rare in elementary schools (Dockrell, Marshall, & Wyse, 2016). There is little evidence about the frequency of touch-typing instruction in low-SES schools, but lower levels of computer access in such schools suggests a lower frequency of touch-typing instruction as well.[2]

Reading is a critical gateway skill for writing. Good readers may not become good writers, but weak reading skills make self-regulation of writing harder to implement.

---

2 The COVID pandemic may have accelerated the acceptance of digital devices even in relatively poorly resourced schools, but so far there is little solid documentation of the long-term consequences. Way and Strain-Seymour (2021) outline a framework for future NAEP data collections that may make it possible to assess this shift more clearly in the future.

Group Differences Mediated by Attention and Working Memory

Given the importance of self-regulation—and its association with working memory—people with shorter working memory spans may encounter greater self-regulation difficulties (Swanson & Berninger, 1996; Van der Steen, Samuelson, & Thomson, 2017).

At the start of formal education, working memory capacity is an important predictor of academic performance (Alloway & Alloway, 2010). Stronger writers often demonstrate greater working memory capacity than weaker writers (Benton, Kraft, Glover, & Plake, 1984; Berninger, Abbott, Swanson, Lovitt, Trivedi, Lin, . . . & Amtman, 2010). Of course, effective working memory capacity is malleable and can be modified by other variables, including motivation and overall cognitive load. However, at any given moment, access to working memory constrains students' ability to handle—and learn from—challenging tasks (Von Bastian & Oberauer, 2014).

Students with attention deficit/hyperactivity disorder (ADHD) are probably the most important group whose performance on academic writing tasks is primarily limited by working memory and attentional processes (Graham, Fishman, Reid, & Hebert, 2016; Rodriguez, Torrance, Betts, Cerezo, & Garcia, 2020). Helping students with attentional challenges requires sustained interventions that target both self-regulation and fluency (Limpo & Alves, 2018).

Group Differences in Working Memory Associated with Gender

In their review of research on verbal working memory, Voyer, Saint Aubin, Altman, & Gallant (2021) found a small gender difference favoring females. Berninger, Whitaker, Feng, Swanson, and Abbott (1996) found a significant female advantage in planning for writing. Zhang and Vukelich (1998) found that girls benefited more from prewriting and planning activities. But several studies that specifically studied relations between working memory, gender, and writing performance found no significant gender effects (Bourke & Adams, 2011; Adams, Simmons, & Willis, 2015). However, Adams and colleagues observed gender differences in the kinds of short-term memory that were most critical for writing. For males, verbal (auditory) short term memory was the better predictor of writing quality, whereas for females, visual short-term memory was better (possibly linked to female skill advantages in reading). Overall, working memory span seems to contribute little to gender differences in writing.

Group Differences in Working Memory Associated with Race and Socioeconomic Status

Low SES is linked to slightly to moderately lower levels of executive function (Lawson, Hook, & Farah, 2018) and moderately lower working memory capacity (Mooney, Prady, Barker, Pickett, & Waterman, 2021). Associations between working memory and SES may be weak or nonexistent among younger children (Alloway, Alloway, & Wootan, 2014), However, there are significant differences in working memory capacity between high- and low-SES young adults (Evans & Schamberg, 2009). Evans and Schamberg (2009) interpret this pattern as the cumulative effect of poverty-related childhood stress.

Emotional factors play a critical causal role linking poverty with reduced working memory capacity (Oshri, Hallowell, Liu, MacKillop, Galvan, Kogan, & Sweet, 2019). Working memory is reduced under conditions of stereotype threat (awareness of negative stereotypes about groups one belongs to) (Beilock, Rydell, & McConnell, 2007). Competition between task-relevant processes and anxiety-related cognition (Moran, 2016) also reduces working memory capacity. Martinie, Olive, and Milland (2010) demonstrated a similar effect specifically for writing.

Table 3.1 Causal Mechanisms Associated with Working Memory

Causal Factor	Gender	SES	Race/Ethnicity
Higher levels of executive control increase self-regulation, and hence writing performance.	Results are mixed.	Average executive function may be somewhat higher among high-SES students.	
Greater working memory span supports more effective executive control and self-regulation, and hence writing performance.	Results are mixed.	Average working memory span may be moderately higher among high-SES students.	
Stress and intense emotion reduce working memory span		Stresses associated with poverty appear to reduce effective working memory capacity.	Stereotype threat reduces effective working memory capacity.

They found that cognitive dissonance during writing also reduced writers' effective working memory capacity.

Table 3.1 summarizes causal mechanisms associated with group differences in writing self-regulation.

Reference List

Adams, A.-M., Simmons, F., & Willis, C. (2010). Undergraduate students' ability to revise text effectively: relationships with topic knowledge and working memory. *Journal of Research in Reading, 33*(1), 54–76. https://doi.org/10.1111/j.1467-9817.2009.01432.x

Ahmed, Y., & Wagner, R. K. (2020). A "simple" illustration of a joint model of reading and writing using Meta-Analytic Structural Equation Modeling (MASEM). In R. A. Alves, R. Malatesha Joshi, & T. Limpo (Eds.), *Reading-Writing Connections* (pp. 55–75). Springer. https://doi.org/10.1007/978-3-030-38811-9

Alamargot, D., Caporossi, G., Chesnet, D., & Ros, C. (2011). What makes a skilled writer? Working memory and audience awareness during text composition. *Learning and Individual Differences, 21*, 505–516. https://doi.org/10.1016/j.lindif.2011.06.001

Alloway, T. P., & Alloway, R. G. (2010). Investigating the predictive roles of working memory and IQ in academic attainment. *Journal of Experimental Child Psychology, 106*(1), 20–29. https://doi.org/10.1016/j.jecp.2009.11.003

Alloway, T. P., Alloway, R. G., & Wootan, S. (2014). Home sweet home: Does where you live matter to working memory and other cognitive skills? *Journal of Experimental Child Psychology, 124*, 124–131. https://doi.org/10.1016/j.jecp.2013.11.012

Beers, S. F. (2004). *Reading Fluency and Adolescent Students' Reading Processes during Writing*. [Doctoral dissertation, University of Washington]. ResearchWorks. https://digital.lib.washington.edu/researchworks/bitstream/handle/1773/7700/3139447.pdf?sequence=1&isAllowed=y

Beers, S., Quinlan, T., & Harbaugh, A. G. (2010). Adolescent students' reading during writing behaviors and relationships with text quality: An eye tracking study. *Reading and Writing, 23*(7), 743–775. https://doi.org/10.1007/s11145-009-9193-7

Beilock, S. L., Rydell, R. J., & McConnell, A. R. (2007). Stereotype threat and working memory: mechanisms, alleviation, and spillover. *Journal of Experimental Psychology: General, 136*(2), 256–276. https://doi.org/10.1037/0096-3445.136.2.256

Bennett, R. E., Zhang, Mo., & Sinharay, S. (2021). How do educationally at-risk men and women differ in their essay-writing processes?. *Chinese/English Journal of Educational Measurement and Evaluation* | 教育测量与评估双语季刊, *2*(1), Article 1. https://www.ce-jeme.org/journal/vol2/iss1/1

Benton, S. L., Kraft, R. G., Glover, J. A., & Plake, B. S. (1984). Cognitive capacity differences among writers. *Journal of Educational Psychology, 76*(5), 820–834. https://doi.org/10.1037/0022-0663.76.5.820

Berninger, V. W. (1999). Coordinating transcription and text generation in working memory during composing: Automatic and constructive processes. *Learning Disability Quarterly, 22*(2), 99–112. https://doi.org/10.2307/1511269

Berninger, V. W., Abbott, R. D., Swanson, H. L., Lovitt, D., Trivedi, P., Lin, S.-J. C., . . . Amtman, D. (2010). Relationship of word- and sentence level working memory to reading and writing in second, fourth, and sixth grade. *Language, Speech, and Hearing Services in Schools, 41*(2), 179–193. https://doi.org/10.1044/0161-1461(2009/08-0002)

Berninger, V. W., & Richards, T. L. (2012). The writing brain: coordinating sensory/motor language, and cognitive writing systems in working memory. In V. W. Berninger (Ed.), *Past, Present and Future Contributions of Cognitive Writing Research to Cognitive Psychology* (pp. 537–566). Psychology Press. https://doi.org/10.4324/9780203805312

Berninger, V. W., Whitaker, D., Feng, Y., Swanson, H. L., & Abbott, R. D. (1996). Assessment of planning, translating, and revising in junior high writers. *Journal of School Psychology, 34*(1), 23–52. https://doi.org/10.1016/0022-4405(95)00024-0

Bourke, L., & Adams, A.-M. (2011). Is it differences in language skills and working memory that account for girls being better at writing than boys? *Journal of Writing Research, 3*(3), 249–277. https://doi.org/10.17239/jowr-2012.03.03.5

Bourke, L., Davies, S. J., Sumner, E., & Green, C. (2014). Individual differences in the development of early writing skills: Testing the unique contribution of visuo-spatial working memory. *Reading and Writing, 27*(2), 315–335. https://doi.org/10.1007/s11145-013-9446-3

Breetvelt, I., Van den Bergh, H., & Rijlaarsdam, G. (1996). Rereading and generating and their relation to text quality: An application of multilevel analysis on writing process data. In G. Rijlaarsdam, H. van den Bergh, & M. Couzijn (Eds.), *Theories, Models & Methodology in Writing Research* (pp. 10–21). Amsterdam University Press.

Deane, P. D., Roth, A., Litz, A., Goswami, V., Steck, F., Lewis, M., & Richter, T. (2018). *Behavioral Differences Between Retyping, Drafting, and Editing: A Writing Process Analysis* (ETS RM-18-06). Educational Testing Service. https://www.ets.org/Media/Research/pdf/RM-18-06.pdf

Deane, P., & Zhang, M. (2015). *Exploring the Feasibility of Using Writing Process Features to Assess Text Production Skills* (RR-15-2). Educational Testing Service. https://doi.org/10.1002/ets2.12071

Dockrell, J. E., Marshall, C. R., & Wyse, D. (2016). Teachers' reported practices for teaching writing in England. *Reading and Writing, 29*(3), 409–434. https://doi.org/10.1007/s11145-015-9605-9

Evans, G. W., & Schamberg, M. A. (2009). Childhood poverty, chronic stress, and adult working memory. *Proceedings of the National Academy of Sciences, 106*(16), 6545–6549. https://doi.org/10.1073/pnas.0811910106

Feit, A. M., Weir, D., & Oulasvirta, A. (2016). How we type: Movement strategies and performance in everyday typing. *Proceedings of the 2016 Chi Conference on Human Factors in Computing Systems* (pp. 4262–4273). https://doi.org/10.1145/2858036.2858233

Fitzgerald, J., & Shanahan, T. (2000). Reading and writing relations and their development. *Educational Psychologist, 35*(1), 39–50. https://psycnet.apa.org/doi/10.1207/S15326985EP3501_5

Flower, L., & Hayes, J. R. (1980). A cognitive process theory of writing. *College Composition and Communication, 32*(4), 365–387. https://doi.org/10.2307/356600

Gillespie, A., & Graham, S. (2014). A meta-analysis of writing interventions for students with learning disabilities. *Exceptional Children, 80*(4), 454–473. https://doi.org/10.1177/0014402914527238

Graham, S., Fishman, E. J., Reid, R., & Hebert, M. (2016). Writing characteristics of students with attention deficit hyperactive disorder: A meta-analysis. *Learning Disabilities Research & Practice, 31*(2), 75–89. https://doi.org/10.1111/ldrp.12099

Guo, H., Zhang, M., Deane, P., & Bennett, R. E. (2019). Writing process differences in subgroups reflected in keystroke logs. *Journal of Educational and Behavioral Statistics, 44*(5), 571–596. https://doi.org/10.3102/1076998619856590

Hacker, D. J. (2018). A metacognitive model of writing: An update from a developmental perspective. *Educational Psychologist, 53*(4), 220–237. https://psycnet.apa.org/doi/10.1080/00461520.2018.1480373

Hayes, J. R. (2012). Modeling and Remodeling Writing. *Written Communication, 29*(3), 369–388. https://doi.org/10.1177/0741088312451260

Hoskyn, M., & Swanson, H. L. (2003). The relationship between working memory and writing in younger and older adults. *Reading and Writing, 16*(8), 759–784. https://doi.org/10.1023/A:1027320226283

Johansson, R., Wengelin, Å., Johansson, V., & Holmqvist, K. (2010). Looking at the keyboard or the monitor: Relationships with text production processes. *Reading and Writing, 23*(7), 835–851. https://doi.org/10.1007/s11145-009-9189-3

Kellogg, R. T. (1996). Attentional overload and writing performance: Effects of rough draft and outline strategies. *Journal of Experimental Psychology: Learning, Memory, and Cognition, 14*(2), 355–365. https://doi.org/10.1037/0278-7393.14.2.355

Kellogg, R. T. (2001a). Competition for working memory among writing processes. *American Journal of Psychology, 114*(2), 175–191. https://doi.org/10.2307/1423513

Kellogg, R. T. (2001b). Long-term working memory in text production. *Memory and Cognition, 29*(1), 43–52. https://doi.org/10.3758/BF03195739

Kellogg, R. T. (2004). Working memory components in written sentence generation. *American Journal of Psychology, 117*(3), 341–361. https://doi.org/10.2307/4149005

Knox, N. S. P. (2003). *Comparison Analysis of Grade Level Implementation of Published Keyboarding Skills Based on International Society for Technology in Education (ITSE) Standards and States in the Southern Association of Colleges and Schools (SACS).* [Doctoral dissertaton, University of Tennessee, Knoxville]. TRACE (Tennessee Research and Creative Exchange). https://trace.tennessee.edu/cgi/viewcontent.cgi?article=3550&context=utk_graddiss

Kuhlfeld, M., Gershoff, E., & Paschall, K. (2018). The development of racial/ethnic and socioeconomic achievement gaps during the school years. *Journal of Applied Developmental Psychology, 57*, 62–73. https://doi.org/10.1016/j.appdev.2018.07.001

Lawson, G. M., Hook, C. J., & Farah, M. J. (2018). A meta-analysis of the relationship between socioeconomic status and executive function performance among children. *Developmental science, 21*(2), Article e12529. https://doi.org/10.1111/desc.12529

Lea, J., & Levy, C. M. (1999). Working memory as a resource in the writing process. In M. Torrance & G. Jeffery (Eds.), *The Cognitive Demands of Writing: Processing Capacity and Working Memory in Text Production* (pp. 63–82). Amsterdam University Press.

Limpo, T., & Alves, R. A. (2018). Tailoring multicomponent writing interventions: Effects of coupling self-regulation and transcription training. *Journal of Learning Disabilities, 51*(4), 381–398. https://doi.org/10.1177/0022219417708170

Logan, G. D., Ulrich, J. E., & Lindsey, D. R. (2016). Different (key) strokes for different folks: How standard and nonstandard typists balance Fitts' Law and Hick's Law. *Journal of Experimental Psychology: Human Perception and Performance, 42*(12), 2084–2102. https://doi.org/10.1037/xhp0000272

Maldarelli, J. E., Kahrs, B. A., Hunt, S. C., & Lockman, J. J. (2015). Development of early handwriting: Visual-motor control during letter copying. *Developmental Psychology, 51*(7), 879–888. https://doi.org/10.1037/a0039424

Martinie, M.-A., Olive, T., & Milland, L. (2010). Cognitive dissonance induced by writing a counterattitudinal essay facilitates performance on simple tasks but not on complex tasks that involve working memory. *Journal of Experimental Social Psychology, 46*(4), 587–594. https://doi.org/10.1016/j.jesp.2009.10.018

McCutchen, D. (1996). A capacity theory of writing: Working memory in composition. *Educational Psychology Review, 8*, 299–325. https://doi.org/10.1007/BF01464076

McCutchen, D. (2000). Knowledge, processing, and working memory: Implications for a theory of writing. *The Educational Psychologist, 35*(1), 13–23. https://doi.org/10.1207/S15326985EP3501_3

McCutchen, D. (2011). From novice to expert: Implications of language skills and writing-relevant knowledge for memory during the development of writing skill. *Journal of Writing Research, 3*(1), 51–68. https://doi.org/10.17239/jowr-2011.03.01.3

Mooney, K. E., Prady, S. L., Barker, M. M., Pickett, K. E., & Waterman, A. H. (2021). The association between socioeconomic disadvantage and children's working memory abilities: A systematic review and meta-analysis. *PloS one, 16*(12), Article e0260788. https://doi.org/10.1371%2Fjournal.pone.0260788

Moran, T. P. (2016). Anxiety and working memory capacity: A meta-analysis and narrative review. *Psychological Bulletin, 142*(8), 831–864. https://doi.org/10.1037/bul0000051

Nottbusch, G. (2010). Grammatical planning, execution, and control in written sentence production. *Reading and Writing, 23*(7), 777–801. https://doi.org/10.1007/s11145-009-9188-4

Olive, T. (2004). Working memory in writing: Empirical evidence from the dual-task technique. *European Psychologist, 9*(1), 32–42. https://psycnet.apa.org/doi/10.1027/1016-9040.9.1.32

Olive, T., & Passerault, J.-M. (2012). The visuospatial dimension of writing. *Written Communication, 29*(3), 326–343. https://doi.org/10.1177/0741088312451111

Oshri, A., Hallowell, E., Liu, S., MacKillop, J., Galvan, A., Kogan, S. M., & Sweet, L. H. (2019). Socioeconomic hardship and delayed reward discounting: Associations with working memory and emotional reactivity. *Developmental cognitive neuroscience, 37*, Article 100642. https://doi.org/10.1016/j.dcn.2019.100642

Piolat, A., Roussey, J.-Y., Olive, T., & Amada, M. (2004). Processing time and cognitive effort in revision: effects of error type and of working memory capacity. In L. Allal, L. Chanquoy, P. Largy, & Y. Rouiller (Eds.), *Revision: Cognitive and Instructional Processes* (pp. 21–38). Kluwer Academic.

Ransdell, S. (1999). Writing, reading, and speaking memory spans and the importance of resource flexibility. In M. Torrance & G. Jeffery (Eds.), *The Cognitive Demands of Writing. Processing Capacity and Working Memory in Text Production* (pp. 99–113). Amsterdam University Press.

Ransdell, S., & Levy, C. M. (2002). The structure of writing processes as revealed by secondary task demands. *L1-Educational Studies in Language and Literature, 2*, 141–163. https://doi.org/10.1023/A:1020851300668

Reilly, D., Neumann, D. L., & Andrews, G. (2019). Gender differences in reading and writing achievement: Evidence from the National Assessment of Educational Progress (NAEP). *American Psychologist, 74*(4), 445–458. https://doi.org/10.1037/amp0000356

Rodríguez, C., Torrance, M., Betts, L., Cerezo, R., & García, T. (2020). Effects of ADHD on writing composition product and process in school-age students. *Journal of Attention Disorders, 24*(12), 1735–1745. https://doi.org/10.1177/1087054717707048

Santangelo, T., Harris, K., & Graham, S. (2016). Self-regulation and writing. In C. A. MacArthur, S. Graham, & J. Fitzpatrick (Eds.), *Handbook of Writing Research* (2nd ed., pp. 174–193). Guilford.

Sita, J. C., & Taylor, K. A. (2015). Eye movements during the handwriting of words: Individually and within sentences. *Human Movement Science, 43*, 229–238. https://doi.org/10.1016/j.humov.2015.01.011

Sommers, N. (1980). Revision strategies of student writers and experienced adult writers. *College Composition and Communication, 31*(4), 378–388. https://doi.org/10.2307/356588

Swanson, H. L., & Berninger, V. W. (1996). Individual differences in children's working memory and writing skill. *Journal of Experimental Child Psychology, 63*(2), 358–385. https://doi.org/10.1006/jecp.1996.0054

Tate, T. P., Warschauer, M., & Abedi, J. (2016). The effects of prior computer use on computer-based writing: The 2011 NAEP writing assessment. *Computers & Education, 101*, 115–131. https://doi.org/10.1016/j.compedu.2016.06.001

Torrance, M., & Jeffery, G. (1999). Writing processes and cognitive demands. In M. Torrance & G. Jeffery (Eds.), *The Cognitive Demands of Writing. Processing Capacity and Working Memory in Text Production* (pp. 1–11). Amsterdam University Press.

Van der Steen, S., Samuelson, D., & Thomson, J. M. (2017). The effect of keyboard-based word processing on students with different working memory capacity during the process of academic writing. *Written Communication, 34*(3), 280–305. https://doi.org/10.1177/0741088317714232

Van Waes, L., Leijten, M., & Quinlan, T. (2010). Reading during sentence composing and error correction: A multilevel analysis of the influences of task complexity. *Reading and Writing, 23*(7), 803–834. https://doi.org/10.1007/s11145-009-9190-x

Vandenberg, R., & Swanson, H. L. (2007). Which components of working memory are important in the writing process? *Reading and Writing, 20*(7), 721–752. https://doi.org/10.1007/s11145-006-9046-6

Von Bastian, C. C., & Oberauer, K. (2014). Effects and mechanisms of working memory training: a review. *Psychological Research, 78*(6), 803–820. https://doi.org/10.1007/s00426-013-0524-6

Voyer, D, Saint Aubin, J, Altman, K, & Gallant, G. (2021, April). Sex differences in verbal working memory: A systematic review and meta-analysis. *Psychol Bull, 147*(4), 352–398. https://10.1037/bul0000320

Way, D., & Strain-Seymour, E. (2021). *A Framework for Considering Device and Interface Features That May Affect Student Performance on the National Assessment of Educational Progress*. NAEP Validity Studies (NVS) Panel. https://www.air.org/sites/default/files/Framework-for-Considering-Device-and-Interface-Features-NAEP-NVS-Panel-March-2021.pdf

Zhang, L., & Vukelich, C. (1998, April 13–17). *Prewriting Activities and Gender: Influences on the Writing Quality of Male and Female Students* [Conference Presentation]. Annual Meeting of the American Educational Research Association, San Diego, CA. https://files.eric.ed.gov/fulltext/ED422297.pdf

Zhang, M., Bennett, R. E., Deane, P., & van Rijn, P. W. (2019). Are there gender differences in how students write their essays? An analysis of writing processes. *Educational Measurement: Issues and Practice, 38*(2), 14–26. https://doi.org/10.1111/emip.12249

Zhang, M., Zhu, M., Deane, P., & Guo, H. (2017, July). Identifying and comparing writing process patterns using keystroke logs. In *Proceedings of the Annual Meeting of the Psychometric Society* (pp. 367–381). Springer. https://doi.org/10.1007/978-3-030-01310-3_32

Zimmerman, B. J., & Risemberg, R. (1997). Becoming a self-regulated writer: A social cognitive perspective. *Contemporary Educational Psychology, 22*(1), 73–101. https://doi.org/10.1006/ceps.1997.0919

CHAPTER FOUR

Writing as the Formulation of Ideas: The Mediating Effects of Prior Content Knowledge

Overview

Novice writers often rely on what Bereiter and Scardamalia (1987) termed *knowledge-telling*, in which writers express ideas that seem relevant as they occur. Knowledge telling can work well when writers know their subject and have already formulated clear, well-focused ideas. It may not work well in academic contexts, where writers must formulate original ideas about new and unfamiliar content. All other things being equal, "stronger" writers may simply be students who know more about their topics and therefore have an easier time generating ideas.

Since people learn differently, depending on situation, life experience, and education, group differences in content knowledge affect literacy achievement. There are powerful effects both for writing and for reading, since reading comprehension depends upon integrating reading content with prior knowledge (Kintsch, 1988). Writing tasks that require students to mobilize knowledge they do not have, based on experiences they do not share, naturally produce worse performance. For this reason, many theorists emphasize the funds of knowledge students bring with them to the classroom and advocate leveraging this knowledge to facilitate learning (Moll & Greenberg, 1990; Flores, 2018).

An influential series of studies examined the effect of content knowledge on writing in a specific domain—baseball—where topic knowledge is easy to measure and unrelated to academic performance. Spilich, Vesonder, Chiesi, and Voss (1979) had students summarize stories about baseball games. They found that high-knowledge students generated more detailed domain-relevant content. Voss, Vesonder, and Spilich (1980) asked students to write their own baseball narratives. High-knowledge students focused on game play, whereas low knowledge students focused on incidental details, such as fan reactions and emotions. These results were confirmed by Mosenthal, Conley, Colella, and Davidson-Mosenthal (1985). DeGroff (1987) examined multiple stages of the writing process—first drafts, writing conferences, and revisions—and showed that at each stage, higher-knowledge students produced richer and more detailed domain-relevant information. Benton, Corkill, Sharp, Downey, and Khramtsova (1995) examined the relationship between prior knowledge about baseball and topic interest. While the two factors were significantly correlated, both contributed independently toward predicting the "thematic maturity" (richness of content development) and interestingness of student narratives. Finally, Kellogg (2001) showed that high-knowledge students put in less effort than low-knowledge students yet produced higher-quality narrative and expository texts.

Similar findings have been adduced across a variety of domains. Topic knowledge is related to topical interest, but only moderately (Tobias, 1994), Both knowledge and interest contribute to writing quality (Olinghouse, Graham, & Gillespie, 2015). Greater topic knowledge leads to higher writing performance (McCutchen, 1986; Rowan, 1990), or to reduced effort to produce texts of similar quality (Kellogg, 1987). Instruction that improves domain-relevant knowledge also improves writing quality (Kim, Relyea, Burkhauser, Scherer, & Rich, 2021), especially if it helps students connect learning with their life outside school (Langer, 2001).

Prior knowledge affects the entire writing process. When students are given topic choice, they choose topics they know better (Gradwohl & Schumacher, 1989). Students who develop deeper knowledge of source materials during prewriting produce higher quality drafts (Proske & Kapp, 2013). Students with higher levels of topic knowledge make more substantive revisions (Butterfield, Hacker, & Plumb, 1994; McCutchen, Francis, & Kerr, 1997), unless their attention is focused on error correction (Adams, Simmons, & Willis, 2010).

McCutchen (2000) and Kellogg (2001) attribute topic knowledge effects to "long-term working memory", which enables rapid retrieval of task-relevant information, reduces idea generation effort, and frees up cognitive resources for other writing processes. As a result, students who score poorly in on-demand writing assessments usually produce shorter texts. If students are relying on knowledge-telling strategies—and most do—they will stop when they run out of easily generated ideas (Bennett, Zhang, Deane, & van Rijn 2020; Fleckenstein, Meyer, Jansen, Keller, & Köller, 2020) Conversely, students who have deeper knowledge about writing and control well-developed prewriting, planning, and revision strategies are better positioned to generate ideas even when they start with relatively weak topic knowledge (de la Paz, 2005; Deane, 2018).

Prior knowledge does not just affect writing performance. It has a pervasive impact on academic and professional achievement. When all else is held equal, individuals with deeper knowledge are also most likely to increase it. Deeper background knowledge also helps adults achieve power and status in mainstream culture, regardless of ethnic background (Hofstetter, Sticht, & Hofstetter, 1999).

Group Differences Mediated by Prior Content Knowledge

Content knowledge is strongly associated with socioeconomic status. However, the relation between content knowledge and gender is relatively weak and variable.

Gender Differences in Prior Content Knowledge

Despite the overall female advantage in writing (and reading) achievement, assessments of general knowledge show an overall male advantage. Specific areas of female advantage are associated with conventional gender norms—advantages in physical sciences, technology, finance, and sports for males; advantages in family, fashion, medicine, literature, and the humanities for females (Ackerman, Bowen, Beier, & Kanfer, 2001). However, meta-analyses by Cole (1997) and Tran, Hofer, and Voracek (2014) measured only small gender-based knowledge differences after accounting for school-related moderators such as school type and selectivity, student age, and parental education. These results are consistent with the gender similarity hypothesis (Hyde, 2005). However, these studies continued to show the same general pattern, in which humanities subjects comprise a specific area of relative female advantage.

Hyland, Hoff, and Rounds (2022) found that gender-linked knowledge differences were associated with specific ability/interest profiles. Males overwhelmingly comprised two of three high-performing profiles (Intellectual/Mathematical and Scientific), while females predominated in a third high-performing profile (Cultural). Low-performing profiles were also differentiated by gender. Each profile showed distinct patterns of knowledge and associated interests.

Gender differences in content knowledge are partly shaped by students' school experience (Booth, 2013). School practices may heighten gender differences by implicitly marking certain genres or subjects as masculine or feminine (Ivinson & Murphy, 2003), though observed differences typically reflect broader societal expectations (Anderson, 2002). To the extent that boys and girls live in different social worlds, they will value different information, prefer different reading experiences, and as a result, develop different knowledge (Newkirk, 2000).

There are important gender-based differences in reading preferences. Though boys are interested in and engaged by narrative (Brown, 2015; Disenhaus, 2015), boys often prefer to read informational texts (Peterson, 2008; Farris, Werderich, Nelson, & Fuhler, 2009; Lepper, Stang, & McElvany, 2022). Boys are also more likely to select texts based on topic (Mohr, 2006). Boys' writing may contain more features characteristic of informational text than narrative, consistent with the hypothesis that they have read more informational texts (Argamon, Koppel, Fine, & Shimoni, 2003).

Overall, the literature suggests multiple paths toward male advantage in prior knowledge, yet females, not males, are advantaged on writing tasks. However, writing is treated as a humanities skill in U.S. schools, and more females are high achieving in language arts and the humanities. In the U.S., elementary education has historically emphasized narrative texts (Moss, 2008; Yopp & Yopp, 2006, 2012), particularly in preschool (Pentimonti, Zucker, Justice, & Kaderavek, 2010) and first grade (Duke, 2000). Reading and writing about informational texts increases significantly only in the upper elementary grades (Ness, 2011). While recent educational reforms such as the Common Core State Standards initiative (2010) emphasize informational texts, the preference for narrative in the early grades remains entrenched (Dreher & Kletzien, 2016). This pattern suggests that in the early grades, where foundational literacy skills are acquired, boys may often discover that the texts and topics that they prefer are less valued and perceive classroom literacy tasks as favoring the other gender.

Socioeconomic and Cultural Differences in Prior Content Knowledge

Lower-SES students often enter school with less school-relevant background knowledge than higher-SES students. These differences are largely driven by malleable social factors (Neuman, 2006; Pinkham, Kaefer, & Neuman, 2012)[1]. Content knowledge is so important in reading that comprehension differences

---

1 There is little published information on differences in interests or knowledge among racial and ethnic, as opposed to socioeconomic, groups, but presumably, such differences exist, given the emphasis advocates of culturally responsive pedagogy place upon paying attention to the funds of knowledge specific to particular communities.

associated with SES disappear when literacy tasks are manipulated to eliminate knowledge-based inference (Neuman, Kaefer, & Pinkham, 2014). It is common for schools with large numbers of low-SES students to focus on skills instruction; but this emphasis, by not addressing group differences in content knowledge, can reinforce existing inequities (Hirsch, 2007; Kato & Manning, 2007).

Initial studies of Sesame Street, an educational TV program begun in the 1960s, suggested that it increased knowledge differences between high- and low-SES students, partly because higher-SES students were more prepared to acquire the knowledge *Sesame Street* offered, and partly because affluent parents more often encouraged their students to watch it (Ball, 1970; Bogatz & Ball, 1971). Celano and Neuman (2008) observed that in the Philadelphia schools they studied, differences in school-relevant knowledge grew over the summer, mostly because high-SES parents and community leaders devoted more resources to involving their children in reading challenging texts for pleasure. More generally, background knowledge is strongly tied to print exposure (Stanovich, West, & Harrison, 1995). Prior knowledge has a powerful positive effect on memory for content (Recht & Leslie, 1988) and increases individual interest, another important factor in knowledge acquisition (Alexander, Kulikowich, & Schulze, 1994).

A major concern in 21st-century literacy is the differential socioeconomic impact of digital devices and the internet. Online media are associated with greater knowledge differences than traditional media because internet use is strongly associated with high SES (Bonfadelli, 2002; Wei & Hindman, 2011). This "digital divide" is not solely driven by access to digital devices and the Internet, but also depends on how socioeconomic groups take up specific literacy practices. In low-SES communities, computer use may lead to replacement of reading by other leisure activities, whereas high-SES communities tend to have strong social supports that encourage online and digital reading and writing (Warschauer, 2017).

Throughout this section, I have avoided the term, "knowledge gap", which historically was used to describe measured differences in student content knowledge. This term may encourage deficit-based, rather than asset-based approaches (Janks, 2010; Hattan & Lupo, 2020). Hattan & Lupo argue that a focus on content knowledge can devalue other forms of knowledge, including cultural knowledge, critical to participation in a diverse society (Smith & Wilhelm, 2002; Au, 2016). However, there is evidence that a knowledge-building curriculum can improve literacy achievement (Coleman & Concannon, 2022; Hwang, Cabell, & Joyner, 2022).

These considerations raise serious issues for writing instruction and assessment. Low-SES writers may experience significant learning challenges, due to a relative lack of academic content knowledge and a tendency for schools to assign

Table 4.1 Causal Mechanisms Associated with Group Differences in Content Knowledge

Causal Factor	Gender	SES Race/Ethnicity
Students from different communities and social backgrounds enter school with different interests and funds of knowledge.	Interests and funds of knowledge tend to be differentiated by gender.	Interests and funds of knowledge are differentiated across socioeconomic, ethnic, and racial boundaries. Academic content knowledge tends to be more strongly developed outside of school in high-SES communities, where parental and community resources more easily can be dedicated to that purpose
Students learn more if schools help them make meaningful connections between what they are learning and their lived experiences and funds of knowledge.	Language arts classes often focus on narrative texts and analyze literary and cultural themes, which align well with the interests and funds of knowledge characteristically associated with female gender identity.	Schools often presume that their students are drawing on the funds of knowledge with which (typically White and upper-middle-class) teachers and curriculum instructors are most familiar, making it easier for students from high-SES communities to develop knowledge of school-relevant content.
Students rely on knowledge-telling strategies to generate ideas for writing. As a result, students with less knowledge are likely to stop writing before they have met reasonable strategies for writing quality.	Higher-ability females tend to have stronger knowledge about and interest in the literary and cultural topics that tend to be emphasized in ELA classes, resulting in more fluent, often higher-quality writing.	Students from high-SES backgrounds tend to have higher levels of academic content knowledge, resulting in more fluent, often higher-quality writing.

literacy tasks that fail to connect with their existing funds of knowledge. There is an obvious fairness issue here, but also a fundamental challenge for education. Students write well when they know what they are talking about -- but writing also helps them learn. Without instruction that builds knowledge and helps students see why that knowledge matters, inequitable patterns of writing achievement are more-or-less guaranteed.

Table 4.1 summarizes the causal mechanisms by which content knowledge appears to affect writing achievement.

Reference List

Ackerman, P. L., Bowen, K. R., Beier, M., & Kanfer, R. (2001). Determinants of individual differences and gender differences in knowledge. *Journal of Educational Psychology, 93*(4), 797–825. https://doi.org/10.1037/0022-0663.93.4.797

Adams, A.-M., Simmons, F., & Willis, C. (2010). Undergraduate students' ability to revise text effectively: Relationships with topic knowledge and working memory. *Journal of Research in Reading, 33*(1), 54–76. https://doi.org/10.1111/j.1467-9817.2009.01432.x

Alexander, P. A., Kulikowich, J. M., & Schulze, S. K. (1994). How subject-matter knowledge affects recall and interest. *American Educational Research Journal, 31*(2), 313–337. https://doi.org/10.3102/00028312031002313

Anderson, D. D. (2002). Casting and recasting gender: Children constituting social identities through literacy practices. *Research in the Teaching of English, 36*(3), 391–427.

Argamon, S., Koppel, M., Fine, J., & Shimoni, A. R. (2003). Gender, genre, and writing style in formal written texts. *Text, 23*(3), 321–346. https://doi.org/10.1515/text.2003.014

Au, K. H. (Ed.) (2016). *Multicultural Issues and Literacy Achievement*. Lawrence Erlbaum. https://doi.org/10.4324/9781315045450

Ball, S. (1970). *The First Year of Sesame Street: An Evaluation*. Educational Testing Service. https://files.eric.ed.gov/fulltext/ED047823.pdf

Bennett, R. E., Zhang, M., Deane, P., & van Rijn, P. W. (2020). How do proficient and less proficient students differ in their composition processes?. *Educational Assessment, 25*(3), 198–217. https://doi.org/10.1080/10627197.2020.1804351

Benton, S. L., Corkill, A. J., Sharp, J. M., Downey, R. G., & Khramtsova, I. (1995). Knowledge, interest, and narrative writing. *Journal of Educational Psychology, 87*(1), 66–79. https://doi.org/10.1037/0022-0663.87.1.66

Bereiter, C. B., & Scardamalia, M. (1987). *The Psychology of Written Composition*. Lawrence Earlbaum.

Bogatz, G. A., & Ball, S. (1971). *The Second Year of Sesame Street: A Continuing Evaluation*. Educational Testing Service. https://files.eric.ed.gov/fulltext/ED122800.pdf

Bonfadelli, H. (2002). The Internet and knowledge gaps: A theoretical and empirical investigation. *European Journal of Communication, 17*(1), 65–84. https://doi.org/10.1177/0267323102017001607

Booth, D. (2013). Literacy education and gender. In C. Kosnik, J. Rowsell, P. Williamson, R. Simon, & C. Beck (Eds.), *Literacy Teacher Educators: Preparing Teachers for a Changing World* (pp. 21–34). Sense Publishers.

Brown, D. W. (2015). *These Heads Are Packed with Stories: The Out-of-School Writing Experiences of Elementary Age Boys.* [Doctoral dissertation, Georgia State University]. Scholarworks. http://scholarworks.gsu.edu/cgi/viewcontent.cgi?article=1007&context=mse_diss

Butterfield, E. C., Hacker, D. J., & Plumb, C. S. (1994). Topic knowledge, linguistic knowledge, and revision skill as determinants of text revision. In E. C. Butterfield (Ed.), *Children's Writing: Toward a Process Theory of the Development of Skilled Writing* (pp. 83–141). JAI.

Celano, D., & Neuman, S. B. (2008). When schools close, the knowledge gap grows. *Phi Delta Kappan, 90*(4), 256–262. https://doi.org/10.1177/00317217089000406

Cole, N. S. (1997). *The ETS Gender Study: How Females and Males Perform in Educational Settings.* Educational Testing Service. https://files.eric.ed.gov/fulltext/ED424337.pdf

Coleman, A. E., & Concannon, J. P. (2022). The impact of knowledge-building curricula on reading achievement: Closing the poverty gap. *Creative Education, 13*(11), 3663–3689. https://doi.org/10.4236/ce.2022.1311233

Common Core State Standards Initiative. (2010). *State standards for English Language Arts & Literacy in History/Social Studies, Science, Common Core and Technical Subjects.* CCSSO. https://learning.ccsso.org/wp-content/uploads/2022/11/ADA-Compliant-ELA-Standards.pdf

De La Paz, S. (2005). Effects of historical reasoning instruction and writing strategy mastery in culturally and academically diverse middle school classrooms. *Journal of Educational Psychology, 97*(2), 139–156. https://psycnet.apa.org/doi/10.1037/0022-0663.97.2.139

Deane, P. D. (2018). The challenges of writing in school: Conceptualizing writing development within a sociocognitive framework. *Educational Psychologist, 53*(4), 280–300, https://doi.org/10.1080/00461520.2018.1513844

DeGroff, L.-J. C. (1987). The influence of prior knowledge on writing, conferencing, and revising. *The Elementary School Journal, 88*(2), 105–118. https://doi.org/10.1086/461527

Disenhaus, N. (2015). *Boys, Writing, and the Literacy Gender Gap: What We Know, What We Think We Know.* [Doctoral dissertation, The University of Vermont]. ScholarWorks. https://scholarworks.uvm.edu/cgi/viewcontent.cgi?article=1329&context=graddis

Dreher, M. J., & Kletzien, S. B. (2016). Have recommended book lists changed to reflect current expectations for informational text in K-3 classrooms? *Reading Psychology, 37*(3), 371–391. https://doi.org/10.1080/02702711.2015.1055871

Duke, N. K. (2000). 3.6 minutes per day: The scarcity of informational texts in first grade. *Reading Research Quarterly, 35*(2), 202–224. https://doi.org/10.1598/RRQ.35.2.1

Farris, P. J., Werderich, D. E., Nelson, P. A., & Fuhler, C. J. (2009). Male call: Fifth-grade boys' reading preferences. *The Reading Teacher, 63*(3), 180–188. https://doi.org/10.1598/RT.63.3.1

Fleckenstein, J., Meyer, J., Jansen, T., Keller, S., & Köller, O. (2020). Is a long essay always a good essay? the effect of text length on writing assessment. *Frontiers in Psychology*, 11, Article 562462. https://doi.org/10.3389/fpsyg.2020.562462

Flores, T. T. (2018). Breaking silence and amplifying voices: Youths writing and performing their worlds. *Journal of Adolescent & Adult Literacy, 61*(6), 653–661. https://doi.org/10.1002/jaal.733

Gradwohl, J. M., & Schumacher, G. M. (1989). The relationship between content knowledge and topic choice in writing. *Written Communication, 6*(2), 181–195. https://doi.org/10.1177/0741088389006002003

Hattan, C., & Lupo, S. M. (2020). Rethinking the role of knowledge in the literacy classroom. *Reading Research Quarterly, 55*(S1), S283–S298. https://doi.org/10.1002/rrq.350

Hirsch, E. D. (2007). *The Knowledge Deficit: Closing the Shocking Education Gap for American Children.* Houghton Mifflin Harcourt.

Hofstetter, C. R., Sticht, T. G., & Hofstetter, C. H. (1999). Knowledge, literacy, and power. *Communication Research, 26*(1), 58–80. https://doi.org/10.1177/009365099026001004

Hwang, H., Cabell, S. Q., & Joyner, R. E. (2022). Does cultivating content knowledge during literacy instruction support vocabulary and comprehension in the elementary school years? A systematic review. *Reading Psychology, 44*(2), 145–174. https://doi.org/10.1080/02702711.2022.2141397

Hyde, J. S. (2005). The gender similarities hypothesis. *American Psychologist, 60*(6), 581–592. https://doi.org/10.1037/0003-066x.60.6.581

Hyland, W. E., Hoff, K. A., & Rounds, J. (2022). Interest-ability profiles: An integrative approach to knowledge acquisition. *Journal of Intelligence, 10*(3), 43. https://doi.org/10.3390/jintelligence10030043

Ivinson, G., & Murphy, P. (2003). Boys don't write romance: The construction of knowledge and social gender identities in English classrooms. *Pedagogy, Culture and Society, 11*(1), 89–111. https://doi.org/10.1080/14681360300200162

Janks, H. (2010). *Literacy and Power.* New York: Routledge. https://doi.org/10.1080/1554480X.2012.657780

Kato, T., & Manning, M. (2007). Teaching strategies: Content knowledge—The real reading crisis. *Childhood Education, 83*(4), 238–239. https://doi.org/10.1080/00094056.2007.10522922

Kellogg, R. T. (1987). Effects of topic knowledge on the allocation of processing time and cognitive effort to writing processes. *Memory and Cognition, 15*(3), 256–266. https://doi.org/10.3758/BF03197724

Kellogg, R. T. (2001). Long-term working memory in text production. *Memory and Cognition, 29*(1), 43–52. https://doi.org/10.3758/BF03195739

Kim, J. S., Relyea, J. E., Burkhauser, M. A., Scherer, E., & Rich, P. (2021). Improving elementary grade students' science and social studies vocabulary knowledge depth, reading comprehension, and argumentative writing: A conceptual replication. *Educational Psychology Review, 33*(4), 1935–1964. https://doi.org/10.1007/s10648-021-09609-6

Kintsch, W. (1988). The role of knowledge in discourse comprehension: A construction-integration model. *Psychological Review, 95*(2), 163–182. https://doi.org/10.1037/0033-295X.95.2.163

Langer, J. A. (2001). Beating the odds: Teaching middle and high school students to read and write well. *American Educational Research Journal, 38*(4), 837–880. https://doi.org/10.3102/00028312038004837

Lepper, C., Stang, J., & McElvany, N. (2022). Gender differences in text-based interest: Text characteristics as underlying variables. *Reading Research Quarterly, 57*(2), 537–554. https://doi.org/10.1002/rrq.420

McCutchen, D. (1986). Domain knowledge and linguistic knowledge in the development of writing ability. *Journal of Memory and Language, 24*(4), 431–444. https://doi.org/10.1016/0749-596X(86)90036-7

McCutchen, D. (2000). Knowledge, processing, and working memory: Implications for a theory of writing. *The Educational Psychologist, 35*(1), 13–23. https://doi.org/10.1207/S15326985EP3501_3

McCutchen, D., Francis, M., & Kerr, S. (1997). Revising for meaning: Effects of knowledge and strategy. *Journal of Educational Psychology, 89*(4), 667–676. https://psycnet.apa.org/doi/10.1037/0022-0663.89.4.667

Mohr, K. A. (2006). Children's choices for recreational reading: A three-part investigation of selection preferences, rationales, and processes. *Journal of Literacy Research, 38*(1), 81–104. https://doi.org/10.1207/s15548430jlr3801_4

Moll, L. C., & Greenberg, J. B. (1990). Creating zones of possibilities: Combiningsocial context for instruction. In L. C. Moll (Ed.), *Vygotsky and Education: Instructional Implications and Applications of Sociohistorical Psychology*. Cambridge University Press. https://doi.org/10.1017/CBO9781139173674

Mosenthal, P. B., Conley, M. W., Colella, A., & Davidson-Mosenthal, R. (1985). The influence of prior knowledge and teacher lesson structure on children's production of narratives. *The Elementary School Journal, 85*(5), 621–634. https://psycnet.apa.org/doi/10.1086/461425

Moss, B. (2008). The information text gap: The mismatch between non-narrative text types in basal readers and 2009 NAEP recommended guidelines. *Journal of Literacy Research, 40*(2), 201–219. https://doi.org/10.1080/10862960802411927

Ness, M. (2011). Teachers' use of and attitudes toward informational text in K–5 classrooms. *Reading Psychology, 32*(1), 28–53. https://doi.org/10.1080/02702710903241322

Neuman, S. B. (2006). The knowledge gap: Implications for early education. In D. K. Dickinson & S. B. Neuman (Eds.), *Handbook of Early Literacy Research* (Vol. 2, pp. 29–40). Guilford.

Neuman, S. B., Kaefer, T., & Pinkham, A. (2014). Building background knowledge. *The Reading Teacher, 68*(2), 145–148. https://doi.org/10.1002/trtr.1314

Newkirk, T. (2000). Misreading masculinity: Speculations on the great gender gap in writing. *Language Arts, 77*(4), 294–300. https://www.jstor.org/stable/41483068

Olinghouse, N. G., Graham, S., & Gillespie, A. (2015). The relationship of discourse and topic knowledge to fifth graders' writing performance. *Journal of Educational Psychology, 107*(2), 391–406. https://psycnet.apa.org/doi/10.1037/a0037549

Pentimonti, J. M., Zucker, T. A., Justice, L. M., & Kaderavek, J. N. (2010). Informational text use in preschool classroom read-alouds. *The Reading Teacher, 63*(8), 656–665. https://doi.org/10.1598/RT.63.8.4

Peterson, J. A. (2008). *Checking out or checking into reading? The borrowing habits of elementary school children in relation to gender, age, and reading ability.* [M.A. Thesis, University of North Carolina Chapel Hill]. Carolina Digital Repository. https://cdr.lib.unc.edu/concern/masters_papers/f1881q91d

Pinkham, A. M., Kaefer, T., & Neuman, S. B. (Eds.). (2012). *Knowledge Development in Early Childhood: Sources of Learning and Classroom Implications.* Guilford.

Proske, A., & Kapp, F. (2013). Fostering topic knowledge: Essential for academic writing. *Reading and Writing, 26*(8), 1337–1352. https://doi.org/10.1007/s11145-012-9421-4

Recht, D. R., & Leslie, L. (1988). Effect of prior knowledge on good and poor readers' memory of text. *Journal of Educational Psychology, 80*(1), 16–20. https://doi.org/10.1037/0022-0663.80.1.16

Rowan, K. E. (1990). Cognitive correlates of explanatory writing skill: An analysis of individual differences. *Written Communication, 7*(3), 316–341. https://doi.org/10.1177/0741088390007003002

Smith, M., & Wilhelm, J. D. (2002). *Reading Don't Fix No Chevys: Literacy in the Lives of Young Men.* Heineman.

Spilich, G. J., Vesonder, G. T., Chiesi, H. L., & Voss, J. F. (1979). Text processing of domain-related information for individuals with high and low domain knowledge. *Journal of Verbal Learning and Verbal Behavior, 18*(3), 275–290. https://doi.org/10.1016/S0022-5371(79)90155-5

Stanovich, K. E., West, R. F., & Harrison, M. R. (1995). Knowledge growth and maintenance across the life span: The role of print exposure. *Developmental Psychology, 31*(5), 811–826. https://doi.org/10.1037/0012-1649.31.5.811

Tobias, S. (1994). Interest, prior knowledge, and learning. *Review of Educational Research, 64*(1), 37–54. https://doi.org/10.2307/1170745

Tran, U. S., Hofer, A. A., & Voracek, M. (2014). Sex differences in general knowledge: Meta-analysis and new data on the contribution of school-related moderators among high-school students. *PloS One, 9*(10), Article e110391. https://doi.org/10.1371/journal.pone.0110391

Voss, J. F., Vesonder, G. T., & Spilich, G. J. (1980). Text generation and recall by high-knowledge and low-knowledge individuals. *Journal of Verbal Learning and Verbal Behavior, 18*(6), 651–667. https://doi.org/10.1016/S0022-5371(80)90343-6

Warschauer, M. (2017). Addressing the social envelope: Education and the digital divide. In C. Greenhow, J. Sonnevend, & C. Agur (Eds.), *Education and Social Media: Toward a Digital Future* (pp. 29–48). MIT Press. https://doi.org/10.7551/mitpress/9780262034470.001.0001

Wei, L., & Hindman, D. B. (2011). Does the digital divide matter more? Comparing the effects of new media and old media use on the education-based knowledge gap. *Mass Communication and Society, 14*(2), 216–235. https://doi.org/10.1080/15205431003642707

Yopp, R. H., & Yopp, H. K. (2006). Informational texts as read-alouds at school and home. *Journal of Literacy Research, 38*(1), 37–51. https://doi.org/10.1207/s15548430jlr3801_2

Yopp, R. H., & Yopp, H. K. (2012). Young children's limited and narrow exposure to informational text. *The Reading Teacher, 65*(7), 480–490. https://doi.org/10.1002/TRTR.01072

CHAPTER FIVE

Writing as Verbal Self-Expression: The Causal Role of Oral Language Skills

Writing depends on fluency and accuracy in verbal expression (Shanahan, 2006). Anything that undermines fluency and accuracy—including the dysfluency and discomfort of communicating in an unfamiliar language, style, or register—necessarily also undermines writing performance.

Group Differences Mediated by Oral Language Skills

Even for native speakers of prestige dialects, oral language skills affect writing achievement. Especially in the early grades, oral language fluency is an important predictor of writing quality (Abbott & Berninger, 1993; Kim, Al-Otaiba, Puranik, Folsom, Greulich, & Wagner, 2011) . Fluent speakers can easily produce long bursts of text without a pause (Connelly, Dockrell, Walter, & Critten, 2012). Group differences in oral language—whether in vocabulary, syntax, and overall fluency, or in the extent to which students are comfortable using their home language in school settings—are therefore likely to lead to group differences in writing performance.

Gender-Based Similarities and Differences in Oral Language Skills

There is a complex relation between language skills and gender. Gender differences in verbal reasoning and vocabulary are very small (effect size <.05) or nonsignificant

(Hyde, 2005, 2014). Meaningful effects are restricted to verbal fluency (as measured by tasks that require production of content meeting specific criteria, typically under a time limit) and verbal memory (as measured by tasks that measure memory for orally presented information).

While Hyde and Linn (1988) found a medium effect size (d=0.33) for verbal fluency, Hirnstein, Stuebs, Moe, and Hausman (2022)'s recent, much larger meta-analysis found smaller and more contingent effects. A small overall female advantage in verbal fluency (d=.07) consisted mostly of an advantage in phonemic fluency (fluency at reproducing sounds, d=0.13). There were only contingent effects in semantic fluency (fluency at producing words meeting semantic criteria), with males being more fluent at naming some categories, such as animals (d= −0.13), and females being more fluent at naming other categories, such as fruits, vegetables, and food (d=0.31). There was no significant interaction between gender and age.

There appear to be somewhat larger gender differences in verbal memory. Asperholm, Högman, Rafi, and Herlitz (2019)'s meta-analysis found a small female advantage on memory for verbally presented content (d=0.28), versus a male advantage in remembering routes and abstract images. Hirnstein, Stuebs, Moe, and Hausman (2022)'s meta-analysis focused specifically on verbal-episodic memory (memory for orally presented information about people and events), where they found a small female advantage (overall d=0.23) that was somewhat larger for recall (d=0.28) than for recognition (ds=0.12–0.17). There was no significant interaction between gender and age.

Overall, these results indicate slight advantages for females in repeating sounds (possibly related to early reading advantages) and in remembering information about people, events, and specific categories such as food, compared to a male advantage remembering spatial and abstract information. The latter differences could arguably be consequences of gender-linked differences in knowledge and motivation. It thus seems unlikely that oral language ability has a major effect on relative gender performance in writing.

Differences in Writing Achievement Mediated by the Stigmatization of Dialect Features and the Cost of Code-Switching

In an everyday context, writers may use any dialect that is acceptable to them and their interlocutors, but in school, students are expected to conform to educator expectations. In practice, that means using Standard American English (SAE). This situation raises various ethical and practical issues (Sweetland & Wheeler, 2014).

Specific varieties of English, such as African American Vernacular English (AAVE), are rule-governed language systems with their own regularities and patterns (Labov, 1972; Redd & Webb, 2005). But well-entrenched attitudes in society and the educational system stigmatize AAVE and other language varieties (Blake & Cutler, 2003; Craft, Wright, Weissler, Queen, 2020). Pre-service teachers often entertain negative attitudes toward AAVE (Newkirk-Turner, Williams, Harris, & McDaniels, 2013), classroom teachers are likely to treat AAVE textual features as errors (Ball, 1999; Dyson & Smitherman, 2009; Smitherman, 2017), and when students are formally assessed, use of AAVE may be penalized (Johnson & Van Brackle, 2012). Students who speak AAVE in school contexts may experience other cognitive costs. These may include difficulty spelling or understanding SAE words whose form or meaning conflicts with AAVE usage (Edwards, Gross, Chen, MacDonald, Kaplan, Brown, & Seidenberg, 2014). Since use of AAVE is strongly linked to African American identity, student resistance to teacher enforcement of norms that privilege SAE may complicate student/teacher relations (Ferguson, 2003; Godley & Escher, 2012). Similar issues arise with working-class forms of English (Snell, 2013). Critics of practices that privilege SAE characterize them as *raciolinguistic* ideologies, on the grounds that discrimination against linguistic variants is functionally equivalent to racial and ethnic discrimination (Flores, 2020; Cushing, 2022).

When schools require students to read SAE texts and enforce SAE norms for writing, some students may adapt quickly and learn to switch between SAE and AAVE, depending on context. But others may not. As a result, many students will be disadvantaged by their continued use of AAVE. Students who display fewer AAVE (and more SAE) features in their speech and writing tend to obtain higher reading comprehension and writing scores on standardized assessments (Charity, Scarborough, & Griffin, 2004; Puranik, Branum-Martin, & Washington, 2020).

Contrastive studies of how students use English in oral and written contexts indicates that many AAVE-speaking students learn to code-switch, using AAVE in oral and informal contexts, and SAE where a more formal, written register is expected. These are typically, though not exclusively, among the strongest academic performers (Connor & Craig, 2006; Craig, Kolenic, & Hensel, 2014), characterized by strong metalinguistic skills (Campbell, 2018).

The ability to avoid AAE features in writing directly predicts reading and writing performance, especially on standardized assessments (Thompson, Craig, & Washington, 2004; Campbell, 2018; Craig, Zhang, Hensel, & Quinn, 2009), suggesting the acquisition of SAE as a written (not just an oral) code. Craig et al. (2014) found no interaction between grade level and the number of students who code-switch, suggesting that AAVE speakers who learn to code-switch do so very early. Code-switching between AAVE and SAE may occur more frequently among girls than boys (Washington & Craig, 1998; Connor & Craig, 2006).

While many AAVE-speaking students learn to code-switch, their effective working memory capacity may be reduced, due to the cognitive load imposed by code-switching (Terry, Hendrick, Evangelou, & Smith, 2010). Students with weaker metalinguistic skills who fail to acquire tacit code-switching skills are multiply penalized: by lower comprehension and writing fluency, higher cognitive loads, and negative interactions with teachers.

Some scholars have argued that AAVE-speaking students will benefit from pedagogies that increase teacher awareness of sociolinguistic variation, gives them practical ways to affirm (rather than stigmatize) students' everyday speech, and explicitly teaches code-switching (Godley, Sweetland, Wheeler, Minnici, & Carpenter, 2006; Hill, 2009; Fisher & Lapp, 2013). Pearson, Conner, and Jackson (2013) review a range of studies based upon this approach. Most notably, Wheeler and Swords (2010) report major improvements in standardized writing test scores in a school where this approach was implemented.

However, code-switching pedagogies have been criticized as an implicit concession to structural racism (Committee on CCCC Language Statement, 1975; Delpit, 2006; Young, 2009). Advocates of "code-meshing", rather than code-switching, argue that educators should work toward acceptance of multiple varieties of English, rather than continued enforcement of a single cultural standard (Young & Barrett, 2018). Whether or not one accepts this critique, the fundamental issue is clear: students who are most comfortable using a nonstandard dialect of American English do not demonstrate their full potential when they are required to write in SAE. It is worth noting, however, that all students—not just minority students—will benefit from developing the ability to read (and produce) texts reflecting (and exploiting) the diversity of language forms present in our society (Snell, 2013; Snell & Cushing, 2022).

Differences in Writing Achievement Mediated by Second Language Status

English language learners also experience academic difficulties linked to language difference. Oral language proficiency is significantly associated with academic performance for ESL students (Hoff, 2013). Such students can take several years to achieve full English proficiency (Slama, 2012), resulting in lower writing performance (August & Shanahan, 2006). However, once ESL students achieve English language fluency, residual differences are small or absent (Perin, De La Paz, Piantedosi, & Peercy, 2016; Huang, Davis, & Ngamsomjan, 2017).

However, some students become long-term English learners or LTELs (defined as students still classified as English learners five or more years after school entry.) Such students are particularly at risk on literacy tasks (Shin, Kao, Keum, Sato, and Choi, 2022). They typically demonstrate higher proficiency with oral than with written English, suggesting overidentification and inappropriate tracking (Clark-Gareca, Short, Lukes, and Sharp-Ross, 2019). Such students may have similar profiles to low-performing native speakers: proficient in everyday English but unfamiliar with SAE and demotivated by typical school practices.

Differences in Writing Achievement Mediated by Socioeconomic Differences in Linguistic Knowledge

Language differences are associated with socioeconomic differences. In fact, socioeconomic differences account for more variance in language tasks than in tasks associated with other major cognitive systems (Noble, McCandliss, & Farah, 2007). As measured by standardized tests, students from low-SES backgrounds enter school with (on average) less exposure to academic language and weaker academic language skills. During the school years, they tend to remain or fall further behind high-SES students (Huttenlocher, Waterfall, Vasilyeva, Vevea, & Hedges, 2010; Fernald & Weisleder, 2015). There are significant differences in average vocabulary size (Farkas & Beron, 2004; NCES, 2012) and, to a somewhat lesser extent, in syntactic complexity (Vasilyeva, Waterfall, & Huttenlocher, 2008).

That linguistic differences exist is incontrovertible. What they mean has been the subject of controversy. Hart and Risley (1995) presented evidence that preschool children receive less direct speech from low-SES than from high-SES parents. They argued that the amount of verbal interaction between parents and children has a powerful impact on their linguistic development. This theory has been extensively debated. Advocates include Rowe and Goldin-Meadow (2009), Weisleder and Fernald (2013), and Golinkoff, Hoff, Rowe, Tamis-LeMonda, and Hirsh-Pasek (2019). Critics include Dudley-Marling and Lucas (2009), Miller (2012), Michaels (2013), Sperry, Sperry, and Miller (2019), and Kuchirko and Nayfeld (2020).

Proponents of Hart & Risley's vocabulary gap hypothesis argue that family interventions can significantly improve the academic prospects of low-SES children. Opponents consider it a classic example of deficit thinking that blames parents for circumstances beyond their control. Kuchirko and Nayfeld (2020) present a particularly clear version of this critique:

- They criticize proponents of the vocabulary gap hypothesis for privileging one particular style of verbal interaction, characteristic of parents in White, educated, industrialized, rich, and democratic populations, who treat children as if they were equal conversational partners.
- They criticize proponents of the vocabulary gap hypothesis for privileging oversimplified measures of linguistic sophistication, such as vocabulary size, ignoring the role of social/cultural context and purpose.
- Finally, they criticize proponents of the vocabulary gap hypothesis for assuming that between-group variation is more important and meaningful than within-group variation.

These criticisms vary in their efficacy. Regardless of cultural preferences, one approach to child rearing may (or may not) be more effective than another in inducing learning, just as one approach to farming may (or may not) be more effective than another in producing crops. That is an empirical question, one that remains hotly contested. However, it would be a mistake for educators to ignore or devalue community norms and culture. As Heath (1983) observes, sociolinguistic differences reflect contrasting social norms and expectations (Gee, 2015). When school and home cultures clash, issues of motivation and engagement are likely to trump everything else.

Similarly, it is fair to point out that there is more to language learning than vocabulary size. Yet vocabulary size is important. It is hard to read, or write, or think about a subject if you do not have the vocabulary (Olinghouse & Wilson, 2013; Wang, O'Reilly, Sabatini, McCarthy, & McNamara, 2021).

It is Kuchiro and Nayfeld's third point that is critical. Children—and their parents—differ on dimensions other than socioeconomic class or conversational style, and these differences matter for academic achievement. For instance, Sullivan, Moulton, and Fitzsimons (2021) found that the size of *parents'* vocabularies mediated the effects of SES on children's vocabularies. In their study, drawn from a sample of British students, there were no vocabulary gaps between high- and low-SES children whose parents had similar levels of vocabulary knowledge.

The implications for understanding achievement gaps in writing are worth spelling out. Students from high-SES backgrounds are more likely to have parents (and other caregivers) with large academic vocabularies and control of formal, written registers, and are therefore likely to acquire similar linguistic skills. Possession of these skills is an advantage in school because they make it easier to learn to read, to learn from reading, and to formulate ideas for writing. It is a good thing if parents invest in developing these skills in their children. But that is the exactly the problem. There are many ways that schools can help parents empower

Table 5.1 Causal Mechanisms Associated with Group Differences in Working Memory

Causal Factor	English Learners	Race/Ethnicity	SES
Parents and caregivers differ in linguistic knowledge and habits, resulting in students entering school with different vocabularies and communicative styles, and varying ability to communicate in SAE and formal, academic registers. These differences tend to be correlated with social markers of race and class.	Students need to learn English while they are attending school, which reduces their academic performance	African American and students from other stigmatized groups use language and communication styles that teachers respond to negatively.	Students from low-SES backgrounds are more likely to enter school lacking vocabularies and linguistic repertoires that make it easier to excel on school literacy tasks.
Teachers treat language that deviates from SAE patterns as errors.	Students learn to focus on avoiding and correcting errors as the most important criteria for school writing, which is likely to reduce their academic performance.		
Students who have not yet developed sufficient metacognitive and metalinguistic awareness may not learn to code-switch when teachers expect them to.	Students who have learned to use English orally, but have not mastered written English, may be tracked and treated as long-term English learners, reducing their opportunities to learn.	Students who persist in producing non-standard English may be tracked or otherwise treated as less capable than they are, reducing their opportunity to learn.	
Students who have richer vocabularies and better control over academic language will find it easier to learn.	There may be persistent and increasing gaps in writing and other literacy tasks between students who have larger and smaller vocabularies, or who display other differences in linguistic knowledge.		
Code-switching is effortful and requires higher levels of self-monitoring	Students who learn to code-switch to SAE may have lower effective working memory capacity when writing in a less-familiar mode, resulting in lower performance on writing and other literacy tasks compared to students who speak SAE at home.		

their children, but it is a bit much to put the primary responsibility on working-class parents to introduce their children to a world from which they themselves are excluded.

Table 5.1 outlines the causal mechanisms that link linguistic knowledge and habits to writing performance.

Reference List

Abbott, R. D., & Berninger, V. W. (1993). Structural equation modeling of relationships among developmental skills and writing skills in primary-grade and intermediate-grade writers. *Journal of Educational Psychology, 85*(3), 478–508. https://doi.org/10.1037/0022-0663.85.3.478

Asperholm, M., Högman, N., Rafi, J., & Herlitz, A. (2019). What did you do yesterday? A meta-analysis of sex differences in episodic memory. *Psychological Bulletin, 145*(8), 785–821. https://doi.org/10.1037/bul0000197

August, D., & Shanahan, T. (2006). *Developing Literacy in Second-language Learners: Report of the National Literacy Panel on Language-Minority Children and Youth*. Lawrence Erlbaum. https://doi.org/10.4324/9781315094922

Ball, A. F. (1999). Evaluating the writing of culturally and linguistically diverse students: The case of the African American vernacular English speaker. In C. R. Cooper & L. Odell (Eds.), *Evaluating Writing* (pp. 225–248). National Council of Teachers of English.

Blake, R., & Cutler, C. (2003). AAE and variation in teachers' attitudes: A question of school philosophy? *Linguistics and Education, 14*(2), 163–194. https://doi.org/10.1016/S0898-5898(03)00034-2

Campbell, D. (2018). *Identifying the Relationship between Frequency and Variety in Relation to Dialect Awareness: AAE to SAE* [Doctoral dissertation, The Florida State University]. Diginole. https://diginole.lib.fsu.edu/islandora/object/fsu:647198

Charity, A. H., Scarborough, H. S., & Griffin, D. M. (2004). Familiarity with school English in African American children and its relation to early reading achievement. *Child Development, 75*(5), 1340–1356. https://doi.org/10.1111/j.1467-8624.2004.00744.x

Clark-Gareca, B., Short, D., Lukes, M., & Sharp-Ross, M. (2020). Long-term English learners: Current research, policy, and practice. *TESOL Journal, 11*(1), Article e00452. https://doi.org/10.1002/tesj.452

Committee on CCCC Language Statement. (1975). Students' right to their own language. *College English, 36*(6), 709–726. https://doi.org/10.2307/374965

Connelly, V., Dockrell, J. E., Walter, K., & Critten, S. (2012). Predicting the quality of composition and written language bursts from oral language, spelling, and handwriting skills in children with and without Specific Language Impairment. *Written Communication, 29*(3), 278–302. https://doi.org/10.1177/0741088312451109

Connor, C. M., & Craig, H. K. (2006). African American preschoolers' language, emergent literacy skills, and use of African American English: A complex relation. *Journal of Speech, Language, and Hearing Research, 49*(4), 771–792. https://doi.org/10.1044/1092-4388(2006/055)

Craft, J. T., Wright, K. E., Weissler, R. E., & Queen, R. M. (2020). Language and discrimination: Generating meaning, perceiving identities, and discriminating outcomes. *Annual Review of Linguistics, 6,* 389–407. https://doi.org/10.1146/annurev-linguistics-011718-011659

Craig, H. K., Kolenic, G. E., & Hensel, S. L. (2014). African American English–speaking students: A longitudinal examination of style shifting from kindergarten through second grade. *Journal of Speech, Language, and Hearing Research, 57*(1), 143–157. https://doi.org/10.1044/1092-4388(2013/12-0157)

Craig, H. K., Zhang, L., Hensel, S. L., & Quinn, E. J. (2009). African American English–speaking students: An examination of the relationship between dialect shifting and reading outcomes. *Journal of Speech, Language, and Hearing Research, 52*(4), 839–855. https://doi.org/10.1044/1092-4388(2009/08-0056)

Cushing, I. (2022). Raciolinguistic policy assemblages and White supremacy in teacher education. *The Curriculum Journal, 34*(1), 43–61. https://doi.org/10.1002/curj.173

Delpit, L. D. (2006). *Other People's Children: Cultural Conflict in the Classroom.* The New Press.

Dudley-Marling, C., & Lucas, K. (2009). Pathologizing the language and culture of poor children. *Language Arts, 86*(5), 362–370.

Dyson, A. H., & Smitherman, G. (2009). The right (write) start: African American language and the discourse of sounding right. *Teachers College Record, 111*(4), 973–998. https://doi.org/10.1177/016146810911100408

Edwards, J., Gross, M., Chen, J., MacDonald, M. C., Kaplan, D., Brown, M., & Seidenberg, M. S. (2014). Dialect awareness and lexical comprehension of Mainstream American English in African American English–speaking children. *Journal of Speech, Language, and Hearing Research, 57*(5), 1883–1895. https://doi.org/10.1044/2014_JSLHR-L-13-0228

Farkas, G., & Beron, K. (2004). The detailed age trajectory of oral vocabulary knowledge: Differences by class and race. *Social Science Research, 33*(3), 464–497. https://doi.org/10.1016/j.ssresearch.2003.08.001

Ferguson, R. F. (2003). Teachers' perceptions and expectations and the Black-White test score gap. *Urban Education, 38*(4), 400–507. https://doi.org/10.1177/0042085903038004006

Fernald, A., & Weisleder, A. (2015). Twenty years after "Meaningful Differences," It's time to reframe the "Deficit" debate about the importance of children's early language experience. *Human Development, 58*(1), 1–4. https://doi.org/10.1159/000375515

Fisher, D., & Lapp, D. (2013). Learning to talk like the test: Guiding speakers of African American Vernacular English. *Journal of Adolescent & Adult Literacy, 56*(8), 634–648. https://doi.org/10.1002/JAAL.198

Flores, N. (2020). From academic language to language architecture: Challenging raciolinguistic ideologies in research and practice. *Theory into Practice, 59*(1), 22–31. https://doi.org/10.1080/00405841.2019.1665411

Gee, J. (2015). *Social Linguistics and Literacies: Ideology in Discourses* (5th ed.). Routledge. https://doi.org/10.4324/9780203944806

Godley, A. J., & Escher, A. (2012). Bidialectal African American adolescents' beliefs about spoken language expectations in English classrooms. *Journal of Adolescent & Adult Literacy, 55*(8), 704–713. https://doi.org/10.1002/JAAL.00085

Godley, A. J., Sweetland, J., Wheeler, R. S., Minnici, A., & Carpenter, B. D. (2006). Preparing teachers for dialectally diverse classrooms. *Educational Researcher, 35*(8), 30–37. https://doi.org/10.3102/0013189X035008030

Golinkoff, R. M., Hoff, E., Rowe, M. L., Tamis-LeMonda, C. S., & Hirsh-Pasek, K. (2019). Language matters: Denying the existence of the 30-million-word gap has serious consequences. *Child development, 90*(3), 985–992. https://doi.org/10.1111/cdev.13128

Hart, B., & Risley, T. R. (1995). *Meaningful Differences in the Everyday Experience of Young American Children*. Paul H Brookes.

Heath, S. B. (1983). *Ways with Words: Language, life, and Work in Communities and Classrooms*. Cambridge University Press. https://doi.org/10.1017/CBO9780511841057

Hill, K. D. (2009). Code-switching pedagogies and African American student voices: Acceptance and resistance. *Journal of Adolescent & Adult Literacy, 53*(2), 120–131. https://doi.org/10.1598/JAAL.53.2.3

Hirnstein, M., Stuebs, J., Moè, A., & Hausmann, M. (2022). Sex/gender differences in verbal fluency and verbal-episodic memory: A meta-analysis. *Perspectives on Psychological Science, 18*(1), 67–90, https://doi.org/10.1177/17456916221082116

Hoff, E. (2013). Interpreting the early language trajectories of children from low-SES and language minority homes: Implications for closing achievement gaps. *Developmental Psychology, 49*(1), 4–14. https://doi.org/10.1177/17456916221082116

Huang, B. H., Davis, D. S., & Ngamsomjan, J. R. (2017). Keeping up and forging ahead: English language outcomes of proficient bilingual adolescents in the United States. *System, 67,* 12–24. https://doi.org/10.1016/j.system.2017.04.002

Huttenlocher, J., Waterfall, H., Vasilyeva, M., Vevea, J., & Hedges, L. V. (2010). Sources of variability in children's language growth. *Cognitive Psychology, 61*(4), 343–365. https://doi.org/10.1016/j.cogpsych.2010.08.002

Hyde, J. S. (2005). The gender similarities hypothesis. *American Psychologist, 60*(6), 581–592. https://doi.org/10.1037/0003-066x.60.6.581

Hyde, J. S., & Linn, M. C. (1988). *Gender Differences in Verbal Ability: A Meta-Analysis*. Paper presented at the Annual Meeting of the American Educational Research Association, New Orleans, LA. https://files.eric.ed.gov/fulltext/ED294919.pdf

Johnson, D., & VanBrackle, L. (2012). Linguistic discrimination in writing assessment: How raters react to African American "errors," ESL errors, and standard English errors on a state-mandated writing exam. *Assessing Writing, 17*(1), 35–54. https://doi.org/10.1016/j.asw.2011.10.001

Kim, Y.-S., Al-Otaiba, S., Puranik, C., Folsom, J. S., Greulich, L., & Wagner, R. K. (2011). Componential skills of beginning writing: An exploratory study. *Learning and Individual Differences, 21*(5), 517–525. https://doi.org/10.1016/j.lindif.2011.06.004

Kuchirko, Y., & Nayfeld, I. (2020). Language gap: Cultural assumptions and ideologies. In C.-A. Huertas-Abril & M. E. Gómez-Parra (Eds.), *International Approaches to Bridging the Language Gap* (pp. 32–53). IGI Global. https://doi.org/10.4018/978-1-7998-1219-7

Labov, W. (1972*). Language in the Inner City: Studies in the Black English Vernacular*. University of Pennsylvania Press.

Michaels, S. (2013). Commentary: Déjà Vu all over again: What's wrong with Hart & Risley and a "Linguistic Deficit" framework in early childhood education? *Learning Landscapes, 7*(1), 23–41. https://doi.org/10.36510/learnland.v7i1.627

Miller, P. J. (2012). Déja vu: The continuing misrecognition of low-income children's verbal abilities. In Fiske, S. T. & Markus, H. R. (Eds.), *Facing Social Class: How Societal Rank Influences Interaction* (pp. 109–130). Russell Sage Foundation.

NCES. (2012). *The Nation's Report Card: Vocabulary Results from 2009 and 2011 NAEP Reading Assessments* (NCES 2013–452). U.S. Department of Education, National Center for Education Statistics. https://nces.ed.gov/nationsreportcard/pdf/main2011/2013452.pdf

Newkirk-Turner, B. L., Williams, M. C., Harris, T., & McDaniels, P. E. W. (2013). Pre-service teachers' attitudes toward students' use of African American English. *Researcher: An Interdisciplinary Journal, 26*(2), 41–57. https://www.jsums.edu/researcher/files/2014/02/Special-Issue-CUR-Complete-Summer-2013.pdf

Noble, K. G., McCandliss, B. D., & Farah, M. J. (2007). Socioeconomic gradients predict individual differences in neurocognitive abilities. *Developmental Science, 10*(4), 464–480. https://doi.org/10.1111/j.1467-7687.2007.00600.x

Olinghouse, N. G., & Wilson, J. (2013). The relationship between vocabulary and writing quality in three genres. *Reading and Writing, 26*(1), 45–65. https://doi.org/10.1007/s11145-012-9392-5

Pearson, B. Z., Conner, T., & Jackson, J. E. (2013). Removing obstacles for African American English-speaking children through greater understanding of language difference. *Developmental Psychology, 40*(1), 31–44. https://doi.org/10.1037/a0028248

Perin, D., De La Paz, S., Piantedosi, K. W., & Peercy, M. M. (2016). The writing of language minority students: A literature review on its relation to oral proficiency. *Reading & Writing Quarterly, 33*(5), 465–483. https://doi.org/10.1080/10573569.2016.1247399

Puranik, C., Branum-Martin, L., & Washington, J. A. (2020). The relation between dialect density and the codevelopment of writing and reading in African American children. *Child development, 91*(4), e866–e882. https://doi.org/10.1111/cdev.13318

Redd, T. M., & Webb, K. S. (2005). *Teacher's Introduction to African American English, A: What a Writing Teacher Should Know*. National Council of Teachers of English.

Rowe, M. L., & Goldin-Meadow, S. (2009). Differences in early gesture explain SES disparities in child vocabulary size at school entry. *Science, 323*(5916), 951–953. https://doi.org/10.1126/science.1167025

Shanahan, T. (2006). Relations among oral language, reading, and writing development. In C. A. Macarthur, S. Graham, & J. Fitzgerald (Eds.), *Handbook of Writing Research* (pp. 171–183). Guilford.

Shin, N., Kao, J. C., Keum, E., Sato, E., & Choi, K. (2022). How long-term english learners perform on an English language proficiency assessment during grades 2 through 5: An examination of assessment tasks and features. *Journal of Education for Students Placed at Risk (JESPAR), 28*(1), 7–46. https://doi.org/10.1080/10824669.2022.2123329

Slama, R. B. (2012). A longitudinal analysis of academic English proficiency outcomes for adolescent English language learners in the United States. *Journal of Educational Psychology, 104*(2), 265–285. https://psycnet.apa.org/doi/10.1037/a0025861

Smitherman, G. (2017). Raciolinguistics, "mis-education," and language arts teaching in the 21st century. *Language Arts Journal of Michigan, 32*(2), Article 3. https://doi.org/10.9707/2168-149X.2164

Snell, J. (2013). Dialect, interaction, and class positioning at school: From deficit to difference to repertoire. *Language and Education, 27*(2), 110–128. https://doi.org/10.1080/09500782.2012.760584

Snell, J., & Cushing, I. (2022). "A lot of them write how they speak": Policy, pedagogy and the policing of 'nonstandard English. *Literacy, 56*(3), 199–211. https://doi.org/10.1111/lit.12298

Sperry, D. E., Sperry, L. L., & Miller, P. J. (2019). Reexamining the verbal environments of children from different socioeconomic backgrounds. *Child Development, 90*(4), 1303–1318. https://doi.org/10.1111/cdev.13072

Sullivan, A., Moulton, V., & Fitzsimons, E. (2021). The intergenerational transmission of language skill. *The British Journal of Sociology, 72*(2), 207–232. https://doi.org/10.1111/1468-4446.12780

Sweetland, J., & Wheeler, R. S. (2014). Addressing dialect variation in US K–12 schools. In M. Bigelow & J. Ennser-Kananen (Eds.), *The Routledge Handbook of Educational Linguistics* (pp. 446–448). Routledge. https://doi.org/10.4324/9781315797748

Terry, J. M., Hendrick, R., Evangelou, E., & Smith, R. L. (2010). Variable dialect switching among African American children: Inferences about working memory. *Lingua, 120*(10), 2453–2475. https://doi.org/10.1016/j.lingua.2010.04.013

Thompson, C. A., Craig, H. K., & Washington, J. A. (2004). Variable production of African American English across oracy and literacy contexts. *Language, Speech, and Hearing Services in Schools, 35*(3), 269–282. https://doi.org/10.1044/0161-1461(2004/025)

Vasilyeva, M., Waterfall, H., & Huttenlocher, J. (2008). Emergence of syntax: Commonalities and differences across children. *Developmental Science, 11*(1), 84–97. https://doi.org/10.1111/j.1467-7687.2007.00656.x

Wang, Z., O'Reilly, T., Sabatini, J., McCarthy, K. S., & McNamara, D. S. (2021). A tale of two tests: The role of topic and general academic knowledge in traditional versus contemporary scenario-based reading. *Learning and Instruction*, *73*, Article 101462. https://doi.org/10.1016/j.learninstruc.2021.101462

Washington, J. A., & Craig, H. K. (1998). Socioeconomic status and gender influences on children's dialectal variations. *Journal of Speech, Language, and Hearing Research*, *41*(3), 618–626. https://doi.org/10.1044/jslhr.4103.618

Weisleder, A., & Fernald, F. (2013). Talking to children matters early language experience strengthens processing and builds vocabulary. *Psychological Science*, *24*(11), 2143–2152. https://doi.org/10.1177/0956797613488145

Wheeler, R. S., & Swords, R. (2010). *Code-Switching Lessons: Grammar Strategies for Linguistically Diverse Writers: Grades 3–6*. Heinemann.

Young, V. A. (2009). "Nah, We Straight": An Argument Against Code Switching. *JAC*, *29*(1/2), 49–76. https://www.jstor.org/stable/20866886

Young, V. A., & Barrett, R. (2018). *Other People's English: Code-Meshing, Code-Switching, and African American Literacy*. Parlor Press LLC.

CHAPTER SIX

Writing as Getting Words on the Page: The Effects of Transcription Skills on Writing Development

Transcription skills can be roughly divided into *motor skills* (handwriting and keyboarding), where the focus is on the physical act of writing, and *orthographic* skills (including spelling, capitalization, and punctuation), where the focus is on representing linguistic units with visual signs. Transcription can occur in multiple modes, with separate supporting skills. Print writing, with each character written separately, is different from cursive writing, where characters are joined. Keyboarding is different from digital writing with a stylus or on a mobile phone. In early development, different written modes may be only loosely related (Berninger, Abbott, Jones, Wolf, Gould, Anderson-Youngstrom, & Apel, 2006).

During the early grades, instruction emphasizes transcription—so much so, that curriculum-based measurement of writing focuses on fluency (number of words produced) and spelling (number of correct word sequences) (Dockrell, Connelly, Walter, & Critten, 2015). During acquisition, transcription skills require concentration and effort, which limits working memory capacity for other processes (McCutchen, 1996; Berninger, 1999; Hayes & Chenoweth, 2006). This results in significantly lower writing performances for individuals with weak transcription skills (Feng, Lindner, Ji, & Joshi, 2019; Troia, Brehmer, Glause, Reichmuth, & Lawrence, 2020; Skar, Lei, Graham, Aasen, Johansen, & Kvistad, 2022) and in a higher concentration of orthographic errors and transcription dysfluencies among special needs students (Graham, 1990; Connelly, Dockrell, Walter, & Critten, 2012).

Handwriting, keyboarding, and spelling are mutually reinforcing skills (Ouellette & Tims, 2014) that integrate as they mature (Abbott & Berninger, 1993). Handwriting instruction is particularly valuable in the early grades (Wollscheid, Sjaastad, & Tømte, 2016), if motor skills are sufficiently developed (Mangen & Balsvik, 2016), since handwriting supports literacy learning in ways that keyboarding does not (Kiefer, Schuler, Mayer, Trumpp, Hille, & Sachse, 2015; Karavanidou, 2017). By contrast, touch typing may be most effectively taught in the upper elementary grades (Sormunen & Wickersham, 1991), though it can provide an important alternative route to transcription fluency for students who find handwriting difficult (Stevenson & Just, 2014). Other input methods, such as dictation, can also increase fluency for students with special needs (Graham, 1990).

Overview

Handwriting Fluency

Handwriting is the first transcription skill taught, but it develops slowly (Alves & Limpo, 2015). Typically, students do not achieve adult performance until early high school (Graham, Weintraub, Berninger, & Schafer, 1998; Feder & Majnemer, 2007). In the early grades, component handwriting skills, such as individual letter production and speed of pen strokes are important predictors of composition quality (Wagner, Puranik, Foorman, Foster, Wilson, Tschinkel, & Kantor, 2011; Kim, Al-Otaiba, Sidler, & Gruelich, 2013). The variance accounted for by handwriting drops steadily from third or fourth grade, when students begin to write independently, through middle school, high school, and college (Kent & Wanzek, 2016; Feng, Lindner, Ji, & Joshi, 2019). But even adults put more effort into producing words by hand than they do when speaking (Bourdin & Fayol, 2002).

Since handwriting is more difficult for children than for adults, the impact on working memory is larger (Levy & Ransdell, 2001). But when adults were asked to use less-familiar upper-case cursive letters, similar reductions in effective working memory capacity were observed (Connelly, Dockrell, & Barnett, 2005). Other studies suggest there is a handwriting fluency threshold. Students who fall above the threshold achieve higher writing quality scores and are more likely to reach their potential, as measured by external measures such as vocabulary size. Students who fall below the threshold struggle to meet writing quality standards and produce texts with smaller vocabularies than their they use when speaking (Medwell &

Wray, 2014; Roessingh, Nordstokke, & Colp, 2019). Interventions that improve handwriting fluency also improve composition quality (Berninger, Vaughan, Abbott, Abbott, Rogan, Brooks, . . . & Graham, 1997; Jones & Christensen, 1999).

Spelling and Other Orthographic Skills

Spelling is another critical transcription skill, given the irregularities of English spelling. Efficient spelling facilitates fast retrieval of the graphic forms of words (Limpo, Alves, & Connelly, 2017). It is therefore a significant focus of early literacy instruction (Ehri, 2013; Graham & Santangelo, 2014). Spelling achievement is an important predictor of writing quality, especially in the early grades (Graham, Berninger, Abbott, Abbott, & Whitaker, 1997; Salas & Silvente, 2020), though it plays an important role throughout the elementary years (Abbott, Berninger, & Fayol, 2010; Kent & Wanzek, 2016; Troia, Shen, & Brandon, 2019).

Spelling difficulties can seriously disrupt the fluency of sentence- and discourse-level processes (Wengelin, 2007). An additional cognitive load is incurred when text production is interrupted to think about how a word is spelled (or to attempt corrections after a word is fully or partially produced). This results in slower transcription, associated with frequent pauses near misspelled words (Sumner, Connelly, & Barnett, 2016).

Keyboarding Fluency

40 to 50 years ago, keyboarding was a clerical skill. It has now become a general literacy skill. This shift is reflected in the literature. Differences in the efficacy of handwriting and keyboarding diminish as students gain experience (Wolfe, Bolton, Feltovich, & Niday, 1996; Connelly, Gee, & Walsh, 2007).

In relatively early studies, such as Haas (1989a), writers were more fluent with pen and paper than on a keyboard, an advantage that has persisted in the early grades (probably because digital writing tools have been less broadly used in those grades). Connelly, Gee, and Walsh (2007) found that elementary school students were worse at keyboarding than handwriting. Berninger, Abbott, Augsburger, and Garcia (2009) showed that elementary school writing quality was higher in handwritten than in typed texts. Alstad (2015) found that cursive writing predicted composition quality across the elementary and middle grades. However, Alstad found that keyboarding fluency only predicted composition quality in grades 5–7, when digital writing tasks are typically introduced. Adult studies do not consistently show differences between keyboarding and handwriting fluency. While Chen, White, McCloskey, Soroui, and Chun (2011) found that adults produced higher-quality handwritten texts, other recent studies showed no significant effects (King, Rohani, Sanfilippo, & White, 2008; Mogey, Paterson, Burk, & Purcell, 2010).

Keyboarding also involves interactions between working memory and transcription fluency (Connelly, Gee, & Walsh, 2007). Among adults, but not children, typing can be so completely automated that it does not reduce working memory capacity (Kellogg, 1999a). Gong, Zhang, and Li (2022) identified keyboarding speed thresholds for online essay-writing tasks. Middle-school students whose keyboarding fluency fell below the threshold produced shorter essays that fell within a restricted score range. Only students whose keyboarding skills fell above the threshold produced high scoring essays.

Keyboarding and handwriting require different motor skills and are only moderately correlated, suggesting that keyboarding may be an alternate route to writing fluency for students struggling with handwriting (Horne, Ferrier, Singleton, & Read, 2011). Keyboarding (especially if combined with use of word processing software) also offers significant general advantages. Faster adult typists type faster and with less effort than they can write by hand (Weintraub, Gilmour-Grill, & Weiss, 2010). Even in college, handwriting speed can limit writing performance. Lovett, Lewandowski, Berger, and Gathje (2010) found that college students who produced texts on a keyboard wrote longer (and higher quality) essays than students who wrote their essays by hand, and that this advantage increased when students were given more time to write.

This result is consistent with Haas (1989b). Haas found that writers did more advance planning and less revision when handwriting (since revision was relatively effortful, involving erasure or recopying). They did more revision and less advance planning when keyboarding (since revision was a much more straightforward process.) Keyboarding in a digital environment offers multiple advantages: an easier, less taxing process, increased legibility, the availability of spellcheckers and other digital tools, and easy sharing with collaborators and online audiences (Yackanicz, 2000; MacArthur, 2006). Teaching students to write in a word-processing environment significantly improves students' writing fluency, willingness to revise, and composition quality (Goldberg, Russell, & Cook, 2003; Morphy & Graham, 2012).

Group Differences Mediated by Transcription Skills

In the early grades, writing instruction is transcription instruction. Transcription difficulties affect writers' performance both directly (by slowing them down and forcing them to pause to correct errors, cf. Perl, 1979) and indirectly (by increasing cognitive load.) Students who struggle to get words on the page may feel that they are bad writers. If students continue to struggle, this feeling may persist, undermining their confidence and willingness to write. Group differences in transcription skills are thus likely to have a disproportionate impact on writing achievement.

Group Differences in Handwriting

A large minority of students (roughly 12–34 % depending on age and school) encounter handwriting difficulties (Rubin & Henderson, 1982; Smits-Engelsman, Schomaker, Van Galen, & Michels, 1996; Rosenblum, Weiss, & Parush, 2004). Students from disadvantaged (predominantly low-SES) schools often have significantly slower handwriting rates than the general population (O'Mahony et al., 2008). Boys also show higher incidence of handwriting difficulties than girls (Graham & Weintraub, 1996; Berninger, Nielsen, Abbott, Wijsman, & Raskind, 2008a). Handwriting fluency may be particularly strongly related to composition quality in the intermediate grades (Berninger, 1999; Wagner et al., 2011), when students start producing extended compositions. Group differences in handwriting fluency may therefore be a significant source of inequities in writing achievement.

Differences in fine motor skill development may help cause these group differences. Fine motor skills, particularly visuospatial integration skills, are associated with early writing achievement (Carlson, Rowe, & Curby, 2013). Lower fine motor skill readiness can negatively impact low-SES student performance in the early grades (Liu, Hoffman, & Hamilton, 2017). Carsone, Green, Torrence, and Henry (2021) review multiple studies that suggest that females may enter school with higher fine motor skill readiness levels than males, though the evidence is not definitive.

Differences in primary-level writing instruction, such as classroom time devoted to handwriting instruction, are also likely to affect writing achievement (Santangelo & Graham, 2016; Lopez-Escribano, Martin-Babarro, & Perez-Lopez, 2022). For instance, Molyneaux (2019) found that handwriting outcomes were related to the amount of teacher-generated, teacher + child generated, and child-generated writing produced. Positive outcomes were associated with larger amounts of teacher + child generated writing—that is, with instructionally meaningful writing activities such as note-taking and question-answering in which the child generated text in response to content supplied by the teacher. Group differences might arise from such effects if schools that serve low-SES populations rely on rote handwriting instruction methods, such as filling out workbooks or copying a set text (Purcell-Gates & Dahl, 1991).

Group Differences in Spelling

There are significant group differences in spelling achievement. Nonstandard spelling appears more commonly among low-SES students and boys (Allred, 1990; Babayigit, 2015; Lee & Al-Otaiba, 2015) and among speakers of AAVE and other nonstandard language variants (Terry, 2006; Terry & Connor, 2010). In a study of more than 800,000 students, grades 3–12, in a U.S. state, Foorman and Petscher (2010) found significant effects of gender, ESL status, race, and SES, with the usual patterns of advantage for high-SES, native-speaker, White and female students. These effects were significantly larger than growth effects observed in the same study, which were small in the primary grades and very small or nonsignificant thereafter.

For an important subgroup (dyslexic students, 5–10 % of the population), spelling problems may persist (Shaywitz, Shaywitz, Fletcher, & Escobar, 1990), resulting in reading and writing difficulties (Berninger, Nielsen, Abbott, Wijsman, & Raskind, 2008b). Dyslexic writing tends to be less fluent and more error-prone, due to difficulties accessing orthographic information. Dyslexia constrains writing quality even for college students (Connelly, Sumner, & Barnett, 2014). However, explicit spelling and morphology instruction is an effective intervention (Berninger, Winn, Stock, Abbott, Eschen, & Lin ... Nagy, 2008).

Spelling is strongly related to the development of word reading skills (Kim, Petscher, Wanzek, & Al-Otaiba, 2018), including decoding and morphological analysis (Goodwin & Ahn, 2013; Moats, 2019). However, much depends on whether schools and teachers are organized and prepared to motivate students to excel. Acujo, Fruehwirth, Kelly, and Mozenter (2020) argue that teacher expectations and feedback may account for most of the gender gap in reading. Terry (2021) makes a similar point about reading achievement gaps.

Group Differences in Keyboarding

Keyboarding skills also demonstrate group differences in gender, race/ethnicity, and SES.

Zhang, Bennett, Deane, and van Rijn (2019) found that females in a middle-school sample entered text more fluently, engaged in more macro and local editing, and paused less at sentence boundaries or between bursts of text production. Gong, Zhang, and Li (2022) found that females had significantly higher keyboarding fluency than males in a measure of typing speed that focused on keyboarding fluency. On the writing section of a high school equivalency test, Bennett, Zhang, and Sinharay (2021) significant differences in fluency favoring females, even after controlling for language arts writing score, age, and essay prompt

Guo, Zhang, Deane, and Bennett (2019) examined the writing processes of a sample of American middle-school students. Group differences persisted even after students were matched on essay length and score. Low-SES students had slower typing speeds and engaged in more typo correction than high-SES students matched on score. Between bursts of text production, they paused more often but with shorter latencies. African American students engaged in significantly more typo correction than White students who showed similar writing outcomes. They also paused more often but showed shorter latencies. Male students showed slower keystrokes and spent more time editing than female students with similar scores.

Explicit touch-typing instruction improves writing quality (Van Weerdenburg, Tesselhof, & van der Meijden, 2019). But children's keyboarding fluency may be driven primarily by access to digital devices. For instance, Deane, Wilson, Zhang, Li, Guo, … and Richter (2021) observed significant increases in keyboarding fluency after a two-month instructional period that gave students multiple opportunities to write in a digital environment.

However, there are significant gaps between high- and low-SES schools in access to digital devices and the internet (Monroe, 2004; Paul, 2016), reflecting the so-called "digital divide" (Norris, 2001). Valadez and Duran (2007) document the consequences: increased computer access, higher internet and computer use, and more creative and experimental use of computers in high-resource, suburban schools. These in-school differences compound SES-driven differences in extracurricular ownership and use of digital devices (Greenhow, Walker, & Kim, 2009; Tate, Warschauer, & Abedi, 2016; Warschauer, 2017). Low-SES students may therefore particularly benefit from instruction in keyboarding, word processing, and computer use.

Table 6.1 summarizes the causal mechanisms that appear to be be responsible for group differences in transcription skills.

Table 6.1 Causal Mechanisms Associated with Group Differences in Transcription Skills

Causal Factor	Gender	Race/Ethnicity	SES
Students with stronger fine visual-motor integration are better prepared to learn how to form letters, which may result in faster acquisition of fluent handwriting skills.	Females may show stronger visual-motor integration before school entry, resulting in stronger handwriting skills.		Students from high-SES families may show stronger visual-motor before school entry, which may result in stronger handwriting keyboarding skills.
Positive student/teacher interaction, combined with high expectations, causes faster learning. Negative interactions and low expectations reduce learning rates. Transcription instruction in the early grades establishes patterns that are likely to persist through later years of schooling.		Teacher acceptance of gender, racial, or social stereotypes about student behavior may produce higher or lower expectations and result in different feedback and encouragement for students who belong to distinct social groups. For example: "Boys usually have messy handwriting".	
Students who pursue literacy activities outside of school develop stronger reading and writing skills (including spelling, handwriting, and keyboarding)	Reading and writing for pleasure are more stereotypically female interests, which may lead to higher female participation in reading and writing activities outside of school.	Historically, mainstream media represent the perspectives of high-SES White communities, which may lead to less interest and participation in these activities from members of other social groups.	Digital and print books, personal computers, and laptops are more readily available for leisure-time use by students in high-SES families, which may lead to higher participation by high-SES students in reading and writing activities outside school.
Handwriting and spelling skills develop better when explicit instruction is combined with meaningful contexts for practice.			School in low-SES and minority communities may provide less effective reading and writing instruction due to staff turnover, lack of resources, and other issues.

Reference List

Abbott, R. D., & Berninger, V. W. (1993). Structural equation modeling of relationships among developmental skills and writing skills in primary-grade and intermediate-grade writers. *Journal of Educational Psychology, 85*(3), 478–508. https://doi.org/10.1037/0022-0663.85.3.478

Abbott, R. D., Berninger, V. W., & Fayol, M. (2010). Longitudinal relationships of levels of language in writing and between writing and reading in grades 1 to 7. *Journal of Educational Psychology, 102*(2), 281–298. https://psycnet.apa.org/doi/10.1037/a0019318

Acujo, E. M., Fruehwirth, J. C., Kelly, S., & Mozenter, Z. (2020). Teachers and the gender gap in reading achievement. *Journal of Human Capital, 16*(3). https://doi.org/10.1086/719731

Allred, R. A. (1990). Gender differences in spelling achievement in grades 1 through 6. *The Journal of Educational Research, 83*(4), 187–193. https://doi.org/10.1080/00220671.1990.10885955

Alstad, Z. (2015). Modes of alphabet letter production during middle childhood and adolescence: Interrelationships with each other and other writing skills. *Journal of Writing Research, 6*(3), 199–231. https://doi.org/10.17239/jowr-2015.06.03.1

Alves, R. A., & Limpo, T. (2015). Progress in written language bursts, pauses, transcription, and written composition across schooling. *Scientific Studies of Reading, 19*(5), 374–391. http://dx.doi.org/10.1080/10888438.2015.1059838

Babayigit, S. (2015). The dimensions of written expression: Language group and gender differences. *Learning and Instruction, 35*, 33–41. https://doi.org/10.1016/j.learninstruc.2014.08.006

Bennett, R. E., Zhang, Mo., & Sinharay, S. (2021) How do educationally at-risk men and women differ in their essay-writing processes?. *Chinese/English Journal of Educational Measurement and Evaluation | 教育测量与评估双语季刊, 2*(1), Article 1. https://www.ce-jeme.org/journal/vol2/iss1/1

Berninger, V. W. (1999). Coordinating transcription and text generation in working memory during composing: Automatic and constructive processes. *Learning Disability Quarterly, 22*(2), 99–112. https://doi.org/10.2307/1511269

Berninger, V. W., Abbott, R. D., Augsburger, A., & Garcia, N. (2009). Comparison of pen and keyboard transcription modes in children with and without learning disabilities. *Learning Disability Quarterly, 32*(3), 123–141. https://doi.org/10.2307/27740364

Berninger, V. W., Abbott, R. D., Jones, J., Wolf, B. J., Gould, L., Anderson-Youngstrom, M., ... Apel, K. (2006). Early development of language by hand: Composing, reading, listening, and speaking connections; Three letter-writing modes; and fast mapping in spelling. *Developmental Neuropsychology, 29*(1), 61–92. https://doi.org/10.1207/s15326942dn2901_5

Berninger, V. W., Nielsen, K. H., Abbott, R. D., Wijsman, E., & Raskind, W. (2008a). Gender differences in severity of writing and reading disabilities. *Journal of School Psychology, 46*(2), 151–172. https://doi.org/10.1016/j.jsp.2007.02.007

Berninger, V. W., Nielsen, K. H., Abbott, R. D., Wijsman, E., & Raskind, W. (2008b). Writing problems in developmental dyslexia: Under-recognized and under-treated. *Journal of School Psychology, 46*(1), 1–21. https://doi.org/10.1016%2Fj.jsp.2006.11.008

Berninger, V. W., Vaughan, K. B., Abbott, R. D., Abbott, S. P., Rogan, L. W., Brooks, A., . . . Graham, S. (1997). Treatment of handwriting problems in beginning writers: Transfer from handwriting to composition. *Journal of Educational Psychology, 99*(4), 652–666. https://psycnet.apa.org/doi/10.1037/0022-0663.89.4.652

Berninger, V. W., Winn, W. D., Stock, P., Abbott, R. D., Eschen, K., Lin, S.-J. C., . . . Nagy, W. (2008). Tier 3 specialized writing instruction for students with dyslexia. *Reading and Writing, 21*(1–2), 95–129. https://doi.org/10.1007/s11145-007-9066-x

Bourdin, B., & Fayol, M. (2002). Even in adults, written production is still more costly than oral production. *International Journal of Psychology, 37*(4), 219–227. https://doi.org/10.1080/00207590244000070

Carlson, A. G., Rowe, E., & Curby, T. W. (2013). Disentangling fine motor skills relations to academic achievement: The relative contributions of visual-spatial integration and visual-motor coordination. *The Journal of Genetic Psychology, 14*(5), 514–533. https://doi.org/10.1080/00221325.2012.717122

Carsone, B., Green, K., Torrence, W., & Henry, B. (2021). Systematic review of visual motor integration in children with developmental disabilities. *Occupational Therapy International, 2021*, Article 1801196. https://doi.org/10.1155/2021/1801196

Chen, J., White, S., McCloskey, M., Soroui, J., & Chun, Y. (2011). Effects of computer versus paper administration of an adult functional writing assessment. *Assessing Writing, 16*(1), 49–71. https://doi.org/10.1016/j.asw.2010.11.001

Connelly, V., Dockrell, J. E., & Barnett, J. (2005). The slow handwriting of undergraduate students constrains overall performance in exam essays. *Educational Psychology, 25*(1), 97–105. https://doi.org/10.1080/0144341042000294912

Connelly, V., Dockrell, J. E., Walter, K., & Critten, S. (2012). Predicting the quality of composition and written language bursts from oral language, spelling, and handwriting skills in children with and without Specific Language Impairment. *Written Communication, 29*(3), 278–302. https://doi.org/10.1177/0741088312451109

Connelly, V., Gee, D., & Walsh, E. (2007). A comparison of keyboarded and handwritten compositions and the relationship with transcription speed. *British Journal of Educational Psychology, 77*(2), 479–492. https://doi.org/10.1348/000709906X116768

Connelly, V., Sumner, E., & Barnett, A. L. (2014). Dyslexia and writing: Poor spelling can interfere with good quality composition. *Brookes eJournal of Learning and Teaching, 6*(2). https://discovery.ucl.ac.uk/id/eprint/1541258

Deane, P. D., Wilson, J., Zhang, M., Li, C., van Rijn, P., Guo, H., ... & Richter, T. (2021). The sensitivity of a scenario-based assessment of written argumentation to school differences in curriculum and instruction. *International Journal of Artificial Intelligence in Education, 31*(1), 57–98. https://doi.org/10.1007/s40593-020-00227-x

Dockrell, J. E., Connelly, V., Walter, K., & Critten, S. (2015). Assessing children's writing products: The role of curriculum- based measures. *British Educational Research Journal, 41*(4), 575–595. https://doi.org/10.1002/berj.3162

Ehri, L. C. (2013). Grapheme—Phoneme knowledge is essential for learning to read words in English. In J. Metsala & L. C. Ehri (Eds.), *Word Recognition in Beginning Literacy* (pp. 3–40). Lawrence Erlbaum. https://doi.org/10.4324/9781410602718

Feder, K. P., & Majnemer, A. (2007). Handwriting development, competency, and intervention. *Developmental Medicine & Child Neurology, 49*(4), 312–317. https://doi.org/10.1111/j.1469-8749.2007.00312.x

Feng, L., Lindner, A., Ji, X. R., & Joshi, R. M. (2019). The roles of handwriting and keyboarding in writing: A meta-analytic review. *Reading and Writing, 32*(1), 33–63. https://doi.org/10.1007/s11145-017-9749-x

Foorman, B. R., & Petscher, Y. (2010). Development of spelling and differential relations to text reading in grades 3–12. *Assessment for Effective Intervention, 36*(7), 7–20. https://doi.org/10.1177/1534508410379844

Goldberg, A., Russell, M., & Cook, A. (2003). The effect of computers on student writing: A meta-analysis of studies from 1992 to 2002. *The Journal of Technology, Learning and Assessment, 2*(1). https://ejournals.bc.edu/index.php/jtla/article/view/1661

Gong, T., Zhang, M., & Li, C. (2022). Association of keyboarding fluency and writing performance in online-delivered assessment. *Assessing Writing, 51*, Article 100575. https://doi.org/10.1016/j.asw.2021.100575

Goodwin, A. P., & Ahn, S. (2013). A meta-analysis of morphological interventions in English: Effects on literacy outcomes for school-age children. *Scientific Studies of Reading, 17*(4), 257–285. https://doi.org/10.1080/10888438.2012.689791

Graham, S. (1990). The role of production factors in learning disabled students' compositions. *Journal of Educational Psychology, 82*(4), 781–791. https://doi.org/10.1037/0022-0663.82.4.781

Graham, S., Berninger, V. W., Abbott, R. D., Abbott, S. P., & Whitaker, D. (1997). Role of mechanics in composing of elementary school students: A new methodological approach. *Journal of Educational Psychology, 89*(1), 170–182. https://doi.org/10.1037/0022-0663.89.1.170

Graham, S., & Santangelo, T. (2014). Does spelling instruction make students better spellers, readers, and writers? A meta-analytic review. *Reading and Writing, 27*(9), 1703–1743. https://doi.org/10.1007/s11145-014-9517-0

Graham, S. & Weintraub, N. (1996). A review of handwriting research: Progress and prospects from 1980 to 1994. *Educational Psychology Review, 8*(1), 7–87. https://doi.org/10.1007/BF01761831

Graham, S., Weintraub, N., Berninger, V. W., & Schafer, W. (1998). Development of handwriting speed and legibility in grades 1–9. *The Journal of Educational Research, 92*(1), 42–52. https://doi.org/10.1080/00220679809597574

Greenhow, C., Walker, J. D., & Kim, S. (2009). Millennial learners and net-savvy teens? Examining Internet use among low-income students. *Journal of Computing in Teacher Education, 26*(2), 63–68.

Guo, H., Zhang, M., Deane, P., & Bennett, R. E. (2019). Writing process differences in subgroups reflected in keystroke logs. *Journal of Educational and Behavioral Statistics, 44*(5), 571–596. https://doi.org/10.3102/1076998619856590

Haas, C. (1989a). Does the medium make a difference? Two studies of writing with pen and paper and with computers. *Human-Computer Interaction, 4*, 149–169. https://doi.org/10.1207/s15327051hci0402_3

Haas, C. (1989b). How the writing medium shapes the writing process: Effects of word processing on planning. *Research in the Teaching in English, 23*(2), 181–207. https://files.eric.ed.gov/fulltext/ED309408.pdf

Hayes, J. R., & Chenoweth, N. A. (2006). Is working memory involved in the transcribing and editing of texts? *Written Communication, 23*(2), 135–149. https://doi.org/10.1177/0741088306286283

Horne, J., Ferrier, J., Singleton, C., & Read, C. (2011). Computerised assessment of handwriting and typing speed. *Educational and Child Psychology, 28*(2), 52–66. https://doi.org/10.53841/bpsecp.2011.28.2.52

Jones, D., & Christensen, C. A. (1999). Relationship between automaticity in handwriting and students' ability to generate written text. *Journal of Experimental Psychology, 91*(1), 44–49. https://doi.org/10.1037/0022-0663.91.1.44

Karavanidou, E. (2017). Is handwriting relevant in the digital era? *Antistasis, 7*(1), 153–167. Retrieved from https://journals.lib.unb.ca/index.php/antistasis/article/view/25104

Kellogg, R. T. (1999a). Components of working memory in text production. In M. Torrance & G. Jeffery (Eds.), *The Cognitive Demands of Writing* (Vol. 3, pp. 43–61). Amsterdam University Press.

Kent, S. C., & Wanzek, J. (2016). The relationship between component skills and writing quality and production across developmental levels: A meta-analysis of the last 25 years. *Review of Educational research, 86*(2), 570–601. https://doi.org/10.3102/0034654315619491

Kiefer, M., Schuler, S., Mayer, C., Trumpp, N. M., Hille, K., & Sachse, S. (2015). Handwriting or typewriting? The influence of pen-or keyboard-based writing training on reading and writing performance in preschool children. *Advances in Cognitive Psychology, 11*(4), 136–146. https://doi.org/10.5709/acp-0178-7

Kim, Y.-S., Al-Otaiba, S. A., Sidler, J. F., & Gruelich, L. (2013). Language, literacy, attentional behaviors, and instructional quality predictors of written composition for first graders. *Early Childhood Research Quarterly, 28*(3), 461–469. https://doi.org/10.1016/j.ecresq.2013.01.001

Kim, Y.-S., Petscher, Y., Wanzek, J. & Al-Otaiba, S. (2018). Relations between reading and writing: a longitudinal examination from grades 3 to 6. *Reading and Writing, 31*(7), 1591–1618. https://doi.org/10.1007/s11145-018-9855-4

King, F. J., Rohani, F., Sanfilippo, C., & White, N. (2008). *Effects of handwritten versus computer-written modes of communication on the quality of student essays* (CALA Report 20). Center for Advancement of Learning and Assessment, Florida State University. https://citeseerx.ist.psu.edu/document?repid=rep1&type=pdf&doi=60a04e1c193d29bcca8ef501e4aa64a6f6231ac4

Lee JA, Otaiba SA. Socioeconomic and gender group differences in early literacy skills: a multiple-group confirmatory factor analysis approach. Educ Res Eval. 2015;21(1):40-59. doi: 10.1080/13803611.2015.1010545. PMID: 25750582; PMCID: PMC4349494.

Levy, C. M., & Ransdell, S. (2001). Writing with concurrent memory loads. In T. Olive & C. M. Levy (Eds.), *Contemporary Tools and Techniques for Studying Writing* (pp. 9–29). Kluwer Academic. http://dx.doi.org/10.1007/978-94-010-0468-8

Limpo, T., Alves, R. A., & Connelly, V. (2017). Examining the transcription-writing link: Effects of handwriting fluency and spelling accuracy on writing performance via planning and translating in middle grades. *Learning and Individual Differences, 53*, 26–36. https://doi.org/10.1016/j.lindif.2016.11.004

Liu, T., Hoffman, C., & Hamilton, M. (2017). Motor skill performance by low SES preschool and typically developing children on the PDMS-2. *Early Child Education Journal, 45*, 53–60. https://doi.org/10.1007/s10643-015-0755-9

Lopez-Escribano, C., Martin-Babarro, M., & Perez-Lopez, R. (2022). Promoting handwriting fluency for preschool and elementary-age students: Meta-analysis and meta-synthesis of research from 2000 to 2020. *Frontiers in Psychology, 13*. Article 841573. https://doi.org/10.3389/fpsyg.2022.841573

Lovett, B. J., Lewandowski, L. J., Berger, C., & Gathje, R. A. (2010). Effects of response mode and time allotment on college students' writing. *Journal of College Reading and Learning, 40*(2), 64–79. https://doi.org/10.1080/10790195.2010.10850331

MacArthur, C. A. (2006). The effects of new technologies on writing and writing processes. In C. A. MacArthur, S. Graham, & J. Fitzgerald (Eds.), *Handbook of Writing Research* (pp. 248–262). Guilford.

Mangen, A., & Balsvik, L. (2016). Pen or keyboard in beginning writing instruction? Some perspectives from embodied cognition. *Trends in Neuroscience and Education, 5*(3), 99–106. https://doi.org/10.1016/j.tine.2016.06.003

McCutchen, D. (1996). A capacity theory of writing: Working memory in composition. *Educational Psychology Review, 8*, 299–325. https://doi.org/10.1007/BF01464076

Medwell, J., & Wray, D. (2014). Handwriting automaticity: The search for performance thresholds. *Language and Education, 28*(1), 34–51. https://doi.org/10.1080/09500782.2013.763819

Moats, L. (2019). Structured Literacy: Effective instruction for students with dyslexia and related reading difficulties. *Perspectives on Language and Literacy, 45*(2), 9–11. https://www.idaontario.com/wp-content/uploads/2019/10/Moats-2019-Structured-Literacy_-Effective-Instruction-for-Students-with-dyslexia-and-related-reading-difficulties.pdf

Mogey, N., Paterson, J., Burk, J., & Purcell, M. (2010). Typing compared with handwriting for essay examinations at university: letting the students choose. *Research in Learning Technology, 18*(1), 29–47. https://doi.org/10.1080/09687761003657580

Molyneaux, A. M. (2019). *Teaching and Learning Writing at Primary School* [Doctoral dissertation, Oxford Brookes University]. RADAR (Institutional Repository of Oxford Brookes University). https://radar.brookes.ac.uk/radar/file/8d6cba9e-70da-4eb7-ab0e-ea0f088df9eb/1/Molyneaux.pdf

Monroe, B. J. (2004). *Crossing the Digital Divide: Race, Writing, and Technology in the Classroom.* Teachers College Press. http://dx.doi.org/10.15365/joce.1102152013

Morphy, P., & Graham, S. (2012). Word processing programs and weaker writers/readers: A meta-analysis of research findings. *Reading and Writing, 25*(3), 641–678. https://doi.org/10.1007/s11145-010-9292-5

Norris, P. (2001). *Digital Divide: Civic Engagement, Information Poverty, and the Internet Worldwide.* Cambridge University Press. https://doi.org/10.1017/CBO9781139164887

O'Mahony, P., Dempsey, M., & Killeen, H. (2008). Handwriting speed: duration of testing period and relation to socio-economic disadvantage and handedness. *Occupational Therapy International, 15*(3), 165–177. https://doi.org/10.1002/oti.255

Ouellette, G., & Tims, T. (2014). The write way to spell: Printing vs. typing effects on orthographic learning. *Frontiers in Psychology, 5,* Article 117. https://doi.org/10.3389/fpsyg.2014.00117

Paul, D. G. (2016). The Millennial Morphing of the Digital Divide and Its Implications for African American Youngsters in a New Literacies Era (Commentary). *The Journal of Negro Education, 85*(4), 407–415. https://doi.org/10.7709/jnegroeducation.85.4.0407

Perl, S. (1979). The composing processes of unskilled college writers. *Research in the Teaching of English, 13*(4), 317–336.

Purcell-Gates, V., & Dahl, K. L. (1991). Low-SES children's success and failure at early literacy learning in skills-based classrooms. *Journal of Reading Behavior, 23*(1), 1–34. https://doi.org/10.1080/10862969109547725

Roessingh, H., Nordstokke, D., & Colp, M. (2019). Unlocking academic literacy in grade 4: The role of handwriting. *Reading & Writing Quarterly, 35*(2), 65–83. https://doi.org/10.1080/10573569.2018.1499160

Rosenblum, S., Weiss, P. L., & Parush, S. (2004). Handwriting evaluation for developmental dysgraphia: Process versus product. *Reading and Writing, 17*(5), 433–458. https://doi.org/10.1023/B:READ.0000044596.91833.55

Rubin, N., & Henderson, S. E. (1982). Two sides of the same coin: variations in teaching methods and failure to learn to write. *Special Education: Forward Trends, 9*(4), 17–24.

Salas, N., & Silvente, S. (2020). The role of executive functions and transcription skills in writing: A cross-sectional study across 7 years of schooling. *Reading and Writing, 33*(4), 877–905. https://doi.org/10.1007/s11145-019-09979-y

Santangelo, T., & Graham, S. (2016). A comprehensive meta-analysis of handwriting instruction. *Educational Psychology Review, 28*(2), 225–265. https://doi.org/10.1007/s10648-015-9335-1

Shaywitz, S. E., Shaywitz, B. A., Fletcher, J. M., & Escobar, M. D. (1990). Prevalence of reading disability in boys and girls. Results of the Connecticut Longitudinal Study. *JAMA: Journal of the American Medical Association, 264*(8), 998–1002. https://doi.org/10.1001/jama.1990.03450080084036

Skar, G. B., Lei, P. W., Graham, S., Aasen, A. J., Johansen, M. B., & Kvistad, A. H. (2021). Handwriting fluency and the quality of primary grade students' writing. *Reading and Writing*, 1-30.

Smits-Engelsman, B. C., Schomaker, M. M., Van Galen, G. P., & Michels, C. J. M. (1996). Physiotherapy for children's writing problems: Evaluation study. In M. L. Simner, C. G. Leedham, & A. J. W. M. Thomassen (Eds.), *Handwriting and Drawing Research: Basic and Applied Issues* (pp. 227–240). IOS Press.

Sormunen, C., & Wickersham, G. (1991). Language arts and keyboarding skill development: A viable approach for teaching elementary school students. *Journal of Research on Computing in Education, 23*(3), 463–469. https://doi.org/10.1080/08886504.1991.10781974

Stevenson, N. C., & Just, C. (2014). In early education, why teach handwriting before keyboarding? *Early Childhood Education Journal, 42*(1), 45–56. https://doi.org/10.1007/s10643-012-0565-2

Sumner, E., Connelly, V., & Barnett, A. L. (2016). The influence of spelling ability on vocabulary choices when writing for children with dyslexia. *Journal of Learning Disabilities, 4*(3), 293–304. https://doi.org/10.1177/0022219414552018

Tate, T. P., Warschauer, M., & Abedi, J. (2016). The effects of prior computer use on computer-based writing: The 2011 NAEP writing assessment. *Computers & Education*, (101), 115–131. https://doi.org/10.1016/j.compedu.2016.06.001

Terry, N. P. (2006). Relations between dialect variation, grammar, and early spelling skills. *Reading and Writing, 19*(9), 907–931. https://doi.org/10.1007/s11145-006-9023-0

Terry, N. P. (2021). Delivering on the promise of the science of reading for all children. *The Reading Teacher, 75*(1), 83–90. https://doi.org/10.1002/trtr.2031

Terry, N. P., & Connor, C. (2010). African American English and spelling: How do second graders spell dialect-sensitive features of words? *Learning Disability Quarterly, 33*(3), 199–210. https://doi.org/10.1177/073194871003300308

Troia, G. A., Brehmer, J. S., Glause, K., Reichmuth, H. L., & Lawrence, F. (2020). Direct and indirect effects of literacy skills and writing fluency on writing quality across three genres. *Education Sciences, 10*(11), Article 297. https://doi.org/10.3390/educsci10110297

Troia, G. A., Shen, M., & Brandon, D. L. (2019). Multidimensional levels of language writing measures in grades four to six. *Written Communication, 36*(2), 231–266. https://doi.org/10.1177/0741088318819473

Valadez, J. R., & Duran, R. (2007). Redefining the digital divide: Beyond access to computers and the internet. *The High School Journal, 90*(3), 31–44. https://www.jstor.org/stable/40364198

Van Weerdenburg, M., Tesselhof, M., & van der Meijden, H. (2019). Touch-typing for better spelling and narrative-writing skills on the computer. *Journal of Computer Assisted Learning, 35*(1), 143–152. https://doi.org/10.1111/jcal.12323

Wagner, R., Puranik, C. S., Foorman, B., Foster, E., Wilson, L. G., Tschinkel, E., & Kantor, P. T. (2011). Modeling the development of written language. *Reading and Writing, 24*(2), 203–220. https://doi.org/10.1007%2Fs11145-010-9266-7

Warschauer, M. (2017). Addressing the social envelope: Education and the digital divide. In C. Greenhow, J. Sonnevend, & C. Agur (Eds.), *Education and Social Media: Toward a Digital Future* (pp. 29–48). MIT Press. https://doi.org/10.7551/mitpress/9780262034470.001.0001

Weintraub, N., Gilmour-Grill, N., & Weiss, P. L. T. (2010). Relationship between handwriting and keyboarding performance among fast and slow adult keyboarders. *American Journal of Occupational Therapy, 64*(1), 123–132. https://doi.org/10.5014/ajot.64.1.123

Wengelin, Å. (2007). The word-level focus in text production by adults with reading and writing difficulties. In M. Torrance, L. Van Waes, & D. Galbraith (Eds.), *Writing and Cognition: Research and applications* (Studies in Writing, Vol. 20, pp. 67–82). Elsevier. https://psycnet.apa.org/doi/10.1163/9781849508223

Wolfe, E. W., Bolton, S., Feltovich, B., & Niday, D. M. (1996). The influence of student experience with word processors on the quality of essays written for a direct writing assessment. *Assessing writing, 3*(2), 123-147.

Wollscheid, S., Sjaastad, J., & Tømte, C. (2016). The impact of digital devices vs. Pen (cil) and paper on primary school students' writing skills–A research review. *Computers & Education*, (95), 19–35. https://doi.org/10.1016/j.compedu.2015.12.001

Yackanicz, L. (2000). *Reluctant Writers & Writing-Prompt Software.* [M.A. Thesis, Chestnut Hill College]. ERIC. https://files.eric.ed.gov/fulltext/ED440381.pdf

Zhang, M., Bennett, R. E., Deane, P., & van Rijn, P. W. (2019). Are there gender differences in how studentss write their essays? An analysis of writing processes. *Educational Measurement: Issues and Practice, 38*(2), 14–26. https://doi.org/10.1111/emip.12249

CHAPTER SEVEN

How to Achieve Equity in School Writing

The last several chapters may seem like a litany of the ways writing can go wrong. It would be more accurate to say they present a litany of reasons to stop conducting educational business as usual.

Business as usual can mean tolerating administrative procedures that make it hard to recruit or retain effective teachers (Nguyen, Pham, Springer, & Crouch, 2019). It can mean relying on well-established but ineffective instructional methods—or changing the curriculum so often that no method is ever given a chance to succeed—or tracking at-risk students into interventions ostensibly designed to help them, but which have the practical effect of reducing their opportunity to learn (Murphy, 2017). As the preceding chapters documented, business as usual can mean that students compete with their peers with minimal care or support, while juggling multiple forms of financial, physical, and emotional stress. It can mean that students who find school boring at best and alienating at worst may be penalized for acting like they do not want to be there. And it often means that students who enter school less well-prepared than their peers are allowed to fail and that their failures are attributed to a lack of ability.

Most of these problems are not, in the first instance, problems with writing, but unless they are addressed, it may be hard to implement effective writing instruction—and in fact, national surveys suggest that schools frequently fail to do so (Applebee & Langer, 2011; Graham, Capizzi, Harris, Hebert, & Morphy,

2014). Effective writing instruction does not exist in a vacuum. It happens when schools believe in and set high expectations for their students while providing them with the support and instruction that they need (Gorski, 2017).

The introduction presented a general theory of action for equitable writing instruction (see Figure I.1 in the introduction). Achieving equity in writing requires attention to all pathways in this theory of action. It is not enough to address just one mechanism or another, because it is the interactions among the elements in Figure I.1 that leads to either to vicious or beneficial cycles of reinforcing cause and effect. The fundamental instructional problem is to maintain high levels of motivation and engagement for writing while helping students overcome the most critical barriers to achievement, which will often be foundational literacy skills (reading, spelling, handwriting, and keyboarding).

Improve Writing Motivation

The literature on motivation suggests several strategies that might help to reduce inequity in writing outcomes. They mostly involve changes that make writing more meaningful, make students more comfortable in the writing classroom, and encourage them to focus on mastery goals.

Provide Real Audiences and Authentic Purposes for Writing

It is important to establish real audiences and authentic purposes for writing (Bruning & Horn, 2000; Duke, Purcell-Gates, Hall, & Tower, 2006). The audience, context, and purpose for writing are key variables manipulated in holistic classroom interventions, such as process approaches to writing and self-directed strategy instruction, which are discussed in greater detail below..

Graham, Harris, and Santangelo (2015) summarizes several studies of exceptional teachers who appeared to improve their students' writing motivation. These teachers adopted the following strategies:

* taking steps to establish a positive mood in the classroom and communicate enthusiasm about writing as an activity
* making students' writing visible in the classroom, so that the classroom became an effective audience for student writing
* encouraging a positive classroom environment, in which students attributed success to their own effort and the strategies the teacher provided, rather than to ability

* promoting peer interaction and collaboration as part of the writing process
* expecting students to improve over time
* encouraging reflection, and
* encouraging students to do as much work as they can on their own.

The theme that underlies these strategies is a concern with making writing meaningful, or, to express this concept in terms of motivation theory, to increase the perceived value of writing. This conclusion is also supported by De Boer, Donker-Bergstra, and Konstons' (2012) meta-analysis of writing interventions. Graham, Bollinger, Booth Olson, D'Aoust, MacArthur, McCutchen, and Olinghouse (2012) make similar recommendations in their practitioner's guide for elementary writing instruction, which was released as part of the U.S. Education department's What Works Clearinghouse.

Of course, "real audiences and authentic purposes for writing" should be audiences and purposes that resonate with students in their local community context. To make writing instruction equitable, all students need to be engaged.

Make Writing Social and Collaborative

When writing is a social practice, students may be motivated to help one another, which can strengthen motivation for writing. Collaborative writing tasks have been shown to have a motivating effect for important subgroups of students (Morrow & Sharkey, 1993; Langer, 2001; Talib & Cheung, 2017). Thinking about other students' writing and communicating with them about it may also help students to clarify their goals and improve their ability to evaluate their own writing. Graham, Harris, and Santangelo (2015) report an effect size of 0.66, suggesting that collaborative writing may make writing instruction significantly more effective.

Since collaboration is a social process, how it is implemented matters. Inappropriate social dynamics can make collaboration demotivating. Le, Janssen, and Wubbels (2018) identified several sources of problems: lack of collaborative skills, free riding (where some students do much less work than others), large differences in competence at the assigned task, and friendships (or other social relationships) that conflicted with the roles people needed to play in the group. These problems were related to teacher behaviors that increased the probabilities of such problems, such as a failure to make collaborative goals clear or failure to provide instruction in how to conduct collaborative work effectively. Equitable instruction depends on collaborative activities being structured and implemented in ways that build confidence and self-efficacy in all students.

Encourage Students to Adopt Mastery Goals

When students are given clear goals to accomplish, so that they know what they need to do to succeed at a writing task, they are more likely to believe that success is something they can control, rather than attributing success to ability or other factors outside their control. Graham, Harris, and Santangelo (2015) estimated that there is, overall, a moderate to strong effect size for goal setting (ES=0.80). Graham and Perin (2007)'s estimate of the effect size was slightly smaller (ES=0.70), as was Graham, McKeown, Kiuhara, and Harris (2012)'s estimate for elementary students (ES=0.76), and Gillespie and Graham (2014)'s estimate for learning-disabled students (ES=0.56).

Of course, goal setting is closely related to teacher expectations and how teachers communicate them to students. Equitable writing instruction depends not only on teachers setting high expectations, but in how well the teachers help students set explicit goals for writing, and the extent to which they provide struggling students with the support they need to meet them.

Provide Supportive Feedback

Achievement goals logically form part of a formative assessment cycle, in which students evaluate how close they have come to achieving their goals, either on their own, or with guidance from the teacher or from peers. To the extent that students receive useful feedback about their achievements, they obtain actionable information that can inform future writing efforts. The simplest possible form of feedback involves the use of scales or rubrics that define what goals need to be achieved to reach a specified level of success. Hillocks (1984) reports a significant, positive effect of providing this kind of feedback (ES=0.36). When feedback publicly praises specific, identifiable accomplishments there is an even stronger impact on writing quality (Rogers & Graham, 2008). Graham, Harris, and Hebert (2011) report an overall effect size of 0.77 for feedback, though Graham, McKeown, et al. (2012) report a somewhat smaller effect for elementary students (ES=0.46). Finally, Koster, Tribushinina, de Jong, and van den Bergh (2015) report an effect size of 0.59 for peer assistance.

Feedback can take several forms. It can come from the teacher or another adult; it can be provided by a peer; or it can be provided by the student's own self-evaluation. The literature suggests the strongest effects for adult feedback. Graham, Harris, and Hebert (2011) found strong overall effects for adult feedback (ES=1.01), while Graham, McKeown, et al. (2012) found a slightly smaller effect size for adult feedback to elementary students (ES=0.80). There are somewhat weaker, but still relatively strong effects for peer feedback (ES>0.70, Graham & Perin, 2007; Graham, Harris, & Hebert, 2011). When student self-evaluation is considered, the effect sizes are somewhat smaller, with Graham, Harris, and Hebert (2011) reporting moderate positive effects for teaching students to assess their own writing (ES=0.46), and Graham, McKeown, et al. (2012) reporting a slightly weaker effect for peer or self-evaluation by elementary students (ES=0.37).

Of course, feedback is one of the most sensitive areas of student/teacher interaction. Teacher feedback can reinforce negative expectations and negative stereotypes. Equitable writing instruction requires teachers to reflect on their own practices and change practices that have the potential to discourage or penalize students from backgrounds unlike their own.

Give Students Greater Agency and Choice of Writing Topics

Advocates of authentic writing experience emphasize the importance of topic choice in motivating students to write (Young & Ferguson, 2020). However, as the literature review in Chapter Two indicated, the relationship between topic choice and writing performance can be complex. Students are more likely to be motivated when they have agency and choice, but it is easy for novice writers to bite off more than they can chew—to select a topic about which they may have the interest, but not necessarily the knowledge. Overall, the evidence suggests that giving students a choice what to write about leads to stronger writing, if students are writing in a supportive environment where they can get the help they need to take on more meaningful—but also more ambitious—goals.

Overall, equitable writing instruction depends on structuring instruction in ways that give students greater agency and choice, and therefore more of a stake and sense of ownership over their work.

Welcome Linguistic and Cultural Diversity

Finally, we come to the role of language and culture in writing motivation. Student motivation can be affected very strongly by the attitudes that teachers take toward non-standard forms of English and toward students from diverse cultural backgrounds. The basic motivational cycle is simple: if a student's home language is stigmatized by the teacher, negatively assessed in formal assessments (Enright & Gilliland, 2011), and if school communication is conducted on a different cultural basis than the student has been exposed to in the home community, alienation and disengagement are a natural consequence (Godley & Escher, 2012). Students are most likely to construct an identity in which school performance is valued as part of their identity when school practices are respectful of, and integrate, home and community literacy practices (McCarthy, 2001). Students who transfer their cultural practices effectively into academic settings may be more likely to succeed at otherwise unfamiliar writing tasks (Smitherman, 1993). Recommendations for improved practice focus on improving teachers' awareness of language and cultural diversity and encouraging culturally and linguistically sensitive approaches that support rather than undermine student motivation and affirm their cultural and linguistic identities (Patthey-Chavez & Gergen, 1992; Mehan, Hubbard, & Villanueva, 1994; Wheeler, Swords, & Carpenter, 2004; Horner, Lu, Royster, & Trimbur, 2011).

Yet as Sweetland and Wheeler (2014)'s review indicates, very few teachers have deep understanding of the issues linked with linguistic diversity, and there are few examples of interventions in which teachers are effectively helped to create more positive environments for students from minority backgrounds. The available studies tend to be qualitative in nature. However, Pearson, Connor, and Jackson (2013) reviewed the available pedagogical literature, and concluded that there are at least three approaches that show evidence of success: (i) programs that set high academic expectations even for low-performing students, while providing appropriate scaffolding and support; (ii) programs that encourage culturally sensitive teaching, so that teachers respond positively to students when they make effective use of the communication resources they bring to school from their home environment, while helping students engage with school literacy practices; (iii) programs that explicitly teach students (and teachers) to be aware of (and respectful about) language and cultural differences, while teaching students to switch between different kinds of linguistic and cultural practices as appropriate.

Improve Writing Self-Regulation

Capacity theories of writing suggest that effective self-regulation helps the writer circumvent working memory limitations by dividing the writing process into a series of subtasks, each focusing on a specific goal (McCutchen, 2000; Kellogg, 2001b). Self-regulation thus plays a key role in writing achievement. However, effective self-regulation can be hard to develop. It depends on people being able and willing to focus on a complex task, being aware of appropriate strategies, and knowing how to deploy them. And that may not be easy, since effective writing strategies may be genre-, discipline- or even task-specific, draw upon different funds of knowledge, and presuppose varying levels of metalinguistic and metacognitive awareness (Hyland, 2004).

Self-regulation draws upon a variety of knowledge, skills, or abilities, but self-regulation is about skill coordination. That is the motivation for Self-Regulated Strategy Development, or SRSD (Graham & Harris, 1989). SRSD targets not only self-regulation, but also genre knowledge (through direct instruction), strategy development (through direct instruction and scaffolded learning activities), and motivation (through a gradual release model designed to increase students' self of self-efficacy).

SRSD consistently shows moderate to strong impacts on student learning. Graham and Perin (2007), reported an effect size of 0.82. Gillespie and Graham (2014) reported even larger effects for learning disabled students (ES=1.09). Among elementary students, Graham, McKeown, et al. (2012) also observed a strong effect (ES=1.17). Graham, Harris, and Santangelo (2015) also reported a large overall effect size (ES=1.00), with a particularly strong effect on writing quality (ES=1.24), second only to the impact of word processing.

The most distinctive feature of SRSD is that it focuses on getting students to practice goal setting and self-monitoring during the writing process. Graham, Harris, and Santangelo (2015) report that these two features account for most of the difference in effect size between SRSD and other approaches to strategy instruction. This may explain why SRSD is one of the few writing interventions that has been shown to be particularly beneficial for struggling writers.

That is, higher-achieving writers may high levels of self-efficacy and high levels of implicit knowledge about writing and writing strategies, even without explicit instruction. Conversely, struggling writers are likely to struggle on multiple fronts: With motivation, with strategy selection, and with process management. SRSD simultaneously helps such writers acquire effective writing strategies, improve their ability to self-regulate the writing process, and develop a stronger sense of self-efficacy.

SRSD thus provides an example of the importance of coordinating multiple pedagogical elements to achieve equity in writing instruction.

Develop Deeper Knowledge about Writing and Writing Strategies

SRSD presupposes direct instruction about writing and writing strategies. Not surprisingly, there is evidence that other forms of writing instruction also improve student achievement. Two specific subcases should be singled out: providing models or exemplar texts and familiarizing students with multiple forms of disciplinary writing.

Provide Models to Emulate

When a task is unfamiliar, writers must expend a great deal of energy analyzing task requirements, acquiring necessary background knowledge, and developing strategies for completing the work. Providing models or exemplars to imitate is one of the oldest pedagogical strategies for overcoming this barrier (Corbett, 1971). If writers have a concrete example, or model, in which someone else has attempted a similar writing task, they can imitate it, and minimize the amount of energy and attention that needs to be devoted to prewriting and planning. There is evidence that imitating models can have a positive impact on writing, though the effects generally are small: an effect size of 0.22 in Hillocks (1984) and 0.25 in Steve Graham and Perin (2007), though the most extensive meta-analysis, that provided by Steve Graham, Harris, and Santangelo (2015), estimates an effect size of 0.40

Providing explicit exemplars is an important element of achieving equity in writing instruction. When teachers assume that students will know what good writing is, they are relying on them having implicit knowledge that must necessarily derive from prior exposure to similar texts. Which may be a safe assumption to make about higher-performing students from upper-middle-class backgrounds, but it is not a safe assumption to make about a mixed population of students from diverse communities.

Explicitly Teach Students How to Write in Multiple Genres and Disciplines

Across disciplines and professions, people do not read or write the same texts; and they do not read or write those texts in the same way (Prior, 1998; Hyland, 2004; Beaufort, 2008; Shanahan & Shanahan, 2008; Smagorinsky, 2015). Writing is differentiated into genres that serve the needs of specific communities (Russell, 1995; Bazerman, 2004). Typically, full competence in disciplinary writing is acquired by a form of cognitive apprenticeship within a community of practice (Collins, Brown, & Newman, 1988; Beaufort, 2000). However, the educational system must prepare students to acquire disciplinary literacy. As various recent educational reform efforts emphasize, disciplinary literacy must be developed by providing focused instruction that communicates the kinds of critical reading and writing that are characteristic for each discipline (Moje, 2008; Shanahan & Shanahan, 2008; McConachie & Petrosky, 2009; Brozo, 2017).

A relatively small number of disciplines and genres are prioritized in school writing. English Language Arts instruction tends to prioritize classical purposes and modes, most notably argumentation, narrative, expository writing (including research), and literary analysis (Deane, Sabatini, Feng, Sparks, Song, Fowles, & Foley, 2015) As Deane and colleagues argue, these correspond to "key practices" that show up in more specialized forms in a variety of disciplines. Teaching students how to write in each of the major modes thus teaches them relatively generalizable skills that prepare them for cognitive apprenticeships in specific disciplines.

Most forms of strategy instruction are genre specific. Graham, Harris and Santangelo (2015) found that strategy instruction without the distinctive features of SRSD had an overall effect size of 0.53, similar to the moderate effect (ES= 0.59) of direct instruction in text structure reported by Graham, McKeown, et al. (2012). Among elementary students, Graham, McKeown, et al. (2012) observed a moderate effect of strategy instruction without SRSD (ES=0.59). Philippakos, and MacArthur (2016) provide specific guidelines for providing genre-specific strategy instruction, with a focus on employing appropriate scaffolds for task analysis, planning, evaluation, and revision.

There is, however, more to developing knowledge about writing than strategy instruction. If professional and academic writing is one of the end goals of 21st-century literacy education, then it needs to prepare students to play many different roles. To use language from the book and journal publication industries, professionals may be called upon to act as acquisitions editors (to solicit submissions and determine whether a submission will be accepted), as authors, as reviewers, as development editors (to work with the author and reviewers to get a manuscript ready for publication), as copy editors (to oversee the final preparation of a completed manuscript), or as proofreaders. This specialization is linked with existence of text genres associated with specific points in the publication process, such as a call for papers, a peer review for a journal, or an editorial letter outlining how a manuscript must be revised before it can be published (Greco, Elliott, & Wharton, 2014; Ware & Mabe, 2015).

Only some forms of academic and professional writing have publication processes as elaborate and detailed as is required for publication of a book by a major publisher. However, there are intermediate forms of publication, especially with the advent of online and digital modes of communication (Merchant, 2007), that require less elaborate processes but require a similar differentiation of roles and responsibilities. These include fan fiction sites like fanfiction.net (Black, 2007; Littleton, 2011), story sharing sites like Wattpad (Tarbox, 2014), and mass participatory projects like National Novel Writing Month (Barack, 2009; Campbell, Aragon, Davis, Evans, Evans, & Randall, 2016). Each of these online modes includes peer review and revision without the gatekeeping function performed by of a traditional editor. Participation in such online spaces has significant motivating effects (Curwood, Magnifico, & Lammers, 2013). It thus seems very likely that significant improvements to student motivation and achievement in school writing could be achieved by encouraging and leveraging student participation in such practices.

Opening up school writing to include new modes of communication may play an important role in achieving equity in writing instruction. Popular forms of communication are likely to be more diverse, and more diversely shared, than the academic modes inherited from the past century and a half of Anglo-American education.

Improve Idea Generation by Making Time for Prewriting

When students write, they must first activate the knowledge that they will use and then think about it to generate specific ideas for writing. But idea generation is not an easy task. Students may struggle to recall what they know, or to organize it in ways that make sense in context. They need time to reflect and develop their ideas. But this idea-generation process—often termed invention, or prewriting—is hard to include in a hectic schedule that may see students changing classes every 45 to 50 minutes. Nonetheless, students write more fluently and more effectively when their school writing activities incorporate prewriting as a normal part of the writing process, with effect sizes ranging between 0.32 and 0.54 (Graham & Perin, 2007; Rogers & Graham, 2008; Graham, McKeown, Kiuhara, & Harris, 2012).

Equity in writing instruction is thus more likely to happen if schools make time for prewriting. Otherwise, we can expect to see writing that expresses what students think *before they have had the time to think*. And that will advantage students who have been given more time and leisure to learn, to think, and to reflect on what they have been taught at school.

Develop Deeper Content Knowledge

Obviously, idea generation is facilitated when students write about what they know. But writing also plays a critical role in developing content knowledge. Writing-to-learn activities take advantage of this dynamic by having students write about subjects they are studying. Two specific approaches are worth calling out: writing to learn and inquiry learning.

Implement Writing to Learn

If students write about what they have read, they achieve deeper comprehension and are more likely to remember text content. This, in turn, may improve the quality of student writing. These assumptions are the basis for a set of teaching practices collectively called "writing to learn" (Emig, 1977; Britton, 1982).

Writing to learn may take various forms, including taking notes, writing summaries of individual texts, writing extended texts that synthesize information derived from multiple sources, or it may focus on content derived from lectures and classroom activities. It may also involve reflective forms of writing designed to help students clarify what they know, what they are confused about, and what they need to learn. Ideally, it happens across the curriculum, following the norms and expectations for specific disciplines, including STEAM disciplines (science, technology, engineering, the arts, and mathematics). As students move through college, they are increasingly exposed to such tasks (Ruggles-Gere, 2019), but the more similar tasks are included in elementary and secondary education, the more prepared students will be for disciplinary writing later in life.

There are three major meta-analyses that address writing-to-learn: Bangert-Drowns, Hurley, and Wilkinson (2004), Graham and Hebert (2011), and Graham, Harris, and Santangelo (2015). These studies suggest that writing to learn has relatively small but significant effect sizes on student learning, with estimates ranging from 0.22 to 0.37. However, they also indicate larger effects on reading comprehension, with effect sizes falling around 0.65. Typical writing-to-learn activities, such as writing summaries, may indirectly increase writing quality on extended writing tasks, by building task-relevant content knowledge (Newell, 2006).

Different writing-to-learn activities have different effects on student learning and reading comprehension. Graham and Hebert (2011) and Graham and Perin (2007) found that extended source-based writing tasks had stronger effects on reading comprehension than shorter, more focused writing-to-learn activities. Bangert-Drowns et al. (2004) found the best learning outcomes for writing-to-learn interventions occurred when in-class writing assignments were short (less than 10 minutes, ES=.52), occurred two to three times per week (ES=.32) and were sustained over longer time periods such as a semester (ES=.45). Results were also significantly stronger results if the writing prompts encouraged students to reflect about misunderstandings and sources of confusion.

Writing-to-learn activities are common in school, but far too many of them focus on demonstrating basic comprehension. Equity in writing instruction depends upon students being given writing tasks that encourage them not only to demonstrate understanding, but also to reflect on what they have read.

Incorporate Inquiry Learning Into Writing Tasks

The term "writing to learn" is primarily applied to writing activities that are closely tied to specific, assigned texts. However, as students move toward disciplinary writing, they must also learn how to define research questions, gather useful information, and develop original ideas (Bateman, 1990). As writing-to-learn activities move into this relatively exploratory mode, they partake more strongly of the features of "writing in the disciplines" (Kiefer, Palmquist, Carbone, Cox, & Melzer, 2000–2021).

In the pedagogical literature, these more exploratory occasions for writing arise in the context of what is commonly called *inquiry learning* or *problem-based learning*. Problem-based learning has been shown to have a strong impact on content learning, with effect sizes around 0.71 (Chen & Yang, 2019). Embedding writing within inquiry (and project-based learning) activities produces two specific benefits for writers. First, it increases their funds of domain- and topic-relevant knowledge. Second, it teaches them how to generate original ideas. Both mechanisms are likely to improve student writing.

Hillocks (1984) reported an effect size of 0.56 for inquiry learning, though Graham and Perin (2007) reported a slightly smaller effect (ES=0.32). Some variation in the effect sizes may be related to the existence of a large gray area between writing-to-learn activities that focus on summarization and synthesis of information from specific sources, and broader research and inquiry activities, where students are left free to decide what they want to learn, what they will do to find out more about the subject, and what they have learned as a result.

Far too often, schools from low-SES and minority communities are underfunded yet are simultaneously under the most pressure to achieve higher test scores. But equitable writing instruction is not going to happen when schools focus on test preparation and rote skills practice, to the exclusion of inquiry and project-based learning.

Increase Effective Working Memory Capacity

Working memory plays a crucial mediating role in writing achievement. Whenever students run into trouble during the writing process, the burden on working memory increases and student performance is likely to suffer. It doesn't matter what the source of the problem is: transcription or reading difficulties, uncertainties about writing strategies, or emotional and social stress. The limitations of working memory create the risk of a series of cascading failures, resulting in students performing far below their potential.

Many of the problems with working memory can be addressed by addressing the underlying cause. However, there are several pedagogical strategies that more directly address working memory limitations, either by decreasing the cognitive load of a writing activity, or breaking it up into smaller, more manageable activities.

Provide Frequent Opportunities to Practice Writing

Working memory load is affected by the familiarity of a task (Klingberg, 2010). If a writing task is part of a well-known, regular routine, writers can internalize the steps of the process and can recapitulate them without incurring large working memory loads (Kellogg, 2008). Graham, Harris, and Santangelo (2015) found that providing more-frequent opportunities to write had a small facilitating effect on writing performance (ES=0.24) and also facilitated reading comprehension (ES=0.35). Graham, McKeown, et al. (2012) obtained similar results for a subset of studies focused on elementary students (ES=0.30).

As they say in the proverb, "practice makes perfect". Equitable writing instruction is only going to happen if all students have ample opportunities to write. When student writing performance is assessed, students from low-SES and minority communities may get low scores, which is all too likely to be interpreted as evidence of a lack of ability. But their performance may simply demonstrate that they are writing novices who have been afforded minimal opportunities to learn how to write.

Support Process Writing

When a task is reasonably well understood, it can be broken down into a series of steps. At each step, different sub-goals are in focus, and working memory is only required to accomplish the current task. The so-called "process approach" to writing applies this idea to writing instruction. Process approaches to writing teach a general schema for the writing process, with distinct phases (prewriting, planning, drafting, revising, editing, publishing), and different goals for each phase (Calkins, 1986; Graves, 1983; Pritchard & Honeycutt, 2006). Students are given time to work through each phase and produce intermediate work products along the way.

Meta-analyses indicate that the process approach to writing improves student performance, though the effect sizes are usually small (ES of .32 to .37, cf. Graham and Perin, 2007; Graham and Sandmel, 2011; Graham et al., 2015). The effects may be slightly larger with less-able populations. Graham, McKeown, et al. (2012) reported an effect size of 0.40 for elementary-age students. Gillespie and Graham (2014) reported an effect size of 0.43 for LD students. However, Graham and

Sandmel (2011) found that process-writing approaches did not have a positive impact upon writers' motivation, and concluded that stronger, rather than struggling, writers appeared to benefit most from a pure process writing approach.

Process writing involves a tradeoff between effort and efficiency. An extended writing process, with separate stages for different parts of the writing process, requires the writer to do a lot more work than novice writers are likely to expect. Equity in writing instruction depends upon teaching students how to use elaborated writing processes to improve writing quality, while giving them the fluency and strategic control they need to handle everyday writing tasks.

Support Alternate Input Formats

Transcription can be extremely effortful. However, technological advances support a variety of alternate input methods that can reduce the effective cognitive load of transcription (MacArthur, 1999, 2009). The use of word processing technologies is among the most important. At similar proficiency levels, digital writing is significantly faster than but requires less effort than writing by hand, enables faster revision processes, and simplifies sharing and collaboration. However, other methods, including the use of dictation and speech recognition technologies, may also be valuable for struggling writers.

Research on the use of dictation (either to a person, or by use of a tape recorder) has consistently found that dictation has significant benefits for learning disabled (LD) writers, for whom handwriting or even keyboarding can be extremely effortful and frustrating (De La Paz, 1999; MacArthur & Graham, 1987). Meta-analyses of the use of dictation report moderate effects both for LD writers (ES= 0.55, Gillespie & Graham, 2014; Graham & Harris, 2013) and for the general population (De La Paz & Graham, 1997). Similar results have been obtained for use of speech recognition technologies, or voice to text (Quinlan, 2004; Garrett, Heller, Fowler, Alberto, Fredrick, & O'Rourke, 2011).

Using word processing software not only increases writing productivity and writing quality (Rogers & Graham, 2008; Graham, Harris, & Santangelo, 2015), but also increases motivation to write (Morphy & Graham, 2012). Given a choice, students preferred word processing to writing by hand (ES=0.64). Morphy and Graham also report a very large impact of word processing on student motivation to write (ES=1.42). This is among the largest effect sizes reported in the literature, which is significant, because the effect sizes for struggling writers were larger than for the general population, suggesting that shifting from handwritten to digital approaches to writing instruction may be particularly important for at-risk students (Goldberg et al., 2003).

It remains to be seen whether the adoption of a broader range of devices to support everyday literacy, such as mobile phones and tablets (Norris & Soloway, 2011; Wood, Kemp, & Plester, 2013; Sessions & Kang, 2016), can provide options for increasing transcription fluency among students from disadvantaged backgrounds. In the current school climate texting is more strongly associated with informal writing in social media contexts and not with the acquisition of formal writing ability of the kind measured on standardized tests such as the SAT (Rosen, Chang, Erwin, Carrier, & Cheever, 2010; Wardyga, 2012). There is some evidence that the association may not be positive for older teens in late high school or college (De Jonge & Kemp, 2012), though De Jonge and Kemp's results may be due to frequent use of text messaging with predictive spelling software by weaker writers.

There is much less research on use of on the instructional effects of using newer forms of digital input, such as mobile phones and tablets. However, this research suggests that student writers are more likely to be fluent and motivated when they are able to use the devices to which they are accustomed (Swan, van 'T. Hooft, Kratcoski, & Unger, 2005; Bedesem & Harmon, 2015). In this context, it is important to note that the technologies that support texting, which draw upon auto-completion and word prediction methods to speed up input (Gong & Tarasewich, 2005; Garay-Vitoria & Abascal, 2006), may be particularly helpful for students who have spelling difficulties (Evmenova, Graff, Jerome, & Behrmann, 2010; Silió & Barbetta, 2010).

Given the effect sizes reported for use of computers in writing, schools and teachers should not ignore the potential value in allowing students to use cell phones, text-to-speech, and other supportive technologies to enable more equitable forms of writing instruction

Strengthen Language Skills

As our previous review indicated, oral (and academic) language is one of the largest sources of individual differences in writing performance. It is thus not surprising that interventions focused on improving students' language skills also improves their writing performance.

Increase Vocabulary Knowledge

Considering the importance of vocabulary in accounting for literacy achievement gaps, there are surprisingly few studies that explicitly examine the relationship between vocabulary instruction and writing performance. Graham, Harris, and Santangelo (2015) reviewed three studies that indicated a moderate to strong relationship between teaching topic- and genre-specific vocabulary and improvements in writing quality (ES=0.78).

The word vocabulary is usually used as a mass noun, but that usage may be misleading. There are in fact many vocabularies that people need to acquire. The vocabularies that people use on social media, communicating among members of their own community, may differ considerably from the vocabularies they use in school, and those may differ, in turn, from the vocabularies deployed by members of a specific profession, or the adherents of a particular sport or hobby. The vocabularies that people command are funds of knowledge. Education should increase students' funds of knowledge and give them the flexibility to use them when and where they are needed. Equitable writing instruction needs to start from the presumption that students—and teachers—differ in the vocabularies they know and are able to use fluently. Leveling that playing field requires schools to teach academic vocabulary without stigmatizing the vocabularies that students bring with them from their life outside school.

Develop Syntactic Flexibility

Writing requires writers to find words, phrases, and sentences that accurately express their ideas. This requires writers to develop flexible control over the syntactic resources of the language. The same ideas can be expressed in a variety of ways, supporting different emphases, nuances, and logical connections. Skilled writers need to be able to generate, consider, and select among these options.

Sentence combining, an instructional technique originally deriving from transformational grammar, focuses explicitly on building up this ability. Meta-analyses of writing instruction consistently indicate that sentence combining has a small-to-moderate effect upon student writing. Hillocks (1984) reports a relatively weak effect (ES=0.35), but Graham and Perin (2007) and Graham, Harris, and Santangelo (2015) report moderate effects (ES=0.50 and 0.56, respectively), consistent with the moderate effects also observed by Rogers and Graham (2008).

People have different ways of expressing themselves. But equitable writing instruction should seek to guarantee that students learn how to express themselves flexibly, fitting what they write and how they write it to suit diverse contexts, audiences, and purposes. That requires explicit instruction and constant exposure to a variety of models.

Develop Code-Switching and Code-Meshing Abilities.

As Chapter Five demonstrated, language is not a monolithic entity, but subsists in a complex array of styles, registers, jargons, and dialects. Skilled writers need to be able to choose the form of the language that is most appropriate to their purpose and audience. In academic contexts, that form will usually be some variant of what is usually termed standard English; but skilled writers switch freely between (and often, mix or combine) language variants as needed. We therefore hypothesize that instruction designed to facilitate code switching and code-meshing will improve students' writing, especially if it respects their home languages and cultures. However, while there is strong advocacy for supporting linguistic diversity in education, there are few empirical studies that examine its efficacy. Wheeler and Swords (2010) provides one of the few published studies that also provides empirical evidence of effectiveness.

Equitable writing instruction depends on writers being able to communicate in a variety of modes and being fluent and comfortable in all of them. That requires instruction that exposes students to the diversity of language and shows them how and when to use the resources of the language to best effect.

Cultivate Metalinguistic Awareness

Writing requires a great deal of metacognitive and metalinguistic control over what one writes (Hacker, 2018). Practicing writers develop a rich awareness of the linguistic choices they are making; conversely, it can be very hard to develop effective writing strategies without being able to identify and label the textual and linguistic elements manipulated by specific writing strategies. Newton (2021) found that metalinguistic awareness is weakly predictive of writing performance (R=.34). The emergence of metalinguistic awareness appears to be associated with active problem-solving activities during literacy activities (Flood & Menyuk, 1983; Pittard & Martlew, 2000), and is encouraged by educational activities that require students to collaborate and communicate with one another and the teacher about texts they are reading and writing (Myhill, Jones, & Wilson, 2016).

Metalinguistic awareness is both necessary for, and contributes to, writers' ability to self-regulate their own writing. Teachers play a critical role in this process, especially for students who have less exposure to models of academic talk and text outside of school. Equity in writing thus entails a pedagogical model in which students engage in rich literacy activities that afford frequent opportunities to think and communicate about their own and other people's writing and in which teachers provide explicit instruction in critical metalinguistic concepts and model the use of those concepts as a part of writing strategy instruction.

Improve Transcription Skills

Transcription skills (e.g., spelling, handwriting, and keyboarding) are crucial contributors to overall writing performance. Achievement gaps in writing appear to be strongly linked to gaps in transcription fluency that emerge in the early elementary years and constrain later learning. In the absence of effective early interventions, mitigation may involve providing more opportunities to practice or providing students with multiple alternate input methods that reduce the effort required to produce correctly spelled, legible text.

Meta-analyses generally indicate that interventions designed to improve handwriting have a significant positive impact on student writing. Graham, Harris, and Santangelo (2015) and Graham, McKeown, et al. (2012) reported moderate effects (ES=0.55), though this probably understates the importance of transcription, since failure to fully automatize handwriting and spelling are almost the defining characteristics of struggling writers. According to Santangelo and Graham (2016)'s meta-analysis of handwriting intervention studies, handwriting instruction produces significant gains in the quality (ES=.84), length (ES=1.33) and fluency (ES=.48) of student writing. According to Graham and Santangelo's (2014) meta-analysis, spelling instruction also significantly improves writing performance. The effect size is quite large (ES=0.94). Feng, Lindner, Ji, and Joshi (2019) found somewhat smaller effects. They report an overall effect size of 0.43 for the contribution of handwriting to writing performance. The specific effect of handwriting instruction on writing quality was .399. The impact on writing fluency was slightly larger (ES=0.525) . They found that keyboarding fluency also had a moderate effect on writing quality (ES=0.524).

However, it is also important to note that the intervention literature does not support approaches that emphasize error correction. Hillocks (1984) found significant *negative* effects for instruction focused on correctness of grammar and mechanics (ES=-0.29). Graham and Perin (2007) also obtained a negative average effect size for grammar instruction (ES=-0.41), though this effect was not significant. On the other hand, the effects of error correction for second-language learners seem to be more positive (Kang & Han, 2015).

It is also worth pointing out that minority and low-SES groups may have relatively greater experience and fluency using mobile devices than computer keyboards (Ortlieb, Rozario, & Sasaski, 2014; Lenhart, 2015). Fluency in texting is not strongly correlated with keyboarding fluency (Ortlieb, 2012; Ouellette & Michaud, 2016), though it is positively correlated with general literacy ability (Plester, Wood, & Joshi, 2009; Drouin & Driver, 2014; Kemp, 2010), and therefore may represent an alternative route to transcription fluency.

Equity in writing depends on students being taught the transcription skills they require to produce text fluently and easily. Students who must devote large amounts of time and effort just getting words down on the page will not have the time and energy to learn everything else they need to learn about writing. An instructor focus on error correction compounds these difficulties by encouraging struggling writers to interrupt or delay other writing processes to double-check everything they do.

Improve Reading Skills

Reading plays a critical direct role in the self-regulation of writing. To monitor and evaluate their own writing, students need to read what they have written. Reading also has an indirect effect on writing performance through its impact on language and transcription skills, content knowledge, and knowledge about writing and writing strategies

Graham, Liu, Aitken, Ng, Bartlett, Harris, and Holzapfel's (2017) meta-analysis reviewed how writing performance was affected by *balanced* literacy programs that included large amounts of both reading and writing instruction. Overall, they found that balancing reading and writing instruction had a small positive effect on writing quality (ES=0.37). There were not particularly large differences in effect sizes for different types of reading instruction, though the largest effect size was for reading instruction based upon cooperative learning principles (ES=0.37), and the smallest was for whole language reading instruction (ES=0.20).

Graham, Liu, Bartlett, Ng, Harris, Aitken ... & Talukdar's (2018) meta-analysis reviewed the effects of different reading pedagogies on writing performance. They found a moderate effect of reading instruction overall (ES=0.57) and specifically on writing quality (ES=0.63). When they examined the effects of specific types of reading instruction on writing, they found moderate to strong effects for phonological awareness training (ES=0.69) and reading comprehension instruction (ES=0.66) and weaker effects for phonics instruction (ES=0.39).

Graham, Liu, Bartlett, Ng, Harris, Aitken ... and Talukdar's (2018) meta-analysis also reviewed the effects of increasing the intensity of student interactions with text. The overall effect size was small but significant (ES=0.35). However, they found that giving students opportunities to observe other readers interacting with text had moderate to strong effects on writing quality (ES=0.67). The studies that yielded this effect size involved student observation of published texts being read either by adults or by other students.

Finally, reading for pleasure—and consequently, high levels of print exposure—also improve writing (Clark & Rumbold, 2006; Jouhar & Rupley, 2021). Jouhar and Rupley's results indicated that high levels of print exposure were associated with stronger narrative and descriptive writing. Students who read more demonstrated higher levels of composition fluency, text organization, grammatical accuracy, and adherence to mechanics and spelling conventions. Equitable writing instruction depends on students being able to read and reading frequently. Equitable writing instruction thus depends on schools providing high quality reading instruction that includes both foundational reading skills and reading comprehension, and on their making students' interactions with texts frequent, intense, and meaningful. Lifelong readers develop implicit mental models of texts and text genres that serve them well when they attempt to write texts of their own.

Reference List

Applebee, A. N., & Langer, J. A. (2011). "EJ" Extra: A snapshot of writing instruction in middle schools and high schools. *The English Journal, 100*(6), 14–27. https://www.jstor.org/stable/23047875

Bangert-Drowns, R. L., Hurley, M. M., & Wilkinson, B. (2004). The effects of school-based writing-to-learn interventions on academic achievement: A meta-analysis. *Review of Educational Research, 74*(1), 29–58. https://doi.org/10.3102/00346543074001029

Barack, L. (2009). Pen Ultimate: For kids who take part in National Novel Writing Month--the acid test for would-be authors--it's no guts, no glory. *School Library Journal, 55*(9), 40–41.

Bateman, W. L. (1990). *Open to Question. The Art of Teaching and Learning by Inquiry.* Jossey-Bass.

Bazerman, C. (2004). Speech acts, genres, and activity systems: How texts organize activity and people. In C. Bazerman & P. Prior (Eds.), *What Writing Does and How It Does It: An Introduction to Analyzing Texts and Textual Practices* (pp. 309–339). Lawrence Erlbaum. https://doi.org/10.4324/9781410609d526

Beaufort, A. (2000). Learning the trade A social apprenticeship model for gaining writing expertise. *Written Communication, 17*(2), 185–223. https://doi.org/10.1177/0741088300017002002

Beaufort, A. (2008). Writing in the professions. In C. Bazerman (Ed.), *Handbook of Research on Writing: History, Society, School, Individual, Text* (pp. 221–236). Lawrence Erlbaum. https://doi.org/10.4324/9781410616470

Bedesem, P. L., & Harmon, A. (2015). The use of mobile phones in K-12 education. In Z. Yan (Ed.), *Encyclopedia of Mobile Phone Behavior* (pp. 575–582): IGI Global. https://doi.org/10.4018/978-1-4666-8239-9

Black, R. W. (2007). Fanfiction writing and the construction of space. *E-Learning and Digital Media, 4*(4), 384–397. https://doi.org/10.2304/elea.2007.4.4.384

Britton, J. (1982). Writing to learn and learning to write. In J. Britton & G. M. Pradl (Eds.), *Prospect and Retrospect: Selected Essays of James Britton* (pp. 123–129). Boynton-Cook.

Brozo, W. G. (2017). *Disciplinary and Content Literacy for Today's Adolescents: Honoring Diversity and Building Competence.* Guilford.

Bruning, R. H., & Horn, C. (2000). Developing motivation to write. *Educational Psychology, 35*(1), 25–37. https://doi.org/10.1207/S15326985EP3501_4

Calkins, L. A. (1986). *The Art of Teaching Writing.* Heinemann.

Campbell, J., Aragon, C., Davis, K., Evans, S., Evans, A., & Randall, D. (2016). Thousands of positive reviews: Distributed mentoring in online fan communities. In *Proceedings of the 19th ACM Conference on Computer-Supported Cooperative Work & Social Computing* (pp. 691–704). ACM. https://doi.org/10.1145/2818048.2819934

Chen, C. H., & Yang, Y. C. (2019). Revisiting the effects of project-based learning on students' academic achievement: A meta-analysis investigating moderators. *Educational Research Review, 26,* 71–81. https://doi.org/10.1016/j.edurev.2018.11.001

Clark, C., & Rumbold, K. (2006). *Reading for Pleasure: A Research Overview.* National Literacy Trust. https://files.eric.ed.gov/fulltext/ED496343.pdf

Collins, A., Brown, J. S., & Newman, S. E. (1988). Cognitive apprenticeship: Teaching the craft of reading, writing and mathematics. *Thinking: The Journal of Philosophy for Children, 8*(1), 2–10. https://doi.org/10.5840/thinking19888129

Corbett, E. P. (1971). The theory and practice of imitation in classical rhetoric. *College Composition and Communication, 22*(3), 243–250. https://doi.org/10.2307/356450

Curwood, J. S., Magnifico, A. M., & Lammers, J. C. (2013). Writing in the wild: Writer's motivation in fan-based affinity spaces. *Journal of Adolescent & Adult Literacy, 56*(8), 677–685. https://doi.org/10.1002/JAAL.192

De Boer, H., Donker-Bergstra, A. S., & Konstons, D. D. N. M. (2012). *Effective Strategies for Self-Regulated Learning: A Meta-Analysis.* Gronings Instituut voor Onderzoek van Onderwijs, Rijksuniversiteit Groningen. https://pure.rug.nl/ws/portalfiles/portal/54332660/Effective_Strategies_for_Self_regulated_Learning.pdf

De Jonge, S., & Kemp, N. (2012). Text-message abbreviations and language skills in high school and university students. *Journal of Research in Reading, 35*(1), 49–68. https://doi.org/10.1111/j.1467-9817.2010.01466.x

De La Paz, S. (1999). Composing via dictation and speech recognition systems: Compensatory technology for students with learning disabilities. *Learning Disability Quarterly, 22*(3), 173–182. https://doi.org/10.2307/1511284

De La Paz, S., & Graham, S. (1997). Effects of dictation and advanced planning instruction on the composing of students with writing and learning problems. *Journal of Educational Psychology, 89*(2), 203–222. https://doi.org/10.1037/0022-0663.89.2.203

Deane, P. D., Sabatini, J., Feng, G., Sparks, J., Song, Y., Fowles, M., . . . Foley, C. (2015). *Key Practices in the English Language Arts (ELA): Linking Learning Theory, Assessment, and Instruction* (RR-15-24). Educational Testing Service. https://doi.org/10.1002/ets2.12063

Drouin, M. A., & Driver, B. (2014). Texting, textese and literacy abilities: A naturalistic study. *Journal of Research in Reading, 37*(3), 250–267. https://doi.org/10.1111/j.1467-9817.2012.01532.x

Duke, N. K., Purcell-Gates, V., Hall, L. A., & Tower, C. (2006). Authentic literacy activities for developing comprehension and writing. *The Reading Teacher, 60*(4), 344–355. https://doi.org/10.1598/RT.60.4.4

Emig, J. (1977). Writing as a mode of learning. *College Composition and Communication, 28*(2), 122–128. https://doi.org/10.2307/356095

Enright, K. A., & Gilliland, B. (2011). Multilingual writing in an age of accountability: From policy to practice in US high school classrooms. *Journal of Second Language Writing, 20*(3), 182–195. https://doi.org/10.1016/j.jslw.2011.05.006

Evmenova, A. S., Graff, H. J., Jerome, M. K., & Behrmann, M. M. (2010). Word prediction programs with phonetic spelling support: Performance comparisons and impact on journal writing for students with writing difficulties. *Learning Disabilities Research & Practice, 25*(4), 170–182. https://doi.org/10.1111/j.1540-5826.2010.00315.x

Feng, L., Lindner, A., Ji, X. R., & Joshi, R. M. (2019). The roles of handwriting and keyboarding in writing: A meta-analytic review. *Reading and Writing, 32*(1), 33–63. https://doi.org/10.1007/s11145-017-9749-x

Flood, J. & Menyuk, P. (1983). The development of metalinguistic awareness and its relation to reading achievement. *Journal of Applied Developmental Psychology, 4*(1), 65–80. https://doi.org/10.1016/0193-3973(83)90059-X

Garay-Vitoria, N., & Abascal, J. (2006). Text prediction systems: A survey. *Universal Access in the Information Society, 4*(3), 188–203. https://doi.org/10.1007/s10209-005-0005-9

Garrett, J. T., Heller, K. W., Fowler, L. P., Alberto, P. A., Fredrick, L. D., & O'Rourke, C. M. (2011). Using speech recognition software to increase writing fluency for individuals with physical disabilities. *Journal of Special Education Technology, 26*(1), 25–41. https://doi.org/10.1177/016264341102600104

Gillespie, A., & Graham, S. (2014). A meta-analysis of writing interventions for students with learning disabilities. *Exceptional Children, 80*(4), 454–473. https://doi.org/10.1177/0014402914527238

Godley, A. J., & Escher, A. (2012). Bidialectal African American adolescents' beliefs about spoken language expectations in English classrooms. *Journal of Adolescent & Adult Literacy, 55*(8), 704–713. https://doi.org/10.1002/JAAL.00085

Gong, J., & Tarasewich, P. (2005). Alphabetically constrained keypad designs for text entry on mobile devices. *Proceedings of the SIGCHI Conference on Human Factors in Computing Systems* (pp. 211–220). https://dl.acm.org/doi/pdf/10.1145/1054972.1055002

Gorski, P. C. (2017). *Reaching and Teaching Students in Poverty: Strategies for Erasing the Opportunity Gap.* Teachers College Press.

Graham, S., Bollinger, A., Booth Olson, C., D'Aoust, C., MacArthur, C., McCutchen, D., & Olinghouse, N. (2012). *Teaching Elementary School Students to Be Effective Writers: A Practice Guide (NCEE 2012–4058).* National Center for Education Evaluation and Regional Assistance, Institute of Education Sciences, U.S. Department of Education. https://ies.ed.gov/ncee/wwc/Docs/PracticeGuide/WWC_Elem_Writing_PG_Dec182018.pdf

Graham, S., Capizzi, A., Harris, K. R., Hebert, M., & Morphy, P. (2014). Teaching writing to middle school students: a national survey. *Reading and Writing, 27*(6), 1015–1042. https://doi.org/10.1007/s11145-013-9495-7

Graham, S., & Harris, K. R. (1989). Components analysis of cognitive strategy instruction: Effects on learning disabled students' compositions and self-efficacy. *Journal of Educational Psychology, 81*(3), 353–361. https://doi.org/10.1037/0022-0663.81.3.353

Graham, S., Harris, K. R., & Hebert, M. (2011). *Informing Writing: The Benefits of Formative Assessment. A Carnegie Corporation Time to Act Report.* Alliance for Excellent Education. https://www.carnegie.org/publications/informing-writing-the-benefits-of-formative-assessment/

Graham, S., Harris, K. R., & Santangelo, T. (2015). Research-based writing practices and the common core: Meta-analysis and meta-synthesis. *The Elementary School Journal, 115*(4), 498–522. https://doi.org/10.1086/681964

Graham, S., & Hebert, M. (2011). Writing to read: A meta-analysis of the impact of writing and writing instruction on reading. *Harvard Educational Review, 81*(4), 710–744. https://doi.org/10.17763/haer.81.4.t2k0m13756113566

Graham, S., Liu, X., Aitken, A., Ng, C., Bartlett, B., Harris, K. R., & Holzapfel, J. (2017). Effectiveness of literacy programs balancing reading and writing instruction: A meta-analysis. *Reading Research Quarterly, 53*(3), 279–304. https://doi.org/10.1002/rrq.194

Graham, S., Liu, X., & Talukdar, J. (2018). Reading for writing: A meta-analysis of the impact of reading interventions in writing. *Review of Educational Research, 88*(2), 243–284. https://doi.org/10.3102/0034654317746927

Graham, S., McKeown, D., Kiuhara, S., & Harris, K. R. (2012). A meta-analysis of writing instruction for students in the elementary grades. *Journal of Educational Psychology, 104*(4), 879–896. https://doi.org/10.1037/a0029185

Graham, S., & Perin, D. (2007). A Meta-Analysis of Writing Instruction for Adolescent Students. *Journal of Educational Psychology, 99*(3), 445–476. https://doi.org/10.1037/0022-0663.99.3.445

Graham, S., & Sandmel, K. (2011). The process-writing approach: A meta-analysis. *The Journal of Educational Research, 104*(6), 396–407. https://doi.org/10.1080/00220671.2010.488703

Graves, D. H. (1983). *Writing Teachers and Children at Work*. Heinemann.

Greco, A. N., Milliot, J., & Wharton, R. M. (2014). *The Book Publishing Industry*. Routledge. https://doi.org/10.4324/9780203834565

Hacker, D. J. (2018). A metacognitive model of writing: An update from a developmental perspective. *Educational Psychologist, 53*(4), 220–237. https://psycnet.apa.org/doi/10.1080/00461520.2018.1480373

Hillocks, G., Jr. (1984). What works in teaching composition: A meta-analysis of experimental treatment studies. *American Journal of Education, 93*(1), 133–170. https://doi.org/10.1086/443789

Horner, B., Lu, M.-Z., Royster, J. J., & Trimbur, J. (2011). *Language Difference in Writing: Toward a Translingual Approach*. Faculty Scholarship. https://ir.library.louisville.edu/cgi/viewcontent.cgi?article=1065&context=faculty

Hyland, K. (2004). *Disciplinary Discourses: Social Interactions in Academic Writing* (Michigan Classics Edition). Michigan University Press. https://doi.org/10.3998/mpub.6719

Jouhar, M. R., & Rupley, W. H. (2021). The reading–writing connection based on independent reading and writing: A systematic review. *Reading & Writing Quarterly, 37*(2), 136–156. https://doi.org/10.1080/10573569.2020.1740632

Kang, E., & Han, Z. (2015). The efficacy of written corrective feedback in improving L2 written accuracy: A meta-analysis. *The Modern Language Journal, 99*(1), 1–18. https://doi.org/10.1111/modl.12189

Kellogg, R. T. (2001). Long-term working memory in text production. *Memory and Cognition, 29*(1), 43–52. https://doi.org/10.3758/BF03195739

Kellogg, R. T. (2008). Training writing skills: A cognitive developmental perspective. *Journal of Writing Research, 1*(1), 1–26. https://doi.org/10.17239/jowr-2008.01.01.1

Kemp, N. (2010). Texting versus txtng: Reading and writing text messages, and links with other linguistic skills. *Writing Systems Research, 2*(1), 53–71. https://doi.org/10.1093/wsr/wsq002

Kiefer, K., Palmquist, M., Carbone, N., Cox, M., & Melzer, D. (2000–2021). *An Introduction to Writing across the Curriculum*. The WAC Clearinghouse. https://wac.colostate.edu/resources/wac/intro

Klingberg, T. (2010). Training and plasticity of working memory. *Trends in Cognitive Sciences, 14*(7), 317–324. https://doi.org/10.1016/j.tics.2010.05.002

Koster, M., Tribushinina, E., De Jong, P. F., & Van den Bergh, B. (2015). Teaching children to write: A meta-analysis of writing intervention research. *Journal of Writing Research, 7*(2), 299–324. https://doi.org/10.17239/jowr-2015.07.02.2

Langer, J. A. (2001). Beating the odds: Teaching middle and high school students to read and write well. *American Educational Research Journal, 38*(4), 837–880. https://doi.org/10.3102/00028312038004837

Le, H., Janssen, J., & Wubbels, T. (2018). Collaborative learning practices: Teacher and student perceived obstacles to effective student collaboration. *Cambridge Journal of Education, 48*(1), 103–132. https://doi.org/10.1080/0305764X.2016.1259389

Lenhart, A. (2015). *Teen, Social Media and Technology Overview 2015*. Pew Research Center. https://www.pewresearch.org/internet/2015/04/09/teens-social-media-technology-2015/

Littleton, C. E. (2011). *The Role of Feedback in Two Fanfiction Writing Groups*. [Doctoral dissertation, Indiana University of Pennsylvania].

MacArthur, C. A. (1999). Overcoming barriers to writing: Computer support for basic writing skills. *Reading & Writing Quarterly, 15*(2), 169–192. https://doi.org/10.1080/105735699278251

MacArthur, C. A. (2009). Reflections on research on writing and technology for struggling writers. *Learning Disabilities Research & Practice, 28*(2), 93–103. https://doi.org/10.1111/j.1540-5826.2009.00283.x

MacArthur, C. A., & Graham, S. (1987). Learning disabled students' composing under three methods of text production: Handwriting, word processing, and dictation. *The Journal of Special Education, 21*(3), 22–42. https://doi.org/10.1177/002246698702100304

McCarthy, S. J. (2001). Identity construction in elementary readers and writers. *Reading Research Quarterly, 36*(2), 122–151. https://doi.org/10.1598/RRQ.36.2.2

McConachie, S. M., & Petrosky, A. R. (2009). *Content Matters: A Disciplinary Literacy Approach to Improving Student Learning*. Wiley. https://doi.org/10.1002/9781118269466

McCutchen, D. (2000). Knowledge, processing, and working memory: Implications for a theory of writing. *The Educational Psychologist, 35*(1), 13–23. https://doi.org/10.1207/S15326985EP3501_3

Mehan, H., Hubbard, L., & Villanueva, I. (1994). Forming academic identities: Accommodation without assimilation among involuntary minorities. *Anthropology and Education Quarterly, 25*(2), 91–117. https://doi.org/10.1525/aeq.1994.25.2.05x0904t

Merchant, G. (2007). Writing the future in the digital age. *Literacy, 41*(3), 118–128. https://doi.org/10.1111/j.1467-9345.2007.00469.x

Moje, E. B. (2008). Foregrounding the disciplines in secondary literacy teaching and learning: A call for change. *Journal of Adolescent & Adult Literacy, 52*(2), 96–107. https://doi.org/10.1598/JAAL.52.2.1

Morphy, P., & Graham, S. (2012). Word processing programs and weaker writers/readers: A meta-analysis of research findings. *Reading and Writing, 25*(3), 641–678. https://doi.org/10.1007/s11145-010-9292-5

Morrow, L. M., & Sharkey, E. A. (1993). Motivating independent reading and writing in the primary grades through social cooperative literacy experiences (National Reading Research Center). *Reading Teacher, 47*(2), 162–165.

Murphy, B. G. (2017). *Inside Our Schools: Teachers on the Failure and Future of Education Reform*. Harvard Education Press.

Myhill, D., Jones, S., & Wilson, A. (2016). Writing conversations: fostering metalinguistic discussion about writing. *Research Papers in Education, 31*(1), https://doi.org/10.1080/02671522.2016.1106694

Newell, G. E. (2006). Writing to learn. In MacArthur, C. A., Graham, S., & Fitzgerald, J. (Eds.), *Handbook of Writing Research* (pp. 235–247). Guilford.

Newton, M. E. (2021). *The Nature and Types of Metalinguistic Awareness in Developing Writing* [Doctoral dissertation, University of Auckland]. ResearhSpace. https://researchspace.auckland.ac.nz/bitstream/handle/2292/58150/Newton-2021-thesis.pdf?sequence=4

Nguyen, T. D., Pham, L., Springer, M. G., & Crouch, M. (2019). *The Factors of Teacher Attrition and Retention: An Updated and Expanded Meta-Analysis of the Literature* (Ed Working Paper 19–149). Annenberg Institute at Brown University. https://www.edworkingpapers.com/ai19-149

Norris, C. A., & Soloway, E. (2011). Learning and schooling in the age of mobilism. *Educational Technology, 51*(6), 3–10. http://www.jstor.org/stable/44429965

Ortlieb, E. (2012). Texting fluency: The new measurement of literacy proficiency? In E. Ortlieb & R. Bowden (Eds.), *Educational Research and Innovations* (CEDER Yearbook, 7, pp. 157–176). Center for Educational Development, Evaluation, and Research, Texas A&M University. https://acal.edu.au/14conf/docs/Towards-a-Predictive-Model-for-Texting-Fluency.pdf

Ortlieb, E., Rozario, R., & Sasaski, Y. (2014, October 3–4). *Towards a predictive model of texting fluency* [Conference Presentation]. Australian Council for Adult Literacy Conference, Gold Coast, Australia. https://www.researchgate.net/profile/Roy_Rozario/publication/303222481_Towards_a_Predictive_Model_for_Texting_Fluency/links/57395f1008ae9f741b2bef9a.pdf

Ouellette, G., & Michaud, M. (2016). Generation text: Relations among undergraduates' use of text messaging, textese, and language and literacy skills. *Canadian Journal of Behavioural Science/Revue canadienne des sciences du comportement, 48*(3), 217.

Patthey-Chavez, G. G., & Gergen, C. (1992). Culture as an instructional resource in the multiethnic classroom. *Journal of Basic Writing, 11*(1), 75–96. https://www.jstor.org/stable/43443992

Pearson, B. Z., Conner, T., & Jackson, J. E. (2013). Removing obstacles for African American English-speaking children through greater understanding of language difference. *Developmental Psychology, 40*(1), 31–44. https://doi.org/10.1037/a0028248

Philippakos, Z. A., & MacArthur, C. A. (2016). The use of genre-specific evaluation criteria for revision. *Language and Literacy Spectrum, 26*, 41–52. https://files.eric.ed.gov/fulltext/EJ1108470.pdf

Pittard, V., & Martlew, M. (2000). Socially-situated cognition and metalinguistic activity. In I A. Camps & M. Milian (Eds.), *Metalinguistic Activity in Learning to Write* (pp. 79–102). Amsterdam University Press.

Plester, B., Wood, C., & Joshi, P. (2009). Exploring the relationship between children's knowledge of text message abbreviations and school literacy outcomes. *British Journal of Developmental Psychology, 27*(1), 145–61. https://doi.org/10.1348/026151008x320507

Prior, P. (1998). *Writing/Disciplinarity: A Sociohistoric Account of Literate Activity in the Academy.* Lawrence Erlbaum. https://doi.org/10.4324/9780203810651

Pritchard, R. J., & Honeycutt, R. L. (2006). Process writing. In C. A. MacArthur, S. Graham, & J. Fitzgerald (Eds.), *Handbook of Writing Research* (2nd ed., pp. 275–290). Guilford.

Quinlan, T. (2004). Speech recognition technology and students with writing difficulties: Improving fluency. *Journal of Educational Psychology, 96*(2), 337–346. https://doi.org/10.1037/0022-0663.96.2.337

Rogers, L. A., & Graham, S. (2008). A meta-analysis of single subject design writing intervention research. *Journal of Educational Psychology, 100*(4), 879–906. https://doi.org/10.1037/0022-0663.100.4.879

Rosen, L. D., Chang, J., Erwin, L., Carrier, L. M., & Cheever, N. A. (2010). The relationship between "textisms" and formal and informal writing among young adults. *Communication Research, 37*(3), 420–440. https://psycnet.apa.org/doi/10.1177/0093650210362465

Ruggles-Gere, A. (2019). *Developing Writers in Higher Education.* University of Michigan Press. https://doi.org/10.3998/mpub.10079890

Russell, D. (1995). Activity theory and its implications for writing instruction. In J. Petraglia (Ed.), *Reconceiving Writing, Rethinking Writing Instruction* (pp. 51–77). Routledge. https://doi.org/10.4324/9780203811948

Santangelo, T., & Graham, S. (2016). A comprehensive meta-analysis of handwriting instruction. *Educational Psychology Review, 28*(2), 225–265. https://doi.org/10.1007/s10648-015-9335-1

Sessions, L., & Kang, M. O. (2016). "The Neglected 'R'": Improving writing instruction through iPad apps. *Tech Trends, 60*(3), 218–225. https://doi.org/10.1007/s11528-016-0041-8

Shanahan, T., & Shanahan, C. (2008). Teaching disciplinary literacy to adolescents: Rethinking content-area literacy. *Harvard Educational Review, 78*(1), 40–59. https://doi.org/10.17763/haer.78.1.v62444321p602101

Silió, M. C., & Barbetta, P. M. (2010). The effects of word prediction and text-to-speech technologies on the narrative writing skills of Hispanic students with specific learning disabilities. *Journal of Special Education Technology, 25*(4), 17–32. https://doi.org/10.1177/016264341002500402

Smagorinsky, P. (2015). Disciplinary literacy in English language arts. *Journal of Adolescent & Adult Literacy, 59*(2), 141–146. https://doi.org/10.1002/jaal.464

Smitherman, G. (1993, November 17–22). *"The Blacker the Berry, the Sweeter the Juice": African American Student Writers and the National Assessment of Educational Progress.* [Conference Presentation]. 83rd Annual Meeting of the National Council of Teachers of English, Pittsburgh, PA. https://files.eric.ed.gov/fulltext/ED366944.pdf

Swan, K., van 'T. Hooft, M., Kratcoski, A., & Unger, D. (2005). Uses and effects of mobile computing devices in K–8 classrooms. *Journal of Research on Technology in Education, 38*(1), 99–112. https://doi.org/10.1080/15391523.2005.10782451

Sweetland, J., & Wheeler, R. S. (2014). Addressing dialect variation in US K–12 schools. In M. Bigelow & J. Ennser-Kananen (Eds.), *The Routledge Handbook of Educational Linguistics* (pp. 446–448). Routledge. https://doi.org/10.4324/9781315797748

Talib, T., & Cheung, Y. L. (2017). Collaborative Writing in Classroom Instruction: A Synthesis of Recent Research. *English Teacher, 46*(2), 43–57.

Tarbox, G. A. (2014). Just a figment? Online communities and the future of the young adult novel. In B. Carrington & J. Harding (Eds.), *Beyond the book: Transforming children's literature* (pp. 54–61). Cambridge Scholars.

Wardyga, B. J. (2012). *The Relationship Between Text Message Volume and Formal Writing Performance Among Upper Level High School Students and College Freshmen*. [Doctoral dissertation, Liberty University]. Digital Commonos. https://digitalcommons.liberty.edu/cgi/viewcontent.cgi?article=1577&context=doctoral&httpsredir=1&referer=

Ware, M., & Mabe, M. (2015). *The STM Report: An Overview of Scientific and Scholarly Journal Publishing*. Digital Commons. https://digitalcommons.unl.edu/cgi/viewcontent.cgi?article=1008&context=scholcom

Wheeler, R. S., & Swords, R. (2010). *Code-Switching Lessons: Grammar Strategies for Linguistically Diverse Writers: Grades 3–6*. Heinemann.

Wheeler, R. S., Swords, R., & Carpenter, M. (2004). Codeswitching: Tools of language and culture transform the dialectally diverse classroom. *Language Arts, 81*(6), 470–480.

Wood, C., Kemp, N., & Plester, B. (2013). *Text Messaging and Literacy–The Evidence*: Routledge. https://doi.org/10.4324/9780203693360

Young, R., & Ferguson, F. (2020). *Writing for Pleasure: Theory, Research, and Practice*. Routledge. https://doi.org/10.4324/9780429268984

Conclusion

This book demonstrates that writing is hard—but also, that students from every background can achieve excellence in writing. But excellent writing does not happen by chance. It grows where it is cultivated. Figure I.1 in the introduction presents a theory of action for writing. In other words it describes what kind of garden skilled writers grow in.

In far too many American schools, however, equitable writing instruction is not happening, as evidenced by the size of group differences in writing achievement. This situation seems mostly to be due to institutional and structural factors that limit the resources available to schools that want to make changes, encourage counterproductive attitudes and practices, and make it hard for schools to implement equitable and effective pedagogies. That needs to change, and I hope that this book will help guide policymakers and educators who are working to make meaningful reforms happen.

As I was finishing the final draft of this book, the educational world was rocked by the release of first GPT3 and its more sophisticated sister, ChatGPT, a very large, deep learning-based language model, which is capable of writing better essays than many novice writers (Elkins & Chun, 2020; Gozalo-Brizuela, & Garrido-Merchan, 2023). Tools like ChatGPT are likely to change writing education in ways that are hard to imagine. They may offer opportunities for educators, but they also raise incredible risks. I would like, therefore, to take some time to consider the implications. What kind of world are we going to end up with, when everyone has a writing assistant? Will it result in a more equitable world, or will it serve to entrench existing social and cultural divides?

To get a sense of what ChatGPT is capable of, I applied it to a common ELA writing task. Specifically, I told GPT to write an essay comparing and contrasting the themes in two poems that I posted years ago on my website on alliterative verse (http://alliteration.net):

Freeway Dawn

Stop-and-go traffic staggers along,
bumper-to-bumper past the brink of dawn
till the raw gaze of the ragged sun
    glances off fenders
    and glares on the hills.

The news-anchor's voice keeps nattering on,
like the humming motor or the hissing fan,
and with rapid pulse an arresting tone
    pierces right through
    each portable cell --
There's a public listing for this private hell.

But under the brush on bright-edged hills
where pattering feet turn poised by holes,
and high up in haze where hawk-shadows wheel,
    and cloudbanks mirror
    the colors of dawn,

and even where traffic inches and crawls,
another pulse measures patterns revealed
in balance of limb, in breath held still,
    when a moment freezes,
    moves and is gone
like a sudden deer in the slanting sun.

Welcome to our website.

Welcome to our website.
We are your friends
    (*assembled to serve*
    your every sensed need.)

Fill out our forms,
get freebies galore

> *(our plan is just perfect*
> *for point-and-click greed.)*
>
> But your name and number
> will never be revealed
> > *(except for investors*
> > *with a valid claim.)*
>
> You are the universe,
> our users are legion.
> > *(We count all your clicks,*
> > *and call them by name.)*
>
> Our banners are waving,
> just watch us succeed
> > *(without all your eyeballs*
> > *our IPO ends.)*
>
> Welcome to our website.
> We are your friends.

This is the essay that ChatGPT wrote:

> The two poems, "Freeway Dawn" and "Welcome to our website," are contrasting in their themes. "Freeway Dawn" is a poem about the natural beauty of dawn and the contrast with the modernity of life. It explores the idea of the human experience being both mundane and profound, with the stop-and-go traffic of the freeway representing the monotony of life, but with moments of stillness and beauty in nature.
>
> On the other hand, "Welcome to our website" is a poem about the digital age, with the website serving as a metaphor for the online world. The poem reflects on the idea of how people are reduced to mere data points on a website, with their name, number and clicks being used to serve the interests of the website's owners. The tone is satirical, reflecting on the exploitation of users in the digital age.
>
> In conclusion, the two poems are contrasting in their themes, with "Freeway Dawn" exploring the relationship between nature and the human experience, and "Welcome to our website" exploring the exploitation of individuals in the digital age.

ChatGPT's essay may not be brilliant, but I suspect it would be good enough to get at least a C in many middle school ELA classrooms.

Of course, ChatGPT failed to do one important thing—back up its generalizations with textual evidence, but when I added to the dialogue the instruction, "Revise the essay to provide textual evidence from the poems to support each point", it produced the following output:

> The two poems, "Freeway Dawn" and "Welcome to our website," are contrasting in their themes. "Freeway Dawn" is a poem that explores the relationship between nature and the human experience. The poem starts with a description of the stop-and-go traffic on the freeway, which is described as "staggering along" and "bumper-to-bumper." This is a representation of the monotony of modern life, as the speaker notes "the raw gaze of the ragged sun / glances off fenders / and glares on the hills." The repetition of the news-anchor's voice and the sound of the motor and fan, serve to underscore the monotony of modern life.
>
> However, the poem also highlights moments of stillness and beauty in nature, as seen in lines 13–14 "when a moment freezes, / moves and is gone / like a sudden deer in the slanting sun." The poem therefore presents a contrast between the monotony of modern life and the beauty of nature, suggesting that the human experience is both mundane and profound.
>
> On the other hand, "Welcome to our website" is a poem that reflects on the exploitation of individuals in the digital age. The tone of the poem is satirical, with the website serving as a metaphor for the online world. The poem opens with the line "Welcome to our website. / Welcome to our website." This repetition serves to emphasize the idea of the website being ubiquitous and inescapable.
>
> The poem also highlights the idea of users being reduced to mere data points on the website, as seen in lines 7–8 "Fill out our forms, / get freebies galore / (our plan is just perfect / for point-and-click greed.)" The fact that the users' name and number will never be revealed, except for investors with a valid claim, emphasizes the idea of exploitation and the users being reduced to mere data points. The final line of the poem, "Welcome to our website. / We are your friends," serves to further underscore the idea of exploitation, as the users are being invited to join a system that is ultimately exploitative.
>
> In conclusion, the two poems are contrasting in their themes, with "Freeway Dawn" exploring the relationship between nature and the human experience, and "Welcome to our website" exploring the exploitation of individuals in the digital age. The themes are supported by the use of imagery, repetition and tone in each of the poems.

I suspect 9th-grade English teachers would consider this a more than creditable effort, if it were written by one of their students and not by a computer.

That is not to say that ChatGPT's performance passes the Turing test, and is indistinguishable from a human's. If you press ChatGPT, or ask it to do something that goes well beyond summarization, thematic analysis, and boilerplate, it falls apart quickly. But for better or worse, for the two-thirds of U.S. students who struggle to write, ChatGPT promises a world in which fluency is no longer a problem.

The immediate response to ChatGPT was a furor, followed by efforts to detect and block students from using it or similar systems. But that is certainly not how the story is going to end. In the world we are entering, people will be able to summarize texts without reading them, and will be able to express (someone's) opinions without knowing how to write. The problem is that in such a world, there will be two kinds of people: those who are passive receivers of text automatically produced for their consumption, and people who have the sophistication to actively work with such tools to do work that surpasses what they would otherwise have achieved. Only skilled readers and writers will fall into the second category. But will people do the work to become skilled readers and writers when it no longer seems necessary?

In other words, we are at risk of entering a world that is even more inequitable than the one we live in. Students who are not motivated to learn literacy skills now may be even less motivated in the future—unless we actively work to make them more than passive recipients of the texts and knowledge that computers generate for them. Consider the essay that ChatGPT wrote about my two poems. It is an example of how to explain thematic inferences. As ChatGPT's response demonstrates, teachers can now generate exemplar texts at the push of a button. But that will only help if students are actively engaged in reading and interpreting texts and expressing their thoughts about them. Automated writing tools may make it easier for students to turn initial concepts into polished texts—but it will be *their* work only if they have the skill and knowledge to evaluate and rework the output so that it reflects their creative vision.

In the end, only skilled readers and writers will thrive in a world in which computers make reading and writing look much easier than they are. It is our job, as citizens, as policy makers, as educators, and (in my case), as a scientist, to make sure that everyone gets that chance, and not a privileged few.

Reference List

Elkins, K., & Chun, J. (2020). Can GPT-3 pass a writer's turing test?. *Journal of Cultural Analytics, 5*(2), 17212. https://doi.org/10.22148/001c.17212

Gozalo-Brizuela, R., & Garrido-Merchan, E. C. (2023). ChatGPT is not all you need. A state of the art review of large generative AI models. *arXiv preprint arXiv:2301.04655*. https://doi.org/10.48550/arXiv.2301.04655

Index

21st-Century Skills 1, 12, 25, 97, 143

Achievement Gaps 27, 38–39, 46–49, 95–96, 108–109, 124–125
   Causes 9–11, 39, 40–41, 49–50, 93–95, 110–112, 125–126
ADHD 84
Affinity Spaces 32, 143–144
African American Vernacular English (AAVE) 35, 56, 107–108
   Negative Attitudes 107, 111
Agreeableness *See* Personality
Asset-Based Models 4–5, 22, 59, 97
Attention Deficit Hyperactivity Disorder *See* ADHD
Audience 7, 10, 21, 23, 26, 36, 46, 50–51, 54, 122, 136–137, 150–151
Authentic Tasks 10, 46, 136–137, 139
Autonomy 50, 53–54, 58

Baseball 93–94
Big Five *See* Personality
Boredom 38, 42, 48–49, 57

ChatGPT 163–167
Code-Meshing 10, 108, 151
Code-Switching 10, 59, 106–108, 111–112, 140, 151
Cognitive Apprenticeship 24, 142–143
Cognitive Dissonance 86
Cognitive Factors 7, 9, 11–12, 19–21, 39, 45, 80, 84, 94, 107–109, 111, 121, 123, 147–149
Common Core State Standards 96
Compliance 46–48, 57–58
Conscientiousness *See* Personality
Conventions 19–20, 37, 40, 154 *See also* Transcription Skills
Culturally Responsive Pedagogy 4–5, 9, 44, 53, 56, 58, 59, 96, 139–140
Curriculum-Based Measurement of Writing (CBM-W) 5, 119
Cursive 119–121

Deficit-Based Models 4, 58, 97, 109
Digital Divide 83, 97, 125

Discourse Communities 7, 22, 24–25, 55–59, 142
Dropout Rates 3, 41, 49–50, 57–58

English Language Arts 4, 49–50, 55, 142, 164–165
ESL *See* Language Learners

Feedback 9, 22, 24–25, 39, 45, 124–126, 138–139
    Collaborative 9, 19, 22–25, 51, 122, 137, 148, 151
    Peer Feedback 22, 51, 137, 139, 143–144
    Peer Review 22, 143
    Teacher Feedback 42–43, 124, 126, 138–139
Fine Motor Skills 123

Gender 3, 8, 27, 36, 38, 44, 46–49, 52–53, 54–58, 82, 84, 85, 95–96, 98–99, 105–106, 108, 123–127
    Ability/Interest Profiles 95, 98
    Gender Similarity Hypothesis 95
    Norms 8, 36, 38, 48, 95, 126–127
    Genre preferences by Genre 54–55
    Roles 38, 53, 57–58, 95–96, 98
Genre 7, 10, 21, 23–25, 54–55, 58, 82, 96, 140–144, 150, 154
    Informational 51, 94, 96, 142
    Narrative 8, 55, 58, 82, 94, 96, 98–99, 142, 154
Grade Level
    College 1–3, 5–7, 12, 23–24, 41, 49, 81, 120, 122, 124, 145, 147–149
    Elementary 3, 5–8, 23, 32, 34, 39, 42–45, 48, 83, 96, 105, 119–124, 126, 137, 138, 139, 141, 143, 145, 147, 152
    High School 1–3, 5, 23, 37, 40, 43–44, 83, 120, 149
    Kindergarten 81
    Middle School 5, 23, 43–44, 46, 83, 120, 121–125, 165
    Preschool 96, 109
    Secondary 7, 145
Grading 40–41, 46, 50–52

Humanities Subjects 95–96

Idea Generation 7–9, 20–21, 26–27, 37, 40, 80, 82, 93–95, 98, 110, 144, 146
Identity 4, 7, 34, 36, 41, 47–51, 54–59, 98–99, 107, 139–140
    Formation 7, 48–49, 50–51, 54–59
Internet Use 22–24, 32, 55, 97, 122, 125, 143–144, 164–166
Interventions 9, 37–38, 41, 80, 84, 109, 121, 124, 136–137, 140–141, 145, 149, 152, 154
    Agency and Choice 10, 46, 49, 52–54, 58–59, 94, 139
    Alternate Input Formats 10, 120, 148–149
    Balanced Literacy Instruction 153
    Code-Meshing Instruction 10, 108, 151
    Code-Switching 106–108, 151
    Collaborative Writing 10, 25, 45, 137
    Error Correction 152–153
    Explicit Genre Instruction 10, 141–143
    Focused on Linguistic and Cultural Diversity 4–5, 10, 44, 56–59, 96, 139–140, 151
    Frequent Practice 9, 10, 20, 147, 152
    Goal Setting 44, 79, 81–82, 138, 141
    Grammar Instruction 152
    Handwriting Instruction 10, 39, 120–121, 123, 126–127, 152–153
    Inquiry Learning 10, 144, 146
    Modeling Metalinguistic Talk 10, 151–152
    Models and Mentor Texts 10, 36, 45, 79–81, 141–142, 150–151
    Morphology Instruction 124
    Observing Readers Interacting with Text 153–154
    Peer Feedback 22, 51, 137, 139, 143–144
    Phonics Instruction 153
    Phonological Awareness Training 153
    Prewriting 10, 84, 94–95, 144, 147
    Process Writing 10, 24, 136–137, 147–148
    Reading Comprehension Instruction 153

Reading for Pleasure 10, 95, 125, 127, 154
Rote Learning 123, 146
Self-Evaluation 37, 39, 138–139
Self-Regulated Strategy Development (SRSD) 10, 41, 141–143
Sentence Combining 150
Spelling Instruction 5, 9, 10, 21, 119–120, 124, 152–153
Teacher Feedback 42–43, 124, 126, 138–139
Touch Typing Instruction 10, 83, 120, 125
Vocabulary Instruction 10, 109–111, 149–150
Word Processing 122, 125, 141, 148–149
Writing for Pleasure 144
Writing to Learn 10, 144–146

Knowledge 4, 7–11, 19–21, 23, 26–27, 51–52, 54, 58, 80, 93–99, 106, 109–112, 139–146, 149–153, 167
  About Writing 9, 10, 21, 26, 95, 141–143, 153
  Academic Knowledge 3, 8, 97–99
  Content Knowledge 8–11, 19, 26, 93–99, 144–146, 153
  Funds of Knowledge 4, 58, 93, 96–99, 140, 146, 150
  Inference 39, 97, 167
  Topic Knowledge 8, 10, 23, 25, 27, 51–54, 93–99, 146

Language Learners 8, 32, 36, 40, 56, 108–109, 124, 152
Language Skills 8–10, 26, 40, 81, 105–112, 149–152
  Academic Language 8, 24, 35, 108–111, 149–151
  Accent 12, 56
  Development 12, 56, 108–112, 150–152
  Dialect 4, 8, 12, 56, 105, 106–109, 151
  Diction 20, 24
  Fluency 20, 105–106, 108
  Metacognitive 20, 44, 80, 82, 111, 140, 151

  Metalinguistic 10, 80, 107–108, 140, 151–152
  Multilingualism 108
  Oral Language 8–10, 26, 40, 48, 79, 105–112, 149–152
  Register 4, 8, 105, 107, 110–111, 151
  Style 4, 8, 20–21, 32, 105, 151
  Syntax 10, 11, 20–21, 105, 109, 150–151
  Text Macrostructure 19–22, 39, 81, 144, 154
  Tone 20–21, 165–166
  Verbal Expression 8, 21, 39, 105–112
  Verbal Memory 106
  Verbal Reasoning 21, 105
  Vocabulary 8, 10, 12, 105, 109–112, 120, 149–150
Long-Term Working Memory 94
Long-Term English Learners (LTELs) 109, 111

Matthew Effect 27
Motivation 7, 9, 10, 26–27, 31–59, 79, 84, 106, 110, 136–141, 144, 148
  Achievement Emotions 33, 35, 38, 42–43
  Attainment Value 33–34, 36, 44–45, 54–59
  Avoidance Goals 34, 37, 40, 43, 47, 57, 111
  Beliefs 7, 32–34, 39–42
  Causal Attributions 33, 35, 37, 40–41
  Competition 7, 35–36, 39, 44, 51, 57, 135
  Cost 9, 33–34, 36, 45–46, 106–108
  Extrinsic 43, 50
  Goal Orientation 33–36, 43–45
  Intrinsic Interest in Writing 50–51
  Intrinsic Value 33–34, 36, 43, 45, 50–54
  Mastery Goals 33–36, 40, 43–45, 47, 57, 136
  Motivation-Based Interventions 41
  Performance Goals 34–35, 43, 51, 57
  Self-Efficacy 7, 33–39, 45, 57, 123, 137, 141
  Success Criteria 33, 35, 39–40, 43

Topic Interest 7, 9, 27, 32, 45, 47–49, 50–54, 56, 58, 94, 95–98, 126, 139
Utility Value 33–34, 36, 45–50, 54, 57
Writing Apprehension 36–38, 47, 57
Writing Motivation Scales 35, 37, 41

National Assessment of Educational Progress 1–3, 83

Parental Speech 109
Peer Feedback 22, 51, 137, 139, 143–144
Personality 46–50
Poverty *See* Socioeconomic Status
Principles for the Postsecondary Teaching of Writing 5

Race and Ethnicity 2–3, 7, 38–39, 41, 44, 50, 55–58, 83, 85–86, 95–99, 107, 110–111, 124–126
   African American Culture 55, 57–58, 107
   African American Students 4, 35, 39, 41–42, 44, 49, 57–58, 107, 110–111, 125
   Asian 2, 54
   Hispanic Students 2, 4, 41, 49, 56, 57
   Multiracial 2
Racism 107–108
   Raciolinguistic Ideologies 107
   Structural 108
Reading
   Comprehension 26, 82, 93, 107–108, 145, 147, 153
   Decoding 124
   Morphological Analysis 124
   Print Exposure 38, 96–97, 142, 150–151, 154
Rhetorical Structure 6–7, 19–22, 24, 39, 55
Rubrics 20, 38–39, 138

Self-Regulation 7–11, 26, 33–34, 37, 41, 44–45, 57, 79–85, 140–141, 151, 153
   Environmental Structuring 79, 81
   Goal-Setting 44, 79, 81–82, 138, 141

Mental Imagery 80–81
Monitoring 7, 19–21, 26, 44, 79–83, 111, 141, 153
Planning 7, 9, 19–21, 25–26, 59, 80–81, 83–84, 95, 122, 142–143, 147
Self-Consequenting 79, 81
Self-Evaluation 37, 42, 80–81, 138
Self-Verbalization 79, 81
Strategy Use 10, 26–27, 38, 41, 45, 80–82, 94–95, 98, 136–137, 140–144, 147–148, 151–153
Use of Models 10, 26–27, 38, 41, 45, 80–82, 94–95, 98, 136–137, 140–144, 147–148, 151–153
Sesame Street 97
Sociocultural Theory 22–24
Socioeconomic Status 2, 8, 38, 50, 55–56, 82, 85–86, 95–99, 109–112, 123–125
   Childhood Stress 8, 45, 85, 135, 146
Special Education 49, 120
Stance 20
Standard American English (SAE) 8, 35, 56, 59, 106–111
Standardized Assessments 4, 41, 50, 52, 94, 107–109, 146, 149
Stereotype Threat 8, 85, 126, 139
Suspension Rates 3, 49, 57

Teacher 4, 6, 11, 19, 26, 34–35, 37, 39–43, 46–48, 50, 53, 55–56, 58–59, 82, 98, 107–108, 111, 123–124, 126, 135–140, 142, 149–152, 166–167
   Attitudes 35–36, 40, 47–48, 55, 107, 111, 126, 138–140, 142, 150
   Classroom Practices 5–6, 9, 12, 24, 35, 43, 48–50, 55, 96, 109, 139–140, 145
   Disciplinary Practices 4, 41, 50
   Feedback 42–43, 124, 126, 138–139
   Gender 55, 58
   Grading *See* Grading
   Race 58
   Relationships with Students 31, 39, 42–43, 48, 50, 53, 56, 107–108, 136
   Retention 135

Text Macrostructure 19–22, 39, 81, 144, 154
Theory of Action 10, 11, 39, 136, 163
Traditional Classrooms 40, 55
Transcription Skills 5–11, 20, 26–27, 39–40, 81–82, 119–126, 146, 148–149, 152–153
    Dictation 23, 120, 148
    Fluency 6, 27, 82, 119–126, 149, 152–153
    Handwriting 5, 7–10, 20, 31, 39, 81, 83, 119–123, 126, 136, 148, 152
    Handwriting Fluency Threshold 120
    Keyboarding 7–8, 10, 20–21, 27, 81–83, 119–122, 124–126, 136, 148, 152–153
    Keyboarding Fluency Threshold 122
    On Different Devices or in Different Modalities 83, 97, 119, 125, 149, 152
    Spelling 5, 8–10, 21, 31, 39–40, 81, 107, 110, 119–122, 124, 126, 136, 149, 152, 154
Translingual Pedagogies 59

Vocabulary Gap Hypothesis 4, 109–110

Workforce Readiness 2, 27
Working Memory 7, 9–11, 19–20, 79–86, 94, 108, 111, 119–120, 122, 140, 146–147
Writer's Workshop 24, 51, 147–148
Writing
    Capacity Theory 20, 80–82, 140, 146–147
    Collaborative 10, 19, 22–25, 45, 51, 122, 137, 148, 151–152
    Construct Definition 5, 20, 32, 37
    Development 5–6, 8–12, 19–23, 37, 39, 45, 50–52, 81, 119–126, 140–154
    Disciplinary 24–25, 142–143, 145–146
    Everyday Writing 7–8, 22–23, 27, 55, 148–149
    Expert vs Novice 20, 24–26, 83, 93, 139, 147–148, 163
    Fluency 7–10, 20, 23, 27, 81–82, 98, 105, 108, 122, 144, 148, 152–154, 167

Pedagogy 9–11, 24–25, 44, 56, 59, 97, 108, 135–154, 163
Professional and Technical Writing 1, 7, 22–26, 95, 143
Purpose 7, 10, 21–22, 25–26, 39, 50–51, 54, 59, 136–137, 142, 150–151
Quality 6–7, 20, 26, 31, 37, 39, 42, 51–52, 80, 82–84, 94, 98–99, 105, 107–108, 120–125, 138–139, 141, 145, 147–154
Simple View 40
Strategy Instruction 45, 136, 141, 143, 152
Technical and Professional Writing 1, 7, 22–26, 95, 143
Topic Choice 10, 22, 52–54, 58, 94, 139
Writing Across the Curriculum (WAC) 145
Writing Processes 7, 10–11, 19–27, 37, 44–45, 59, 80–82, 84–85, 94–95, 119, 121–122, 125, 137, 140–148, 151, 153
    Editing 7, 19, 21, 24–25, 82–83, 124–125, 147
    Ideation *See* Idea Generation
    Monitoring 7, 19–21, 26, 44, 79–83, 111, 141, 153
    Planning 7, 9, 19–21, 25–26, 59, 80–81, 83–84, 95, 122, 142–143, 147
    Revision 7, 9, 19, 21, 23–26, 40, 80–82, 94–96, 122, 143–144, 147–148
    Transcription 7 *See* Transcription Skills
    Translation 7, 20–21
Writing Strategies 8, 9–10, 20–21, 25–27, 32, 37–38, 41, 45, 80–82, 94–95, 98, 136, 140–143, 145, 147–148, 151–153
    Instruction 45, 136, 141, 143, 152
    Knowledge Crafting 25–26
    Knowledge Telling 21, 25–27, 93–94
    Knowledge Transforming 25–26
    Planning 7, 20–21
    Reviewing 20, 26, 80, 83
    Revision 7, 9, 19, 21, 23–26, 40, 80–82, 94–96, 122, 143–144, 147–148

www.ingramcontent.com/pod-product-compliance
Lightning Source LLC
Chambersburg PA
CBHW061716300426
44115CB00014B/2711